Shouning Li  Andrea Libovitch  Kevin Lichten  Laurie Li
Tiffany Lin  Lucyna Lis  Julien Liu  Sharon Lobo  John
Loughran  Bryant Lu  Ethan Lu  Linda Lu  Gail Lubin  Phyllis
Karen Lynfield  Jon Maass  F. Daniel MacNelly  Phil Maguire  Christine Maher  Maria
Maldonado  Joseph Mancuso  David Mann  Kate Mann  Lisamarie Manso  Leonard
Manzo  Mark Mariscal  Robert Marnez  Alixa Martinez  Mildred Martinez  Laurie
Marvald  Susan Dunlope Masi  Melida Mason  Elizabeth McClure  Shirley McDougal
Ryan McEnroe  Daniel McKee  Garfield McKenzie  Robin Mclasky  Larry Mebane  Beat
Meier  Lillian Mendez  John Menz  Lisa Merrill  Terese Michaud  Tara Mikolahsi  Tim
Milam  John Miller  Ronald Miranda  Kenichiro Mito  Kevin Miyamura  Scelecina
Mohammed  Kimberly Mok  John Monrose  Johnny Monrose  Colin Montoute  Manny
Morales  Sarael Morales  Ramon Mormes  Douglas Muir  Anne Myers  George Myers
Cornelius Nailis  Kirk Nakahira  Nalina Mosese  Joseph Navarro  Cassandra Nelson  Traci
Nelson  Andy Neuburger  Stuart Nicholl  Christopher Nichols  Stephanie Nigro  Sonya
Nocetti  Carl Nolan  Carla Noriega  Kim Novick  Diana Noya  Aviane Nylfeler  Florian
Oberhuber  Erin O'Keefe  Susan Oldroyd  Majalia Olivares  Ursula Oliver  Peter Olney
Harutaka Oribe  Anna Ortega  Paul Osmolskis  Mehemet Ozpay  Gladys Pagan  Geoffrey
Paine  Donna Paley  Anthony Palladino  Carey Palmer  Edward Pang  Mary Pepchinski
Raphael Pereira  Marc Perotta  Peter Pesce  Roberto Petrucelli  Yvonne Pho  Joseph
Pikiewicz  Stanley Pinska  Linda Pisano  Michael Plofker  James Micha Poindexter  Alan
Polinsky  Vincent Porpora  Richard Potestio  Teresa Pross  Matthew Przystup  Mariana
Ramirez  Rosa Ramos  Karen Randel  Nancy Rankin  Krishna Rao  James Rappa  Timothy
Rasic  Alexander Redfern  Katharine Redfern  Sean Reilly  Rewati Prabhu  Lourdes
Reynafarje  Zena Rhoden  Kathryn Rhodie  Vera Ellen Ricci  William Rice  Kristine Riemer
Jennifer Riggs  Olga Rios  Daisy Rivera  Janice Rivera-Hall  Michael Robins  Aveon
Robinson  DeShawn Robinson  Lynn Robinson  Deborah Rockey  Paul Rodman  Ana
Rodriguez  Lourdes Rodriguez  Ann Rolland  Alexander Rosado  Gerald Rosenfield
Thomas Rosenkilde  Scott Roslyn  Joyce Rotchester  Stephen Roth  Henry Roux  Ieva
Rozens  Randi Rubenstein  Noah Rubin  Mark Rusitzky  Anthony Saby  Jacqueline
Saccocio  Julie Sales  Maritza Salichs  Nadia Samuelson  Priscila Sandler  Nicholas
Saponara  Andrea Saunders  Heidi Sawyer  Christopher Scarpati  Tracy Schaffer  Ann
Marie Schara  John Schliewenz  John Schlinke  Charles Schmitt  Daniel Schmitt  Sinan
Schwarting  John Secreti  Jorge Sein  Naoto Sekiguchi  Catherine Selby  Anabelle Selldorf
Andrew Shadid  Manan Shah  Guobo Shao  Emily Shieh  Shaun Shih  Ivan Shinkar
Hannah Sholl  Mallory Shure  Kirsten Sibilia  Joy Siegel  Thomas Sincavage  Matthew
Smith  Roland St. Aude  Michael Stark  Karen Steifel  Mary Steiner  Karen Stevens  Carl
Stone  Jeann Stoney  Elfriede Stremnitzer  Deborah Stuart  Ramkumar Subramanian
Christie Suddoth  Heidi Sudolsky  William Suk  Christina Sum  Patricia Suplee  Maria Suri
Gerardo Sustalta  Paul Sutliff  Katherine Sutton  Thomas Sze  Michael Szivos  Conrad
Talley  Mauri Tamarin  Dana Tang  Eric Taniguchi  Donald Tapert  Paul Tapogna  Deborah
Taylor  Ericka Temple  Qui Thach  Simon Thackurdhin  Joylyn Thompson  Ana Tishelman
Nicholas Tocheff  Risa Tolin  Laura Tramantano  Dawn Trischitta  Bogue Trondowski
Rosalind Tsang  Stephen Tsou  Wendy Turner  Martin Tuzman  Luke Tyler  Judythe Ucinski
Eric Van Der Sluys  Janet Van Voornis  Andrew Varela  Raquel Vasallo  Nellie Velazquez
Rodney VenJohn  Edgardo Venturanza  Deborah Verne  Manella Villanueva  Senen Vina-
de-leon  Gerda Vlugter  Claudia Vrabie  Erik Wang  Elizabeth Wastler  Lauren Wegel
Peter Weingarten  Timothy Westbrook  Ray Williams  Darrell Wilson  Jason Winstanley
Karla Wishnik  Kevin Wolfe  Andrew Wong  Scott Wood  Audrey Woodhall  Beth Worell
Albert Wu  Sharon Xiaotong Wu  Hui Lay Yeo  Paula Young  Yuan-Sung Yu  Marek
Zamdmer  Chaim Zeitz  Barbara Zeleny  Josette Zeno  Adrienn Zessman  Allison Zucrow

Designing for the Built Realm

# FOX & FOWLE ARCHITECTS

## Designing for the Built Realm  Kira L. Gould   Preface by Thomas Fisher

# FOX & FOWLE ARCHITECTS

Bruce Fowle  Daniel Kaplan  Sudhir Jambhekar  Sylvia Smith  Mark Strauss

*[Handwritten note:]*
Bill —
Hope you enjoy this.
Look forward to many more opportunities to work with you.
Bruce

*[Handwritten note:]*
Bill —
Arnhold Hall was a personal highlight. I enjoyed working with you and the committee!
Sylvia

images
Publishing

Published in Australia in 2005 by
The Images Publishing Group Pty Ltd
ABN 89 059 734 431
6 Bastow Place, Mulgrave, Victoria, 3170, Australia
Telephone: +61 3 9561 5544  Fax: +61 3 9561 4860
Email: books@images.com.au
Website: www.imagespublishing.com

Copyright © The Images Publishing Group Pty Ltd 2005
The Images Publishing Group Reference Number: 540

National Library of Australia Cataloguing-in-Publication entry:

Designing for the built realm: Fox & Fowle Architects.

Bibliography.
Includes index.
ISBN 1 920744 00 2.

1. Fox & Fowle Architects. 2. Architecture, Modern – United States. 3.
Architecture, American. I. Gould, Kira L. (Series: Master architect series VI).

720.973

Coordinating Editor: Fiona Gruber
Designed by The Graphic Image Studio Pty Ltd, Mulgrave, Australia
www.tgis.com.au
Film by Mission Productions Limited
Printed by Everbest Printing Co. Ltd. in Hong Kong/China

IMAGES has included on its website a page for special notices in relation to
this and our other publications. Please visit: www.imagespublishing.com

# Contents

## PROJECTS

# Everything Flows

by Thomas Fisher

## Everything Flows

The ancient Greek philosopher, Heraclitus, observed that "everything flows," and while that idea seems far removed from architecture, the notion of the world as a series of flows has regained currency in modern times. As the physicist Gerald Schroeder puts it, "all matter is both particle-like and wave-like." Some architects have tried to express the wave-like quality of matter literally, with architecture that looks like frozen lava, although in doing so, they have created objects disconnected from the flow of life around them. Fox & Fowle Architects offers another way of thinking about this idea. Its work flows in various ways, sometimes visibly in the objects, materials, and forms it uses, and sometimes invisibly in the flow of relationships, energy, or information that its buildings enclose. At the same time, its architecture relates to what surrounds it—existing urban fabric, other buildings, the natural landscape—reminding us that all things remain discrete as well as connected, particle-like and at the same time wave-like.

## Human Flows

The wave-like character of the world is most obvious when looking at the movement of people and vehicles across space, over roads, and along tracks. In Fox & Fowle's master plan for Buffalo's Inner Harbor, elevated highways, train lines, ship docks, and pedestrian paths overlap, with finger-like open spaces that stitch these various flowing systems together. The firm has also created flows where none existed before, such as the mid-block pedestrian path it has proposed for the Clinton Housing Competition, linking functions that often remain distinct in cities.

The firm's architecture has expressed the flow of human activity as well. The tiny Lehman College Communication Center, with its circular information booth and flared, metal canopy, expresses the flow of people and information in and around this entry to the campus. And the firm's design for a subway station in New York has ceilings that undulate, scallop, angle, and curve, as if flapping in the wake of people rushing to the trains.

## Vehicular Flows

One of the key discoveries of the flowing nature of the world came with Einstein's recognition that matter and energy are related by speed. Fox & Fowle, in a number of transit-oriented projects, has explored the architectural and urban implications of speed, and how vehicular flows affect our perception of the world. In urban design projects such as the Dosflota Master Plan and the East River Development concept, Fox & Fowle has envisioned buildings whose curved, lozenge, or elliptical shapes address how they will look from the fast-moving cars, planes, and boats around them. In other schemes, such as the Huntington Station or Jamaica Station Master Plans, the firm has proposed long, linear buildings along the tracks, like rows of train cars. In one building there, Fox & Fowle has envisioned a tower with staggered, horizontal windows that recall those of passing trains moving at different speeds.

The train stations and platforms Fox & Fowle has designed express these ideas at a smaller scale. The Walter Rand Transportation Center, for example, has a continuous surface that serves as seating, wall, and ceiling, wrapping its way through the terminal and leading the flow of passengers to and from the tracks. The building itself embodies the waves of people within. Other stations express the energy released by moving vehicles. Fox & Fowle has given stations along the Hudson Bergen Light Rail Transit System asymmetrical fabric canopies and streamlined forms, as if shaped by the suction of the passing trains. At the Intermodal Station at Roosevelt Avenue and at the Stillwell Avenue Terminal, the main roofs arc up, as if inflated by the train's piston of air. And, in a competition entry for a canopy over an outdoor subway entrance in Washington DC, the firm has designed a structure that actually moves, swinging up when the station is open and cupping down, like a giant hand, when closed.

In all of these cases, the architecture mediates between the speed of the vehicles and that of pedestrians, between our wave-like movements and our particular selves. Fox & Fowle's proposal for the Gloucester Green Competition takes a different tack. It uses the detritus of transportation—standard steel shipping containers—as the building blocks for housing, offices, hotels, and community activities, stacked in a long, curving structure beside a rail line. In reusing these abundantly available containers, the firm has addressed one of the key problems of our world, our extravagant use of finite energy flows and our wastefulness of finite material flows.

## Material Flows

We waste materials because we don't see the flow of embodied energy in them. The firm has represented that idea in various ways with glass, the building material closest to being a crystallized flow. In a number of office buildings, for example, the fluidity of this material finds expression in glass walls that bow in (Bryant Park Tower), curve out (the American Bible Society), bend back (Avaya) and extend out and up (Dongbu). Corrugated glazing also expresses this idea on a lower budget in the interior partitions in the Barney Skanska New York offices. Material flows, if largely invisible to us, remain a major part of the global economy. In projects such as the East 125th Street Corridor study, Fox & Fowle has sought to integrate the huge material flows of big-box retail into the urban fabric of New York by breaking down the buildings' scale and opening them up to the street with glass entries and canopies. In contrast to this flow of products, the firm also treats materials and physical objects as precious commodities, evident in the design of Herman Miller's Manhattan showroom, where the company's elegant furniture stands out in a spare, day-lit space.

## Energy Flows

If we waste materials because we don't think of them as a flow, we waste energy because we can't see its flow. Fox & Fowle Architects has used, in several projects, architectural means to control the energy flows in buildings and sites. The best known of these is the Condé Nast Building, where the firm deployed everything from recycled materials to photovoltaic curtain-wall panels to motion detectors to save energy, making this a seminal example of how to "green" a tall office building. The designers used strategies to save

energy, improve health, and increase productivity in other tall buildings as well: a high-rise Manhattan apartment building (The Helena, the first private residential building in New York submitted for LEED gold rating), a bank headquarters in China (ICBC), a corporate tower in New Jersey (Merrill Lynch), and with Renzo Piano's office, a newspaper building in New York (The *New York Times*). Smaller, more modest projects have been treated with the same care. In the Black Rock Forest Center, the firm used local and recycled materials, along with an array of mechanical, electrical, and daylighting strategies, as a demonstration of environmentally responsible design. And in their renovation of the Bronx Zoo's Lion House, designers leveraged the need for a natural-appearing interior to maximize daylight and to use the ground for heating and cooling.

## Information Flows

Energy contains information, notes Gerald Schroeder, and several Fox & Fowle projects attend to information flow as carefully as they do that of energy. The firm's competition entries for the Museum of Women and for the Queens Museum of Art treat the flow of information as a mix of order and happenstance, with galleries allowing for a variety of paths and experiences. University projects such as new academic facilities at the New School, Lehman College, and Syracuse University bring innovation to the various ways in which information flows in learning environments, from individual computer screen or book to informal hallway gatherings to formal classes and lectures, with light and views connecting them. The flow of information has even begun to affect the form of secondary schools. Fox & Fowle's competition design for the Perth Amboy High School contains five interlocking "academies" that weave across the site and connect to each other and to a set of support facilities, maximizing the interactions of students. And its master plan for the historic Spence School interlocks diverse learning environments vertically, with mixes of uses on many of the floors, uniquely linked by a central elevator and stair core. The flow of information has also taken over public space. Two of the towers Fox & Fowle has designed for Times Square—3 and 11 Times Square—mix the

flowing forms that have come to characterize the firm's highrises, with the flow of information along their façades in the form of giant electronic screens. While Times Square may be one of the most extreme examples of a public information space, this work suggests that information flows, like those of energy, materials, and movement, have become dominant forces affecting the form of our buildings and cities. Some think that this spells the end of architecture, that buildings will disappear behind the billboards or become indistinguishable from the landscape, or become simply a symbol of flow. But the work of this firm disputes those dire predictions. The work on the following pages suggests that physical form and face-to-face interactions have become even more important in a world awash in the high-speed movement of people, information, and goods. The firm's proactive stance on a range of critical public issues, from environmental sustainability to transit-oriented development to urban revitalization to the pro bono envisioning of Lower Manhattan after 9/11, have resulted in a number of buildings and urban designs that have galvanized people's attention. And the firm's pursuit of a relationship-oriented design process, one that attempts to align the personalities and approaches of clients and design teams, has achieved better buildings with less conflict than often occurs in the construction industry.

One of the dilemmas of a world of flows is that, because of the speed with which people and images move, we tend to categorize work based on appearance, not giving ourselves the time to see beyond the most superficial characteristics of things. The architecture of Fox & Fowle is diverse in form and function and so doesn't lend itself easily to categorization. But that is all the more reason why it deserves more careful study. This work shows how architecture can achieve multiple public purposes and also manifest, in a very concrete way, the often invisible flows that have come to define, for better or worse, modern life.

*Thomas Fisher, former editorial director of* Progressive Architecture, *is Dean of the College of Architecture and Landscape Architecture at the University of Minnesota.*

# Vision and Perspective

by Bruce Fowle LEED, FAIA

This volume, published to mark Fox & Fowle Architects' twenty-sixth year, is an exploration of the firm's work and way of working. Readers familiar with the first monograph will discover new as well as familiar voices—evidence of continuity and change. The many leaders whose voices and ideas fill these pages are diverse in their educational, professional, and personal backgrounds, and they each share an optimism about architecture and planning and the role of these endeavors in the betterment of society.

The firm's commitment is to what Eliel Saarinen called the "next larger context" and what we call "bigger, linked thinking." It is what has enriched and enlivened our work for years. This framework for thought and design drives each project by questioning the nature of relationships from the small scale to the very broad. Such thinking encourages connections among scales and disciplines, supports the integration of new technologies, and ultimately links form making strategies, urban design, and sustainability. Big thinking is an attitude that supports place-making as a comprehensive process. It is influenced by many externalities and results in responsible design.

For me, design entails the creation of environments that seek to fulfill and enlarge the human spirit. Responsible design must foster a symbiotic relationship with its physical, sociological, emotional, and environmental context. While design is essentially human-centered, it must also communicate a sense of its place in the universe. Each component of the built environment, no matter who designs or builds it, must be integral to a greater whole. The vision of that greater whole must come from a holistic understanding of the systems that sustain life.

Almost every aspect of architecture and planning practice has changed in the last quarter century, yet some things about Fox & Fowle's way of working have remained consistent. Through our special alchemy, we continue to strive to educate and elevate our clients' aspirations and expectations while advancing the civic and environmental agenda of architecture. We are motivated and unified by the process of finding innovative ways to connect the environment, context, and culture.

We are in an age when the computer has provided architects and planners boundless opportunities for experimentation and exploration. This technology is in a constant state of change, and while we are incredibly fortunate to be practicing in this exciting time, we are given tremendous responsibility. New ideas that evolve must be rooted in human scale and use patterns, and they must work toward the reconnection of man to our natural systems rather than trying to reinvent or overwhelm them.

Our clients are sophisticated and responsible in their roles as builders, but they are not always prepared to let issues relating to the public good enter into their perception of their needs. We believe it is our professional responsibility to lead them in a thorough and thoughtful consideration of their obligations toward the greater whole. It is imperative that architects and their clients work closely with urban designers, planners, engineers, landscape architects, artists, and others traditionally involved with the design process. This imperative extends to working with environmentalists, ecologists, economists, sociologists, and other experts in our expanding intelligence. Just as no building should be an isolated object, whether in an urban, suburban, or rural context, we as designers must not work in isolation. Our firm nurtures those connections because we feel they are not only indispensable but also integral to serving the public's interest.

In this same view, we have brought urban design and planning together with architecture and interior design under one roof. Our collaborative process has enabled us to engage regularly in a dialogue within the office that challenges all aspects of a project by subjecting them to candid scrutiny. We assign each project to the studio with the typological expertise, experience, and creative talent best suited to satisfy the broadest possible criteria of design excellence.

Each studio is cross-referenced and supported by subgroups of specialists. These include design, technology, quality assurance, interior design, sustainable design (including 37 LEED accredited professionals), management, clerical assistance, and business development. In the critical phases of design and planning, the principals and studios play dual roles in support of each other. Communication through open dialogue, selflessness, a commitment to sharing the work effort, and a willingness to share the credit are the essence of our firm's culture and the key to our collaborative process.

One of the strengths of our structure is its empowerment of associates and other firm leaders who are so critical to Fox & Fowle's short-term effectiveness and long-term success. Leaders at all levels are encouraged to seek new ways to organize teams and to guide the design process, which vary among typologies as well as individual projects.

As the culture of our firm has evolved over the years, there has been a continuing spirit of learning and sharing. The exploration and evaluation of ideas involves all team members. Firm leaders of long standing as well as younger staff members share a mutual commitment to educating each other and ensuring meaningful professional development for everyone. Our work benefits significantly from our insistence on open and frequent communication, both structured and unstructured. We encourage all members of the staff to be assertive in asking questions, suggesting ideas, and pushing our collective effort forward.

To assure professional and personal development of our staff, we run a program of weekly luncheon seminars. Alternating between technical, design, and general interest topics, these keep staff apprised of current technologies and trends and add another layer to our quality assurance. Reaching beyond our industry, the office has maintained an art gallery for over twenty-five years where every three months we have a changing exhibit of young artists' work. These

bring a stimulating and often provocative new dimension to our workplace.

The Fox & Fowle work process is distinctly collective, yet collaboration is not an end in itself. In order for architecture and planning to embody a spirit and convey an emotion that ventures beyond the obvious, individual leadership is necessary to assure that the design evolves with a clarity of vision. Any one of a number of talented individuals at our firm may be best positioned to understand a client's needs and guide the design process in a manner that will responsibly carry forward the integrity of the design, satisfy the collective goals, and clarify the vision.

Like any form of democracy, a collaborative working style is unpredictable and ever-changing, but we believe it is the only enduring method of practice. We embrace the challenge to improve our methodology and structure to ensure it continues to foster new, diverse ideas and support multiple forms of expression.

On several occasions, we have taken collaboration to another level by associating with other architects. In Europe and Asia, many practitioners work in an environment that is more supportive of design innovation and technical advancement than in the United States. By joining forces with several prominent foreign firms, we have broadened our experience and enhanced our expertise.

Our collaborative culture extends to our clients as well. We foster strong relationships and ensure that the client feels a sense of ownership and a personal connection to a realized project. We take care that the client fully understands the design path, embraces it, and is equipped to make decisions in an informed manner. This invariably builds trust that enables us to introduce new ideas effectively.

Much of the credibility we have earned with our clients and the community at large is a consequence of the engagement with, and commitment to, civic and professional activism. That has been the soul of our firm's culture since

*"Always design a thing by considering it in its next larger context—a chair in a room, a room in a house, a house in an environment, an environment in a city plan."*
—Eliel Saarinen
(quoted by Eero Saarinen, *Time* magazine, June 2, 1977).

its founding. Civic and professional engagement enriches our work. It is not enough to shape only buildings or spaces. Architects and planners, in a world of specialized players, are the visionaries who must conduct the "orchestra" that shapes our communities, our cities, and our regions. Embracing and understanding the bigger, linked aspect of all built form is essential, in our view, if we are to consistently design with integrity, meaning, and relevance.

Fox & Fowle has helped shape public policy and has built relationships with community leaders. A further understanding of broader civic issues has been achieved through leadership roles with the American Institute of Architects, the Van Alen Institute, the United States Green Building Council, Architects Designers and Planners for Social Responsibility, Yestermorrow, various academic institutions and other activist groups. Our ongoing participation in social discourse and policy debate has been both professionally important and personally satisfying.

Immediately after 9/11, the firm helped initiate, organize, and support New York New Visions. Responding to the desire to bring the design community to the table with one voice in the planning for rebuilding of the World Trade Center and Lower Manhattan, this volunteer group rapidly grew to more than two-dozen professional and civic groups with some 500 active participants representing 30,000 constituents. The effort was instrumental in setting principles and guidelines for the planning process, creating public awareness of the need for quality design and sustainability, and serving as a sounding board to assist the governing authorities. This was the first time, to my knowledge, that all the design disciplines worked harmoniously together with complete commonality of purpose. It is the pooling of the resources, the power of collective thinking, and the ability to speak with unity that continues to make New York New Visions so effective. We must endeavor to keep this spirit alive.

Our steadfast commitment to change and professional growth within the firm exemplifies our capacity to respond and adapt to a changing world. We have recently experienced a major transition. With mutual good will, my co-founding partner, Robert Fox, Jr., left the firm after 25 years. Since we had shared so many experiences and the joy of building a firm together, parting was not easy. Fortunately we had established a succession plan that was designed to position younger partners to carry the firm forward after the departure of Bob and/or myself.

A merger with Jambhekar Strauss PC in 2000 added professional diversity and strength to the firm and helped solidify our commitment to promoting and nurturing critical connections between architecture and the planning and infrastructure settings that surround it. This was a major step toward ensuring the long-term viability of the firm. Diversity—of backgrounds, of disciplines and of design philosophy—will continue to strengthen the firm. With the success of the merger and the promotion of Dan Kaplan to senior principal, the succession plan has thus far exceeded our expectations.

The five principals—Dan Kaplan, Sudhir Jambhekar, Sylvia Smith, Mark Strauss, and myself—are unified in our approach to responsible design and our commitment to engagement. We have two associate principals, Heidi Blau and Managing Director Tim Milam, 16 associates, and a large group of very talented professionals who are fully integrated into our culture and are energetically pushing us to greater heights—a sure sign of long life.

Today, the world is severely stressed, both politically and ecologically. Its future is perhaps more in doubt now than at any time since World War II. This is the context in which we work to refine and expand responsible design. Perhaps the most tangible threat to the survival of our planet is sprawl and its many side effects.

To discourage uncontrolled destruction
of our landscape, it is essential that we in the
building design and planning industry find ways
to make sustainable high-density living a viable
and desirable lifestyle.

Design professionals cannot disengage themselves
from these realities. We must capitalize on this
moment in history by seizing every opportunity
for architects and planners to leverage our broad
knowledge and effect change. In the coming
years, we at Fox & Fowle Architects look forward
to an increased role in the movement toward a
more livable and sustainable society. We must all
unify our efforts, expand our horizons, and apply
bigger, linked thinking.

# Designing for the Built Realm

by Kira L. Gould

Architects, planners, and urban designers contribute to the built environment by creating opportunities for human experience and engaging in a dialogue with the social and cultural context. At Fox & Fowle, that dialogue is energetic and diverse. The work process is a deep investigation of fit and form. Fit is a broad, comprehensive idea that includes honing project purpose, context, community, and region to achieve a complementary balance; it is intimately bound up with form, which derives from rigorous exploration and reconciliation of diverse ideas about program, spatial relationships, materiality, and sustainability. The end results are places with social, environmental, and aesthetic integrity—responsible contributions to the built environment.

These contributions embody "good design," which Fox & Fowle defines, in general terms, as work that fulfills its purpose, responds to its context, makes optimal use of materials and methods of production, and does so in an artful and inventive way. Bruce Fowle sums it up succinctly: "We advocate solutions that use less, do more, and relate better to their surroundings than their conventional counterparts."

These solutions evolve through a design process that is sensitive to craft and materiality. Sudhir Jambhekar articulates that sensitivity: "We care deeply about the design and about how the parts go together, how it lasts, and how it is used." One consequence of this concern is that much of the work has a quality of simplicity or directness, even where the ideas and building technologies are themselves complex. Attention to the material expression renders a building that seems to "understand" its material and the methods of production and construction that assembled it.

The work represents a synthesis of mid- to late-twentieth-century Modern concepts of function, form making, and place. The firm and its work are influenced by Corbusian notions of rationality and pure form, Colin Rowe's ideas about place and context, and Christian Norbert-Schulz's convictions about the importance of spirit of place. The architects at Fox & Fowle cultivate an ideal of design that encourages positive social and cultural change. They acknowledge an ethical responsibility to the work and to those whose lives are affected by it. Formally, Modernism plays a strong role; a clear expression of material and structure is always evident.

This eclectic reformulation of Modernism focuses on function and the machine in order to celebrate human complexities. In broad terms, the firm's thinking is based on a Modernism expanded to be more humanist, pluralist, and responsive, without relentlessly insisting on repression of history as advocated by orthodox Modernists.

The architectural content may vary for different principals, but there are shared values and common goals among them. Sylvia Smith, alluding to the shared quest for meaningful and responsible design, says, "We each work, in our own ways, to create a simple, declarative aesthetic that is not wasteful of gesture or resource."

This design philosophy, which acknowledges that many roads may lead to the desired end, underlies a commitment to collaboration within the design team and beyond. Bruce, extolling the virtues of teamwork, notes: "We promote collaboration in part because we know there is rarely one definitive answer. Finding the 'obvious' simple solution often takes great effort and comes through debate and reevaluation." The firm celebrates the notion that all design decisions are intertwined and informed by other disciplines. Working closely with other professionals "is an essential part of a truly integrated process," insists Sudhir Jambhekar.

Collaboration is dynamic, animating, and sometimes challenging. When different personalities and design attitudes come together in collaboration, the creative tension pushes exploration ever further and results in strong design. As in formal debate, this design process enables the firm to consider and respond to a multitude of arguments, opinions, and challenges that might not otherwise be addressed at any stage of a project's development. Anticipating and understanding these alternate positions—and calibrating the design in response—infuses the architecture with quality, character, and integrity.

As Bruce puts it, "Design excellence is accomplished through collaboration, which fosters more innovative and enduring solutions." This includes teaming within the office, a strong relationship with the client, partnering with other architects, designers, and planners, and working closely with engineers, contractors, construction managers, artists, and other project consultants. Bruce further insists that building synergistic teams, both internally and externally, "is itself an art form."

Integrating the work of architects and engineers is an aspect of the firm's move toward low-impact, high-performance projects. "Working with talented engineers," Sudhir says, "we are exploring new possibilities of structure, materials, and form that have impact on efficiency and the qualities of architecture that provoke human response."

Collaboration with public officials, agencies, and community groups adds complexity and time to the process. The firm recognizes the critical nature of that complexity; it is a part of the bigger, linked thinking behind program exploration and design. As Mark Strauss explains, "Our design process is exploratory, comparative, and highly iterative, and the journey is shared with the client and stakeholders."

That notion of a collective journey can also be found inside the Fox & Fowle office. The culture is open and inquisitive. There is palpable excitement about the work in progress and the contributions made by team members at all levels. "We are all committed to design excellence, professionalism, and social consciousness. We encourage young people to grow and to lead," Bruce says. "We expect them to contribute, which is a growth process for them and a regeneration process for the firm." Another important aspect of the culture is the healthy symbiosis between design and production. The segregation of departments that seems to rise up as some firms grow has been conspicuously absent at Fox & Fowle.

Dan Kaplan believes this accommodation of diverse talents and perspectives sets the firm culture apart: "The principals are fluent in a wide range of building types and scales. We don't do only one thing, and we don't expect our colleagues to be one-dimensional either. We believe that an exchange of ideas and experiences is important to the continual learning of everyone at the firm; it is a nurturing process for all of us." This office culture results in an architecture that is responsive to the social and cultural context.

## GENESIS OF FORM: PROGRAM

Architecture derives meaning from its circumstances. Program, which entails much more than an exposition of mundane spatial requirements, is fundamental to the conception and construction of meaningful architecture. Whether overtly declared or implied, program can include the clues that allow an architect to enrich a space and form with character. A wide-ranging inquiry into program results in a project that transcends literal requirements and makes a statement about its owner's aspirations. The program reveals opportunities for interpretation and reinvention. These are the seeds from which functional solutions develop into projects with cohesion, balance, relevance, and longevity.

Program is often understood to be little more than the quantitative assessment of a project—lists of rooms, levels, adjacencies, circulation patterns. It is often overlooked as the locus of a project's true intentions. "In the program, we find the poetic aspects of a project that provide the qualitative character. We often rethink program needs," Sylvia says, "to create 'new' experiences within the overlay of rigorous demands of complex projects. We identify the intangibles that breathe life into the projects."

The creation of meaningful places begins with the exploration of project goals and purpose. Bruce and Sylvia aptly summarized the practical, aesthetic, and philosophical ramifications of program in that exploration:

1

2

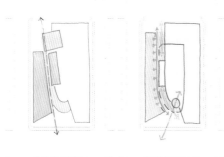

3

*"A building's reason for being is to accommodate human activity. However, while satisfying the functional requirements of a building program, architecture, like art, must also promote endeavors, elicit responses, communicate meaning, and enrich life. The fundamental contribution of art is to deepen the understanding of ourselves and the world in which we live. The artist/architect has the power to convey emotion to others through deep-seated and unchangeable associations created by proportion, scale, mass, rhythm, space, shape, light, shadow, color, and texture. Through shared values, meaning is communicated. This cumulative emotional effect and aesthetic communication must be linked to a building's symbolic and programmatic purpose and contribute to its sense of place."*
– American Craft Museum grand opening presentation, 1985.

## Intentions

*"We find innovative ways of using programmatic elements to enliven space and form."*
– Bruce Fowle

Thorough readings of program reveal clues and point the way to the resolution of apparently conflicting agendas. The program for the new Martin J. Whitman School of Management building (1) at Syracuse University contained clear ideas about how best to keep the school's three departments distinct and yet united. What was not stated in the program was the desire for the school to make a clear statement about its own complex identity. The team was determined that the building, situated at the edge of the campus, would relate to both the campus and the greater community.

Interpreting and synthesizing these discrete goals, Fox & Fowle unfolded the cloistered form of a conventional campus building into a composition of distinct masses, each of which expresses its programmatic function. The team shifted the atrium, programmed as an internal courtyard, to the exterior as the public set piece of the composition. The assemblage is connected by a multi-level transparent circulation spine running the length of the site. This glazed interior street, combined with the courtyard, dynamically animates the building and provides the school with a non-programmed but much desired visual link to the campus.

"We interpreted the program to enhance the functional requirements and to highlight the internal and external orientation," Sylvia explains. As a link between low-rise campus buildings, a commercial retail district, an over-sized hotel, and various medium-scaled academic buildings, the building had to be dynamic, rather than a static, internalized edifice. "The creation of appropriate massing harmonized disparate elements and enabled the building to engage its surroundings, which is how that linkage was realized," she says.

In the School of Management project, space is shaped to create the most value to its occupants while generating a sense of identity and interconnection throughout. In the process, collaboration, "bigger," linked thinking, careful consideration of context, and rigorous exploration of program have led to clear definition and realization of architectural intent.

## Redefinition

*"The program often includes clues about the project that the client has not articulated. These clues can redirect the project, crystallize its concept, or provoke a salient unifying aspect."*
– Dan Kaplan

Study of the program often results in project redefinition and redirection. The American Bible Society (2) came to Fox & Fowle seeking a renewed prominence for their New York City headquarters. The designers' immersion in program intangibles revealed that the Society wanted a visible symbol to signal and signify their commitment to proactive outreach and communication with the public.

The resulting creation is an armature of communication, a transparent glass pavilion etched with "in the beginning" in many languages and backed by video screens. The pavilion, drawing from the internal program, reaches out to the street figuratively and formally. The solution is simple, yet surprising, energetic, and entirely fresh in an established neighborhood. At night, it is a beacon; by day, it invites passersby to pause, read, and come inside. The pavilion embodies the organization's outreach mission and engages its lively street.

In this case, the client wanted a renovation and a new, fresh face. The design team provided that through a pavilion that is a contemporary, enticing expression of mission, message, and presence. "We were able to make a strong, engaging statement that the client had not previously imagined," Sylvia says.

## Reaching beyond

*"Program must be linked to the greater whole. The program for a speculative, high-rise office building, for example, cannot be solely about its tenant space and its lobby. It must deal with the external space it is defining in its urban context, its relation to the public realm, and how it will involve the light and air."*
– Bruce Fowle

High-rise programs contain a unique set of conditions (such as size, scale and visibility) that enable architects to reach beyond program so that they can simultaneously provide a community gesture and increase the value of the project for the client. In the case of the unbuilt Merrill Lynch Headquarters (3) in the Colgate redevelopment area of Jersey City, New Jersey, this meant finding ways for a large new office building to help create a sense of place. Given the remoteness from Manhattan corporate circles and the blandness of the new development setting, it was important that the project help introduce a sense of urbanity to the neighborhood and provide space for interaction between Merrill Lynch entities in adjacent existing buildings. Fox & Fowle's non-programmed intervention was a seven-story public winter garden at the base that allowed the project to contribute to a sense of place on the street. In this way, the project will become a contributing part of its evolving urban neighborhood.

"Merrill Lynch recognizes the value of a good working environment," Dan says, reflecting on the particular requirements of this project. "They wanted this project to express their mandate to provide a healthy, sustainable environment." Working with interior design, human resource, and environmental specialists, the Fox & Fowle team distilled this directive into guidelines for daylighting, air quality, spatial arrangements, functional amenities, and high performance systems. The program that evolved from this exercise ultimately influenced the building form, not just its internal layout, allowing the architects to create a non-conventional iconic building that would add a dynamic presence to both New Jersey's Hudson River skyline and the streetscape.

## Planning

*"We are able to see the bigger picture and provide a comprehensive assessment of what might be possible."*
– Mark Strauss

The search for unwritten aspirations can be complex in planning projects, especially given the large number of stakeholders. Both client and the community are usually involved and their priorities rarely align seamlessly. Program exploration is the first opportunity for the planners and architects to begin balancing the economic, environmental, and social goals of such projects.

In Queens, an ambitious planning project for Jamaica Center (4) is being realized to complement the new Airtrain link from Jamaica Station to the John F. Kennedy International Airport. This will add to the importance of Jamaica Station as an intermodal facility; it already serves Long Island Railroad and New York City subway and bus lines. As a consequence, the area is positioned to become a new commercial center, just an eight-minute ride from the airport. The planning team listened closely to area residents and business owners and created a program of development strategies and design guidelines to both spur growth and control its impact.

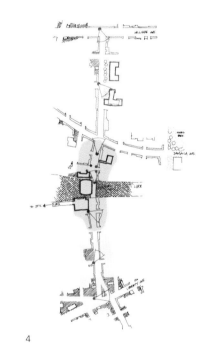

4

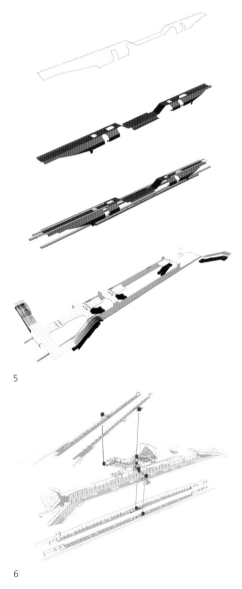

5

6

While it was an unwritten aspiration, it was clear to the planning team that there was a desire to connect the community long divided by the viaduct. The project represents a new kind of "runway city" revitalization model for communities close to transit hubs and the businesses that support them. "Our planning approach went beyond the identification of development sites," Mark says. "We established key linkages between the new terminal and the existing downtown by a series of open spaces, which provided a focus for redevelopment and connections to the community." The plan was the result of a multi-disciplinary process that involved planners, designers, economists, engineers, and others.

## Infrastructure

*"It is important to think about infrastructure as a critical component of the built environment, one that benefits from good design and suffers without it."*
– Sudhir Jambhekar

People have significantly more contact with infrastructure each day than they do with most buildings in their communities. The firm sees infrastructure as intimately interconnected with architecture and equally deserving of attention and care.

For the Second Avenue Subway project (5), important conceptual work has gone into the at-grade points at which the public meets the system. As the team explored the project, they realized that its unwritten aspirations could contribute to the fluidity of the urban experience and substantially improve the commuter experience. "There was no program for the public spaces when we started, only objective criteria for access width, train operation, and other particulars," Sudhir says. Since most transit work in New York City is related to the restoration of a 100-year-old system, there were no guidelines for how the portals and other surface components would interact with the neighborhoods. "We extended the program from the station platforms to the surface environment," he says, "and developed an approach to creating micro places while keeping the macro north/south linkages in mind."

The Roosevelt Avenue Intermodal Station Rehabilitation (6), began as a relatively straightforward project that was to be based on conceptual diagrams previously prepared by the New York City Transit Authority. This Queens station, one of the busiest in the city's transit system, needed a rebuilding of its grade level terminal, a renovation of its connecting underground and elevated rail components, and a shelter for a bus depot. As Fox & Fowle, working with the Vollmer team and the user agencies, explored the program, they discovered an opportunity to establish a grander, more efficient station than had originally seemed possible. "Transit portals can define one's perception of the city," Dan says. "This was a chance to create a space where people want to congregate, not just pass through."

One challenge was to find ways of innovating within the parameters of New York City Transit's long-standing standards. By embracing issues of maintenance, standard parts, safety, wayfinding, and user expectations, the design team drew the authorities into a realm of new ideas. One of these, sustainability, helped inform the design; passive heating and cooling has accomplished a permeable enclosure of the main area, which creates a chimney effect. The resulting form is a soaring space that serves as a neighborhood beacon.

Expressing the sustainable measures helped the team establish aesthetic direction. The two rail lines were built 30 years apart, so their decorative styles were at odds and gave little hint of an appropriate character for the "neutral" zone of the on-grade terminal. "Our solution," Dan says, "was to create this identifiable element, shaped in part by the ventilation strategy, as an iconic form. This station will help give the neighborhood an identity and create a sense of place." Rather than generating a stylistic debate in a diverse community, the Modernist icon gained public support by avoiding historic or ethnic references —another twist of the programmatic concept.

These two projects are typical of how the Fox & Fowle approach weaves program and bigger, linked thinking. The interventions that follow become their site's morphology and fit into the greater systems of sidewalks, roadways, neighborhoods, districts, and regions.

"Throughout our office and among our colleagues, and beyond, we cultivate a critical consciousness of and attentiveness to the built and natural environment," Sudhir says. "This has direct bearing on how we find resolution between the specific program components of the project and issues of form and massing. We vigorously work through the program process, establishing resolutions. Ultimately, these resolutions organize into meaningful built form."

## FORM MAKING

Form making is based on human experience of the built world, relates to multiple contexts, and results in a series of parts that constitute a multi-faceted yet unified whole.

Fox & Fowle takes into account diverse traditional and non-traditional modes of perceiving and understanding form, with particular concern for how form is logically deduced, how its parts relate to each other and to the whole, and how it is experienced. As the discussion moves among these different ways of dealing with form, reference is made to a broad set of aesthetic criteria that includes proportion, scale, order, simplicity, harmony, light, materiality, color, texture, and unity.

"We focus on to the essential and then draw inspiration from a broad array of influences, including the context, the client's vision, and materiality," Sylvia says. "We don't replicate history or layer details for decorative purposes." That essence, Sudhir says, "is based on simplicity and abstraction and informed by functional needs, tectonics, and exploration of new ideas."

The process is centered on the dialogue between people and the built environment they inhabit, and it is full of questions. How will people see, understand, and use the architecture and infrastructure? How do traditional issues of

proportion, scale, and relationship apply? Does form making derive its inspiration from nature, or do designers mimic nature or respond to it in other ways? How do architects deal with the issue of its relationship to the human form?

Here, we explore three ways form is approached and generated at Fox & Fowle: assemblage, metaphor, and balancing of opposites. Implied in each is a keen sense of conscious response and an understanding of how broad planning strategies set the stage for powerful form.

## Assemblage

*"In high-density urban settings, buildings will rarely be seen or experienced as a single composition."*
– Dan Kaplan

In one type of design dialogue, form is generated by an assemblage of different views of the object and its context. This method suits large-scale projects particularly well. "We visualize views or 'cinemagraphic vignettes' of the building—what the entry looks like close up, how the building appears from the opposite corner, and what it looks like from across the river," Dan says.

Exploring these vignettes from various distances and vantage points gives shape to form. Urban high-rise structures are seldom stand-alone elements. Such buildings, Dan says, "should not be designed as precious objects and then inserted into the fabric without consideration of how each view and slice of view functions as a part of the composite whole." Evaluating the views and vistas of the building from several positions, angles, and distances is essential.

Designs for the very dense environment of Times Square in New York illustrate how seldom new buildings there are read as discrete objects. The Reuters Building at 3 Times Square (7) is a composition of interlocking planes and volumes that are understood very differently from the street, a block away, and across town. A lofty, curving glass wall interlocks with masonry base

7

8

9

elements. Commercial signage is linked with the fabric of the architecture. The LED screens at the base are scaled for readability by people on the street; the one on the steel mesh fin at the building's top reads best from afar.

The low-scale elements are accessible and intelligible to people on the street, including a seven-story "drum" at the corner of 42nd Street that is reminiscent of the Rialto Theatre that formerly occupied the site. This shape gives continuity to the abutting complex of historic theatres. The drum's gentle curvature acts as a hinge connecting the 42nd Street venue to the grander-scale Times Square bow-tie area.

"The overall form of the building is an ensemble of ground-based masses supporting a spirited composition of planes that convey a sense of weightlessness," Bruce says. Signage elements are interspersed within the ensemble. Large LED panels suspended from a curvilinear fascia in the lobby and along the street are part of a computer-programmed sequence that moves images horizontally, and up 21 stories at the corner before leap-frogging to the wedge-like fin at the top of the building.

Across the street, the complexity of the Condé Nast Building @ 4 Times Square (8) is concentrated at its base, where dynamic planes and masses intersect. The form becomes more defined, with hard edges delineated, and a crystalline quality. According to Bruce, "The energy of the base is drawn upward through a carefully crafted ensemble of masses and planes that become more composed and vertical as the building rises." Those forces culminate in a tectonic expression at the top where a vibrant 380-foot communication tower marks the skyline.

The design for another neighboring project, Times Square Plaza at 11 Times Square (9), is a composition of set pieces with a highly volumetric result. At the base, large-scale signage dominates; above, a series of volumes, each with its own character, are interlocked into a dynamic arrangement. The dominant volume, a

rectangular glass box that seems stretched to exaggerated angularity, celebrates the corner of the building at Eighth Avenue and 42nd Street, a prominent gateway to the district. Secondary volumes with less permeable skins create the armature.

For the Times Square projects, the intersection of signage and architecture was a key issue. "As the signs, known in Times Square vernacular as 'spectaculars,' became bigger and bigger, they needed to be an integral part of the design," Dan explains. "Integration of visual agendas that are not intrinsically related to the building itself becomes a fundamental principle of form making." Bruce points out that what separated these projects from most of the earlier Times Square architecture was an acceptance of the mandated signage as part of the architecture. "We didn't fight it. We used it to make a kind of Broadway boogie-woogie revival."

For Dan, thinking about views allows the team to tackle the large scale and still think about architectural resolution and detail development. "In dealing with the urban scale, we address the fine-grain experience of it." That fine grain begins in the urban realm, but moves to the interior architecture. The designers envision the views and the "moments" a person would experience when approaching, entering, and moving through the building; these visions shape entry sequences, lobby spaces, and other interiors. In all these projects, the architects sought a formal unity that would hold up when contemplated from any perspective.

## Metaphor

*"Finding the story of a project in its program can be a powerful and poetic way of letting the project goals actually drive the form."*
– Sylvia Smith

After program analysis, Fox & Fowle begins to reveal a project's intrinsic story. Sometimes it is a narrative about form itself, as in the accumulation and release of formal energy that results from the sequence of horizontal and vertical elements of the high-rise buildings discussed above. At other times, the story is a metaphor—the spatial articulation of a direct or indirect message, a mode of expression that invites comparison with the rhetorical strategies of a poetic text.

Sylvia uses this approach, which she finds can be a path to clear architectural articulation "and a result that feels very true to project goals. This approach is really about the deep understanding of the project—letting it be the driver of its own form. The story can be translated into architectural terms. The message is decoded and made accessible and, of course, buildable."

New School University's Arnhold Hall (10) is a good example of metaphor as a form making strategy. A minimal program of meeting and gallery space set the stage for dialogue between client and project team. The project is unified by the use of natural and artificial light as a metaphor for education. Backlit panels, filtered natural light, and other light features lead one through the space, which has a clear sense of sequence and graceful spatial differentiation. One architectural gesture leads to the next and none seems self-conscious.

"We conceived the project as part of the streetscape," Sylvia says. A curved plane draws people and the movement of the street inside. A diagonal plane marks a new zone; this angled wall is continuous from the first to the second floor. A stair between floors is the focal point, and its back wall is awash with light. Visitors are backlit as they ascend and become players in the theatricality of the gallery space. At the entry to the primary space on the upper floor, the sequence is completed by natural light filtering through the wall of windows on the street façade.

A vivid, site-specific mural by Sol LeWitt serves as a connector, visible on both ground and second floors. Working with the artist was central to determining the definition of these planes. Here, art and architecture merge. "You feel like you are in the artwork," Sylvia says. "You discover the composition and sense of wholeness as you move between floors."

Metaphor provides a sense of spatial discovery, not literal storytelling. "We think users will feel that sense as they move through the space and absorb the subtly changing qualities of light from one space to the next," she says. "The experience is neither uniform nor constant. The human body and mind respond to variation."

Wherever you are there is a sense of internal illumination. From place to place that light never vanishes—one's awareness of the luminous glow and physical illumination also suggests a metaphorical passage to enlightenment, as well as the notion of perpetuity implied in the passing on of light from place to place, or, extending the metaphor into the temporal realm, the Platonic vision of a procession of torches passed on from age to age. The nature of the institution, its material requirements, and even the issue of liminality are especially congenial to this metaphorical approach to form making.

In an entirely different context, a statement can be conveyed by deliberately abandoning traditional conventions of signifying and by reformulating typical expectations. Fox & Fowle's concept for a new bank building in Shanghai's new Pudong district is based on the client's desire for an image of accessibility. The design for the Industrial and Commercial Bank of China Headquarters (11) had the unusual condition of establishing rather than addressing context. It was the first of several towers to be built on its block in the new development district. The building is organized into three interlocking masses: two slabs make up the 28-story tower; a low mass at the rear of the site houses retail banking and meeting spaces.

The base of the tower encloses a long banking hall and public space. The glass-clad front slab forms a transparent volume that filters light to the stone central slab—a play on the Chinese vernacular of traceried void juxtaposed with solid.

10

11

12

The banking hall façade of transparent glass with stainless steel banding opens up these public functions to the light and offers views of and from the street, an important goal of the financial institution. Further, it enlivens the street experience. The image and the experience from the street is one of openness and permeability. Bruce notes that this is a stark contrast to much of historic China, "where privacy and opaqueness have ruled for centuries." The client's message of accessibility is dramatically conveyed. The luminous transparency and openness to the street encourage a tantalizing range of metaphorical possibilities. The architecture prompts reflections on the nature of an open society in its infancy.

## Balance

*"Balancing the many opposing forces inherent in each project is an integral component of design inquiry."*
– Sudhir Jambhekar

Oppositions can be found in the program, the site, the building type, the aesthetic context, and many other aspects of a project. The idea of balancing these opposites is integral to the design process as Sudhir sees it. "All elements are part of the larger whole," he says. "Defining those elements, and their relationship to that whole, is most effectively accomplished by considering a series of opposing forces."

Typology brings with it preconceptions and biases that the project teams challenge and explore. Other forces include the urban setting, the shape of the site, its immediate surroundings, the city grid, the social culture, and the community. Each tells something about the place and how the building or buildings can engage it. Negotiating toward balance is a dialogue during which the archetype is challenged, reshaped, and questioned anew.

The identification and balancing of apparent contradictions was especially important in the Queens Museum of Art Competition (12). The contrasting elements were a historic building and

a fast-evolving neighborhood. The Fox & Fowle team, a finalist among 300 entrants, proposed a transformation of the existing steel and concrete Neo-Classical building, sited at a former World's Fair venue, to make a cultural center in an ethnically diverse part of the borough. They stripped it down to the skeleton and wrapped the building with a continuous new skin, which became the building shape. This addresses the critical duality of a historic building and context and an evolutionary institution and community with a solution that appeases both. Another apparent dichotomy was the need for the building image to read at high speeds from the adjacent Grand Central Parkway, as well as from the personal scale of visitors in Flushing Meadows Corona Park. The design resolves this with large, diaphanous "QMA" letters on the side of the building and punched walls that reveal people and activity—another scale of signage—inside.

"Our design for the Queens Museum of Art, like the cultures it represents, is an unfolding story," Sudhir says. "The institution's desire for a metamorphosis from a fine art museum to a cultural arts center led us to design the museum as a celebration of the evolution from past to present and sets a stage for the transition from present to future. As the demographics of the surrounding neighborhood evolve as part of the cityscape in constant flux, so would the Museum."

## Conscious response

*"We create sense of place with buildings that relate to their neighbors through harmony, contrast, invention, or reinvention. Contemporary architecture can not only fit into existing environments, it can enrich them."*
– Bruce Fowle

A common backdrop to the different ways of working at Fox & Fowle is responsiveness to context. A regard for context—site, neighborhood, city, region, climate—encompasses scale, orientation, form, and materiality. It is not a matter of imitating neighbors. Mark puts it in basic terms,

"Buildings relate to each other. This is something that we should embrace, not avoid. That doesn't mean they have to look alike."

For Dan, designing with context in mind is the only way to achieve architecture rather than object: "This can take many forms. You can draw on cues within the context, develop a contrast, complement the context, or create a critical assessment of it. More likely, the response will include more than one of these approaches."

Sudhir puts it another way: "The city is a fabric of strong and neutral elements. You make choices about how to relate form to the surroundings by bringing in additional strong or neutral pieces. Every element is part of a larger whole. Each one has a responsibility to relate to that which is beyond itself. This is what context is really about—not building red brick buildings in red brick neighborhoods."

Engaging context is rife with contradictions, such as the creation of private spaces within the public city. This has repeatedly been addressed in large-scale projects by the introduction of public gathering spaces at the building's base as a means of mediating the two conditions. "Another way to think about this is that nothing in the urban environment is truly private," Sudhir says. "Every time we build under those conditions, we have to think about how the form reads to many more people than those people who will use it every day." At the same time, Bruce adds, "we must invent habitats that satisfy the human need for privacy—places of repose to provide comfort to urban dwellers."

The often abrupt division between public and private space in the urban realm can sometimes be mediated by means of transparency. At the American Bible Society and the Industrial and Commercial Bank of China Headquarters, the firm used this approach to relate projects to their streets. Transparency, even when it encloses an essentially private space that a passerby may never step foot in, can transmit a sense of openness that reads as "good urban neighbor," as in the Reuters Building.

This approach resembles that developed for a vintage Fox & Fowle project, the American Craft Museum (13) in New York City, among the first museums to present an open face to the street from which the collection is visually accessible. Generated by a simple idea about permeability from the street, the sculptural interior space features a broad, curved stair. The design team conceived a 72-foot-long glass wall at the street line, offering a view of the dramatic stairway linking four gallery levels.

"We didn't see the museum as insular," Sylvia says. "We engaged the street. At the time, this was really unusual. But this is the way that we start most projects, with the question 'how does this building live on its street?' " In exploring that question, and answering it with transparency and openness, the team's elegant solution addressed the American Craft Council's two goals: to attract visitors by projecting a distinctive identity to the street, and to create highly flexible galleries adaptable to craft works of many types and scales.

Dealing effectively with context also involves community and regional connectivity. The firm has always viewed buildings as holistic parts of the built environment. Very often, the architecture seeks to blur the boundary between the landscape or cityscape and the interior of the building, heightening this connection. "I see building and designing responsibly as a broad mandate," Sylvia says. "It's part of our sensibility. Buildings should be engaged physically and socially in their communities."

## Setting the stage

*"Our goal is to provide clarity and vision that will support sustainable vitality for the immediate and greater community."*
– Mark Strauss

Urban design and planning set the stage for balanced and responsive form making. The multi-disciplinary nature of Fox & Fowle enables the firm to provide broad, linked thinking while making its practitioners consistently aware of its importance. "As architects, we must think about

13

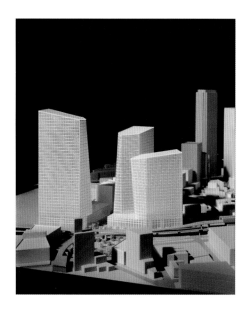

urban design and planning issues," Sudhir says. "That perspective is critical to building responsibly and effectively."

The value of a unified approach is evident in projects such as the Midtown East Development Plan (14), in which a private developer's interest in promoting development in Long Island City, east of Midtown Manhattan in Queens, led to a successful rezoning effort, and a subsequent architectural project. In this case, a multi-disciplinary effort effectively linked political action and community outreach (in the rezoning), economic planning, in tandem with architectural design. The area has a mixed-use character. The plan draws on that character in the development of 4.5 million square feet of commercial space near a transportation hub.

The project also involves major public spaces in Queens Plaza. Development would be concentrated at the two ends of the project area; restrictive zoning between these areas will preserve the scale of Jackson Avenue in response to community concerns. "This will encourage conversion of existing industrial buildings for housing and retail and new construction will be similarly low scale," Mark says. A streetscape with integrated open space will create a recognizable and inviting sense of place. While it is important that the planning of such a place allows it to meld with its surrounding low-rise, quasi-industrial neighborhood, the challenge here was to establish an urban character that it will need for social interaction and pride of place.

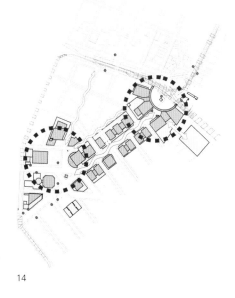

14

Clearly, form making happens in many ways at Fox & Fowle. Balancing opposites, decoding the subtle messages of a project, and assembling and analyzing views of the project and its site, and a thorough consideration of context are all form making techniques. Frequently, these (and other strategies) are used together on the same project. Always, these approaches are overlaid with an awareness of what it means to respond consciously to context and an understanding of the planning framework within which each project exists.

## BEYOND FORM

The intellectual basis of the design and planning process is paired with a dedication to working collectively, building trust-based relationships, engaging in activism, and exploring sustainability strategies. In each of these areas, Fox & Fowle has become a leader.

## Building trust

The trust clients have in Fox & Fowle has allowed the firm to push projects beyond expectations. One might imagine clients bristling at the notion of being "educated" by their design and planning teams. But many clients come to the firm because they want architects and planners who bring leadership and ideas to the table. That trust gives the design and planning teams freedom to innovate. As Bruce points out, "We built that trust by demonstrating that innovative ideas are in their best interests."

With participation of the owner in the design dialogue, new ideas are vetted and preconceptions are challenged. Bruce explains that open communication is what makes it possible to reach a trusted relationship with clients, "We don't 'sell' good, innovative design, but through this style of leadership, we make it possible for clients and owners to 'buy into' it naturally through in-depth understanding and informed decision-making."

Strong relationships forged during some early commissions have enabled the firm to raise the bar on development work in New York. Since the early 1980s, the firm has proven that commercial buildings can be aesthetically powerful benchmarks. The 4 Times Square project for the Durst Organization is the most visible of these, and has become New York's first "green" skyscraper.

"It is very satisfying to be able to create projects that are commercial successes, turn discerning heads with the architecture, and improve the quality of life of a community," Bruce says. "Working within the constraints of urban zoning ordinances, tight site conditions and limited program, while trying to make good architecture is a challenge. With given streetwall heights, set-back lines and sky exposure planes, you are often working with difficult proportions. The trick is to manipulate massing within the rules in a way that creates volumetric harmony without losing square footage or usability." It's important to the firm to understand the project economics and to respond with innovative solutions that take the architecture beyond the "zoning envelope."

At the top of the Condé Nast Building @ 4 Times Square (15), Dan says, "We knew we had to create something to complete the poetry of the architecture. We discovered that the height and relative isolation of the tower was ideal for communication systems. We demonstrated the economic value, which became the foundation for an expressive top." The only architectural move not related to this system is a 60-foot steel cube frame designed to complete the tectonic expression and set a visual framework for the communications element. The architects suggested commercial signage at the top that would culminate in the four vertical faces of the massing, create a burst of energy, enlivening the building and marking Times Square on the skyline.

Trust was at the heart of the Downtown New Rochelle Master Plan (16), which involved close collaboration with public officials and many other community stakeholders. The firm ran workshops with a cross-section of those with interests or ideas about what should (and should not) happen downtown. Mark emphasizes that it was important to meet with local officials and stakeholders prior to developing concepts: "We went to them without preconceived notions. We wanted to know what they thought the strengths and weaknesses of their city were, and what they wanted to see happen." The community identified priorities, including mixed uses, ground floor retail, and walkability. "In subsequent sessions," he continues, "We described what we heard and referred to local issues as we discussed emerging concepts." Four schemes resulted, each with a different goal and

with varying levels of intervention. Features included creating a gateway to downtown, establishing linkages, and public greens.

## Shaping public policy

The firm has a tradition of strong civic involvement. Intimate, personal connections to neighborhoods, communities, and institutions bring richness and relevance to the work. Some firm leaders are educators; they learn through teaching. Many are active in professional associations and public and civic organizations, such as the American Institute of Architects (AIA), the American Planning Association, the US Green Building Council, and Architects, Designers and Planners for Social Responsibility (Bruce helped found the New York chapter).

The firm has been a vocal advocate of policy changes, such as New York State Green Building Tax Credit, which passed in 2000 and has since been used as a model for several other states seeking to encourage sustainable architecture and development.

Several members of the firm have helped increase the role of the New York Chapter of the American Institute of Architects. Fox & Fowle was instrumental in leading several of the AIA's Planning and Urban Design Committee studies of proposed zoning changes in New York City, explorations that were widely recognized as critical to the public dialogue at the time.

After the World Trade Center destruction, the firm was an early initiator of New York New Visions, a coalition of design and planning organizations. "We knew that if such a coalition was not formed, the design/planning profession would lose the opportunity to be part of the process," Bruce says. "The effectiveness exceeded our expectations," Mark adds. "New York New Visions (17) has earned the trust and respect of the policy makers, and we continue to be their sounding board."

15

16

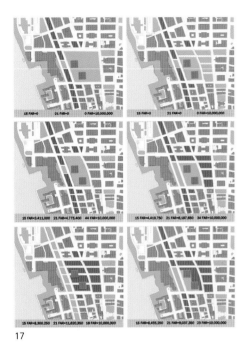

17

## Sustainability

Working toward a more socially, environmentally, and economically sustainable condition has been central to Fox & Fowle since the firm's inception in 1978. The firm has a holistic understanding of sustainability as a social, economic, and ethical pursuit. But they are candid about how far there is to go in this area. "We are finding high-tech and low-tech ways of making buildings more efficient, healthier, and more user-friendly," Dan says. "These are important aspects of sustainability."

But where the recent rise of public awareness about sustainable design gives cause for optimism, there are many hurdles. "The rate of consumption of goods and land has never been higher," Bruce laments. "Until our society is willing to make meaningful changes in lifestyle, real progress is a tremendous challenge. To paraphrase Janine Benyus in *Biomimicry*, we are out of balance with nature."

Fox & Fowle, like many other firms, is exploring architecture that meaningfully expresses its sustainability. "To achieve and maintain a level of design expression where sustainability prevails," Dan says enthusiastically, "is one of the most exciting and serious challenges that we face." He hopes that the dialogue within the firm and beyond will deepen. "Divisions between culture and nature seem to be collapsing. Soon buildings will be able to adapt and 'learn.' These are exciting developments for designers, and they suggest real possibilities for the built environment. We plan to be out front on this and other new manifestations of greener and smarter built form."

What does it mean for people who routinely build big and tall to talk seriously about sustainable design? It means that they become advocates for livable density. Fox & Fowle does this through planning, including the reuse and reclamation of the urban core and brownfields for contemporary uses, and by bringing to bear a deep understanding and appreciation of public transportation infrastructures. It is also effected through the firm's participation in the

stewardship of institutions that make cities strong, and through leadership in integration of architecture, planning, and engineering to achieve an environmentally "light touch."

"We aim to create a dense environment that captures the public imagination, thereby helping serve as a competitor to the entropy of sprawl," Dan says. This kind of thinking highlights the role of reinvention in the work, and how the design teams are constantly interpreting changing social conditions. The firm promotes the positive, humanistic aspects of density through architectural expression that creates great places and memorable forms infused with the vitality of this information-rich, global era.

The firm's Helena project, a 590-unit residential rental building in New York City, is destined to be the first non-mandated building of its type to receive a gold rating under LEED, the U.S. Green Building Council's rating program. The building should set a new standard for high-rise residential construction.

There is a strong role for sustainability in rural settings, too. The Black Rock Forest Center (18), situated in the 3,750-acre Black Rock Forest, needed a setting for environmental study and research for staff, scientific teams, and student groups. The site-sensitive building orientation and form, material use, and energy consumption management make it a model sustainable facility. "The client's mission of environmental monitoring and study allowed us to aggressively introduce sustainable measures, including geothermal heating, composting toilets, and locally harvested materials," explains Sylvia. These measures were seamlessly integrated into a light-filled building that is not only a regional center for environmental study but is also a model of sensitive and sustainable building design. The complex is also designed as an educational tool. There are viewing windows to demonstrate sustainable construction technologies, building systems, and materials.

The firm is a leading advisor on sustainable issues. For the Hugh L. Carey Battery Park City Authority (BPCA), New Jersey Transit, and the

New York City Transit Authority, Fox & Fowle teams crafted guidelines for future sustainable projects and operations. BPCA commissioned the firm to develop the country's first Sustainable Design Guidelines created for high-density residential buildings, followed by Sustainable Design Guidelines for Commercial and Institutional Buildings. These stringent guidelines are being used to select developer/architect teams for new projects. The firm consulted for the New York City Transit Authority's upgrade of existing facilities to make them better neighbors, have healthier indoor environments, and be more operationally efficient. Guidelines for future transit projects (19) address many other issues such as site management, water conservation, construction methodology, and operations.

The firm strongly resists the compartmentalization of sustainability. "Sustainable attributes are not separate from the rest of the process or product," Sylvia says. "Before 'green' was part of the lexicon, we were recycling materials, finding responsible ways to handle construction and demolition waste, and worrying about indoor air quality and other issues that are now identified as green. The sustainable design movement has codified such efforts, but they are, and have always been, really about creating quality environments in a responsible way."

Dan sees sustainability as an integral part of creating architecture. It relates, he says, "To making urban living better than its alternatives, and making architecture and urban spaces healthier and more effective, not only more attractive. It is broad thinking about new ways for people to move about cities. But it is also specific: making a rail station effective and beautiful so that people want to use it…and then maintain and restore it for years."

## Into the future

Fox & Fowle Architects has experienced a significant transformation in the last few years. Beginning with the merger, which strengthened design diversity and leadership at the firm and also bolstered the commitment to an

interdisciplinary approach, the firm has been restructuring and repositioning to allow it to move boldly and effectively forward into the future.

Recent leadership transitions have been an important part of helping to guide the firm into its next form. "Transitions are always a challenge," Bruce says. "I feel lucky that ours are so smooth, in large part because we prepare ahead of time to deal with change. We are already feeling the positive effects of our reorganized structure. Everyone at the firm is energized by what we are doing and where we are going."

Within the firm, the shift is part of a broad, natural evolution that firm leaders see as evidence of the health and vibrancy of the organization. There is a strong commitment to creating a structure that allows the many talented individuals at all levels of the firm to take their own leadership roles. "We recognize that our strongest asset is our people," Bruce says. "This is true no matter how long our history or how strong our last project. We are particularly fortunate in these times to have a very committed and extremely talented staff, and we intend to make sure that they have every opportunity to contribute and to lead."

With a long history of success, excellence, and innovation, Fox & Fowle is today characterized by a strong commonality of purpose among principals and associates. There is a palpable synergy among diverse voices, and the sense of a shared commitment to exploration and pursuit of excellence. Today, the array of projects is a great deal broader than it was ten years ago, in both typology and design approach.

The firm is positioned to respond to a future in which few things are certain. This thoughtful group sees those uncertainties as exciting challenges and opportunities to enrich people's lives and the lives of their communities. They believe that by remaining true to shared values, celebrating diverse ideas and approaches, and being as flexible as twenty-first-century life demands, they will continue to contribute positively and responsibly to the built environment.

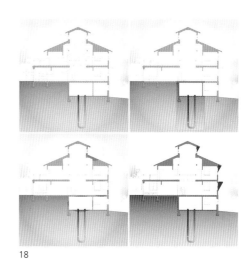

18

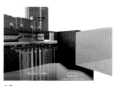

19

*Kira L. Gould is a Boston-based freelance journalist who writes for* Metropolis, The Boston Globe, Architectural Record, *and other publications, and for groups such as the Institute for Urban Design and the American Architectural Foundation. She is a senior associate in communications with Gould Evans and is active in the national American Institute of Architects' Committee on the Environment.*

# SELECTED PROJECTS

1

2

New York City (Manhattan)
Client: American Bible Society
Completion: 1998

# American Bible Society

3

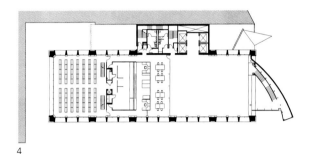

4

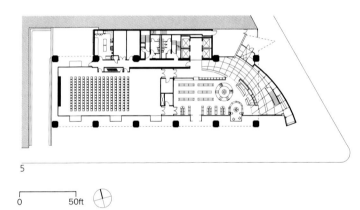

5

1   New entrance canopy and pavilion
2   Concept sketch
3   Pavilion addition from Broadway
4   Plan: second floor
5   Plan: ground floor

0        50ft

The American Bible Society, a publisher of the Bible in many languages, challenged the architectural team to create an addition and renovation which would bring a new presence to the institution's headquarters on Broadway and 61st Street in New York City. The Society requested an architectural design that would convey the organization's mission, improve its accessibility, and engage the public. The design team explored these abstract needs in conjunction with tangible functional requirements, developing a sweeping building form that metaphorically embraces the street and acts as a beacon of light and inspiration.

The building's street presence provided the central project thesis. The design team explored the program for ideas about how to translate the organization's desired posture—a more welcoming profile than the existing facility provided—into a spatial reality. The designers drew on the desire for an increased presence and saw an opportunity to use that presence as a way to demonstrate the institution's message and literally invite passersby inside.

The resulting all-glass sculpted pavilion complements the original 1960s concrete structure. Its glass form begins inside, engaging the new bookstore, concierge desk, and entry area, and flares into a spacious volume on the plaza outside. The pavilion walls are etched with inscriptions of "in the beginning" in many languages, representative of the Bible translations issued by the Society. A 36-screen media wall is integral to the composition.

The transparency and lightness of the pavilion allows the passerby to easily perceive the interior space while leaving the volume somewhat undefined, a complement to the forceful form of the building. The curving pavilion gives the original reserved façade an open and fresh face. This single intervention transforms the building's image.

31

6   Pavilion addition
7   Staircase connecting
    gallery and ground level
8   Gallery and library
9   Bird's-eye view
Opposite
    Soaring view

6

7

8

9

1 New building addition
2 Elevation
3 Reception
4 Transverse section
5 Detail

1

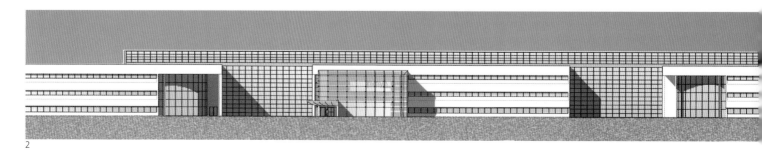

2

# Avaya Headquarters

3

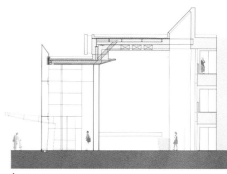

4

To reinvent an early 1980s office building for this international communications company, Fox & Fowle Architects created the arc of suspended glass fins that sweeps across the façade. This three-story lobby space, with a stainless steel and glass canopy—the crisp arc of suspended glass—is an airy welcome to the building. From within, the soaring space offers views and creates a commodious, comfortable portal to the work environment.

A sweeping glass-clad form was used as part of the renovation of the Avaya Headquarters in Basking Ridge, New Jersey. In the suburban context, the glass wall is a kind of catcher's mitt. Whereas the American Bible Society's glass wall was pushing out into its urban neighborhood, this glass wall is a gesture to draw people and attention inward: scaled to be read by drivers passing by, it acts as the building's attractor.

Structural glass fins support the wall, and bands of ceramic frit lend order to the expanse. The glazing is secured to the support members with countersunk precision fittings. During the day, the potentially opaque impression of the glass is softened by ample interior natural lighting from a lobby skylight, and from a suspended Avaya sign (which is readable from both back and front). The effect is simple, elemental, and dynamic. Lightness and technology characterize the renovations throughout the building.

5

1

2

3

4

Sheffield, Massachusetts
Client: Berkshire School
Completion: 2002

# Berkshire School Dormitories

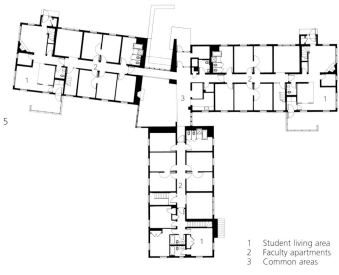

5

1   Student living area
2   Faculty apartments
3   Common areas

1   Southwest campus
2   Site plan
3   MacMillan Hall from northeast
4   MacMillan Hall from southwest
5   Plan: ground floor
6   Crispin-Gordon-Rose Hall faculty unit

6

For the Berkshire School, a private boarding school in Sheffield, Massachusetts, Fox & Fowle Architects created a sensitive student housing addition on the 500-acre campus. The project team examined the program, explored the campus, and listened to the client to uncover possibilities for the new buildings. The design team knew how the buildings would function, but they explored the site and program for clues about how they would fit into the composition of existing structures and the topography of the site. They realized that the exterior spaces created would be as important as the interior ones. These would be the spaces that define the feel and use of the campus neighborhood.

The team proposed two three-wing, 19,000-square-foot dormitories with T-shaped footprints.

The pinwheel plan provided for three separate 10-student "cottages," each with its own faculty unit, interconnected with a common entry. By angling the relationships and offsetting the floor levels, the buildings were nestled into their site. They respond well to the site's hilly topography; the buildings have a feeling of being anchored there.

Beyond the airy central commons, the geometry shifts, providing distinction between public and private spaces. The double-height common space is dynamic; at the second floor, walkways connect the wings. Responding to the emphasis on group activities, the designers created lively, engaging spaces. The lightness of the commons contrasts with the heavy stone pier at the entry

to each dormitory. Moving into the space is a progression from grounded, solid entry into an uplifting, soaring space: a clear interplay between the modernist sculpted space and the more traditional expressions of the cottages.

The new buildings make architectural reference to existing buildings on the 95-year-old campus, providing an aesthetic bridge. The proportions and design of the classic English manor house are evident here; white stucco cladding, pitched metal roofs, and large chimneys create a strong profile visible from the Route 41 approach. While the design draws strongly on the campus vernacular and is defined by clean lines, meticulously detailed, the buildings make a simple, crisp statement.

7

7   Crispin-Gordon-Rose Hall
    from northwest

8   Common area

9   MacMillan Hall entry

8

9

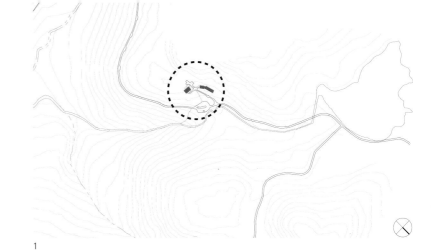

1

2

Cornwall, New York
Client: Black Rock Forest Consortium
Completion: 1999, 2004

# Black Rock Forest Center

3

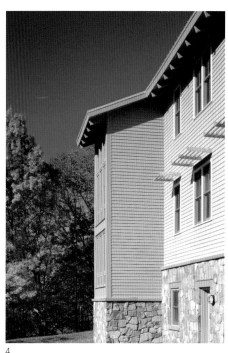

4

After the completion of a comprehensive master plan, Fox & Fowle Architects designed the first phase of the Black Rock Forest Center for Science and Education. This modern research and educational facility is located at the Black Rock Forest Consortium's field station within the 3,750-acre Black Rock Forest. The Center provides a needed setting for environmental study and research for staff, scientific teams, and student groups ranging in age from kindergarten through graduate school.

The Center's site-sensitive design, building form, material use, and energy consumption management make it a model facility in keeping with the sustainable mission of the academic consortium. The cohesive building form and detailing are influenced by local vernacular gabled structures. The rectangular footprint and east/west orientation maximizes solar exposure while minimizing building mass, and individual southern window overhangs minimize summer heat gain.

A central atrium topped by a roof monitor provides internal visual focus for the building while also

bringing natural light and ventilation to the building's center. It is the metaphorical "clearing in the forest." A highly efficient geothermal heat pump system provides heating and cooling within the well-insulated envelope. A composting toilet system replaces a conventional solid waste system. Building materials such as the stone veneer are from local sources; soil, rock, and trees that were disturbed were reused in the new construction. The columns, which frame the atrium, are trees from the surrounding forest, as is the oak paneling. The fine-tuning of the building design was aided by a computer-modeled energy consumption analysis. The final design consumes 45 percent less energy annually compared to a traditional structure meeting all applicable codes.

Phase II of this project, the Lodge, is incorporated into the natural bench that parallels the roadway to the Center, establishing a campus in the forest with minimal impact on the natural setting. The main floor houses four- and six-person sleeping rooms and support space for student

stays in the forest. The building is organized around a floor-to-ceiling glazed central gathering space that is framed by near views of the ridge to the northeast and the long views of the forest to the southwest. Natural light and ventilation are also provided from clerestory windows in the raised gable that crowns the communal space. The central hall to each wing of sleeping rooms is punctuated with operable skylights above each grouping of room entries. Natural light animates the building's logical organization.

The sustainable strategies of the Center are fine-tuned and extended in the Lodge. The high-performance building envelope utilizes dense-pack cellulose and structural insulated roof panels. A greywater recovery system recycles water for site irrigation. Wood and stone from the forest are featured in the building, including the four hemlock columns and pine wainscot in the gathering space. The Center for Science and Education is an ideal venue from which to manage the Black Rock Forest as an interactive part of a larger natural system.

5

6

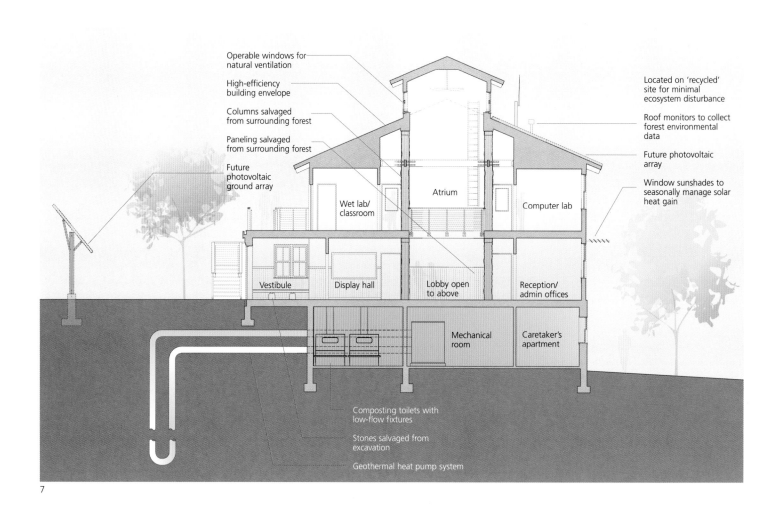

Operable windows for
natural ventilation

High-efficiency
building envelope

Columns salvaged
from surrounding forest

Paneling salvaged
from surrounding forest

Future
photovoltaic
ground array

Located on 'recycled'
site for minimal
ecosystem disturbance

Roof monitors to collect
forest environmental
data

Future photovoltaic
array

Window sunshades to
seasonally manage solar
heat gain

Atrium

Wet lab/
classroom

Computer lab

Vestibule

Display hall

Lobby open
to above

Reception/
admin offices

Mechanical
room

Caretaker's
apartment

Composting toilets with
low-flow fixtures

Stones salvaged from
excavation

Geothermal heat pump system

7

8

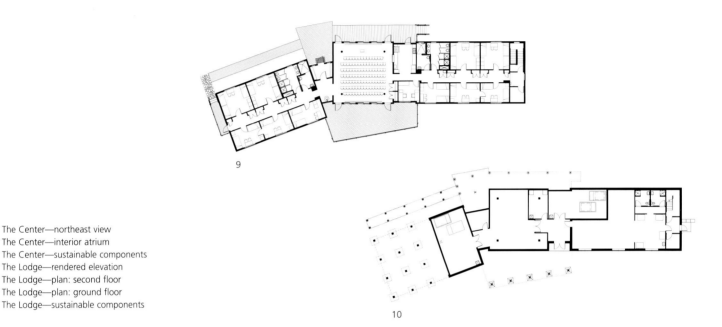

9

10

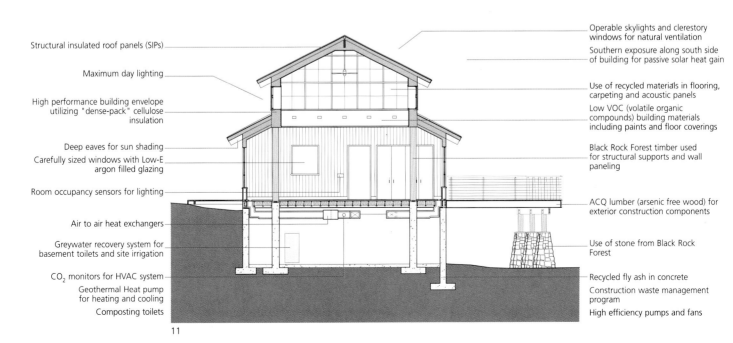

Structural insulated roof panels (SIPs)

Maximum day lighting

High performance building envelope utilizing "dense-pack" cellulose insulation

Deep eaves for sun shading

Carefully sized windows with Low-E argon filled glazing

Room occupancy sensors for lighting

Air to air heat exchangers

Greywater recovery system for basement toilets and site irrigation

$CO_2$ monitors for HVAC system

Geothermal Heat pump for heating and cooling

Composting toilets

Operable skylights and clerestory windows for natural ventilation

Southern exposure along south side of building for passive solar heat gain

Use of recycled materials in flooring, carpeting and acoustic panels

Low VOC (volatile organic compounds) building materials including paints and floor coverings

Black Rock Forest timber used for structural supports and wall paneling

ACQ lumber (arsenic free wood) for exterior construction components

Use of stone from Black Rock Forest

Recycled fly ash in concrete

Construction waste management program

High efficiency pumps and fans

11

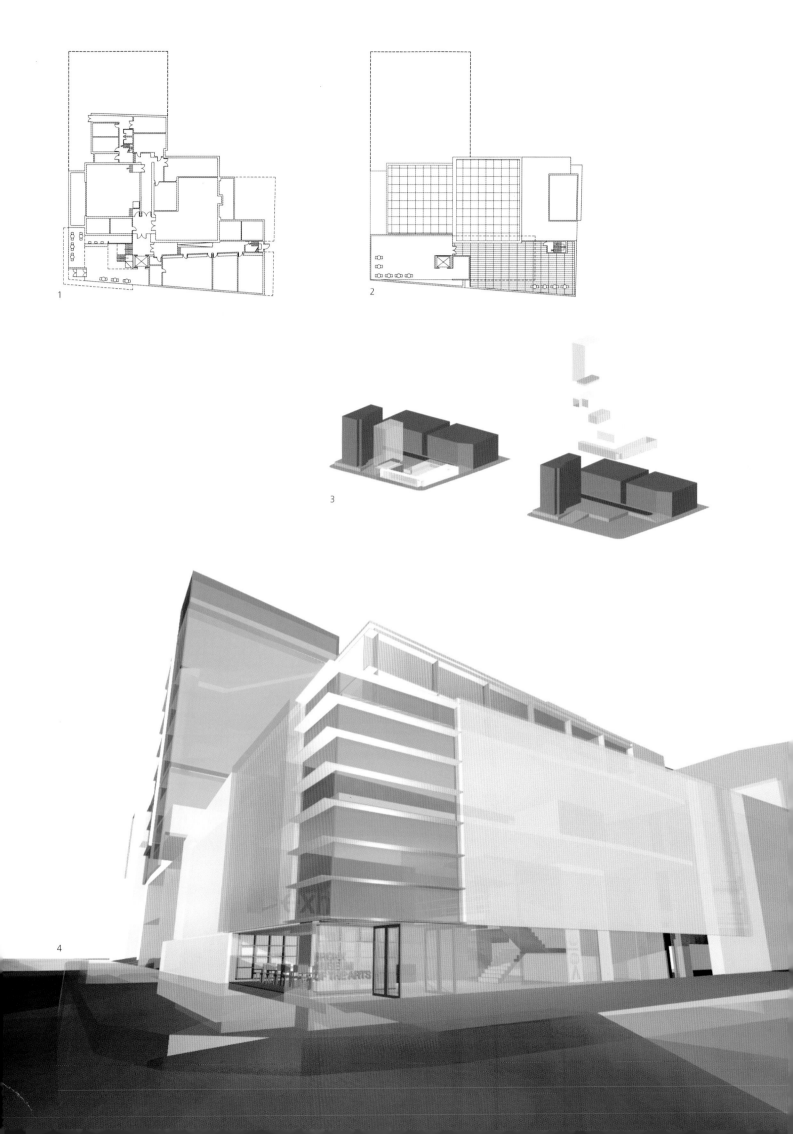

1

2

3

4

New York City (Bronx)
Client: Bronx Museum of the Arts, New York City
Department of Design and Construction
Completion: 2000

# Bronx Museum of the Arts Master Plan

1   Plan: ground floor
2   Plan: fourth floor
3   Program components
4   Final phase
5   Final design
6   Renovation and expansion phases

5

6

 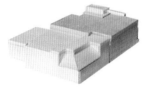 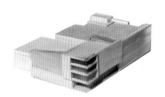 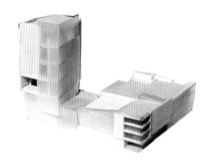

This project began with the identification of the program needs of the Bronx Museum of the Arts. From these, a flexible master plan was developed that addresses both immediate and long-range expansion opportunities and alternatives. The Museum's 10-year master plan is a road map created to guide the institution through a series of physical changes. Rather than an abstract vision, this plan identifies specific development alternatives and phasing strategies to help guide decisions.

The primary goals of the plan include identifying the museum's current and future space requirements, assessing the existing condition of the building, identifying short-term code compliance improvements, and exploring long-range expansion options. Each of these goals was directed toward the overriding effort of the institution to expand its role as community gathering space and cultural center and better serve its visitors.

The plan is based on a theme of linkages. Located on a high point on the Grand Concourse, various points in the museum have views to Manhattan. The plan configures spaces to take advantage of this visual linkage—hinting at the museum's connection to the larger New York art scene. The plan for the new museum also recognizes the institution's linkage to the community as a cultural extension of the neighborhood, creating a new identity and more welcoming entrance.

Recognizing that the museum needed a more contemporary architectural image to complement its thriving cultural events, the design team developed a phased, additive approach that re-skins the outdated building exterior. Two recently renovated large galleries are left untouched through this innovative approach to renovation. The additions and renovations act as a subtle but

strikingly contemporary marker for this contemporary cultural facility.

Programmatic ingenuity makes the museum user-friendly by adding amenities and "destination uses" at various nodes. A public access gallery would be created and all galleries would be reconfigured to smooth circulation between them. Administration offices would be adjusted to better integrate with other spaces and maintenance uses would be consolidated. The education studios would be expanded and reinvented, giving this department a stronger identity. Internal adjustments would be designed to link seamlessly with the future addition of a Children's Art Center to the north of the existing building. Taking advantage of the adjacent vacant site, the expansion plan includes a final phase of private-use development to generate income and help the museum move into the future.

1

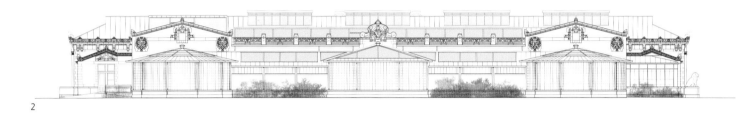

2

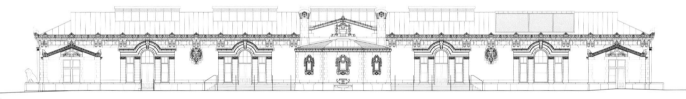

3

4

46

New York City (Bronx)
Client: Wildlife Conservation Society,
New York City Department of Design and Construction
Completion: 2006

# Bronx Zoo Lion House Renovation

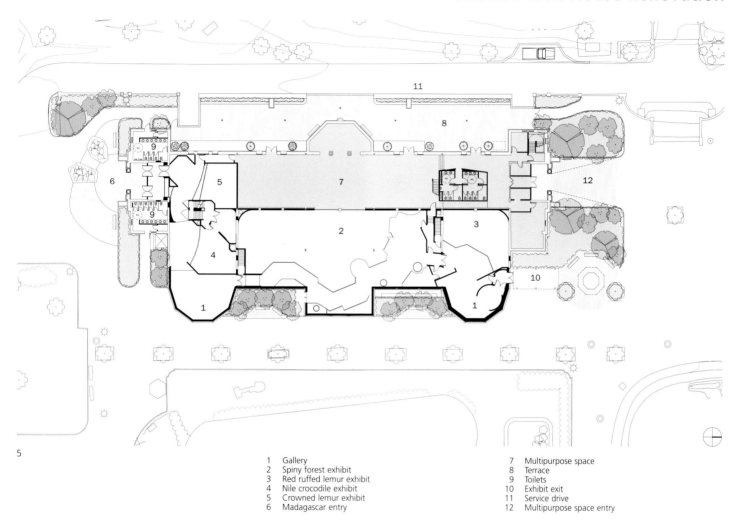

1   Gallery
2   Spiny forest exhibit
3   Red ruffed lemur exhibit
4   Nile crocodile exhibit
5   Crowned lemur exhibit
6   Madagascar entry
7   Multipurpose space
8   Terrace
9   Toilets
10  Exhibit exit
11  Service drive
12  Multipurpose space entry

The Beaux Arts 19,000-square-foot Lion House is the largest structure on the historic Astor Court, the zoo's original assemblage of buildings. Designed by Heins and LaFarge and constructed in 1903, the landmarked building has been closed to the zoo's visitors since the late 1970s when the lions, panthers, and tigers were moved to more expansive and naturalistic settings. One hundred years later, the building will once again house animals. The exhibition will recreate the habitats of the smaller animals native to the endangered landscapes of Madagascar. The adaptive reuse of this structure will transform it into a vital public educational venue and a sustainable, LEED-rated building, emblematic of the Wildlife Conservation Society's mission.

Enlightened thinking led to the creation of the zoo and the construction of the Lion House. The cage configuration and method of enclosure were exemplary for their day. The design approach to articulating the new building uses, image, materials, and systems continues this tradition. The dignity, simplicity, and refinement of this Beaux Arts civic structure are reinterpreted and recreated with contemporary interventions. The planar surfaces, regular rhythms, and reticulated character of the original building complemented its boxy massing and skeletal framing. The new elements do the same without replicating the original.

The new uses fundamentally redefine the building organization. The area of the interior and exterior

cages is combined to create a meandering path surrounded by exhibition habitats. Instead of viewing the animals from the outside of a cage, the public walks "within" the exhibit for a more immediate experience. The once transparent cage now encloses an exhibit experienced from within and is therefore opaque to the exterior. Yet the building must still engage the passerby on Astor Court. This is done by reinterpreting the grid of the cage in a larger scale and modulating its spacing. The grid is backed by a metal panel with the ghosted image of the forests of Madagascar. Its appearance changes as one walks by.

The former long, narrow interior viewing now houses a rentable multipurpose space. Rather

47

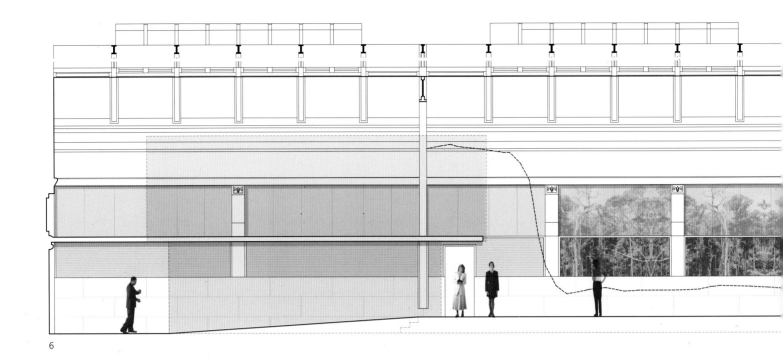

6

than circulating through this space, gathering
is the norm. The problematic proportions are
redefined by the insertion of a two-level glass
and stone box. The body of the building is an
abstract rectangular container. The added
element is its contemporary equivalent.
Under-floor air conditioning and services
allow the original trusses to remain unobstructed
and to maintain the clarity of the space. The
adjacent exterior landscaped terrace is conceived
as an extension of the room and its enclosing
wall is articulated in a manner similar to the

interior wall on the opposite side of the
multipurpose space.

Optimum standards of performance are achieved
through the use of new systems and materials.
The building will have a recycled greywater
system, a fuel cell, and geothermal wells. The
indigenous plant materials within the exhibits will
require high quantities of UV light, yet the
building envelope must thermally perform. An
innovative skylight system has been incorporated
into the shallow pitch of the original metal roofs.

6   Section: interior
7   Sustainable components

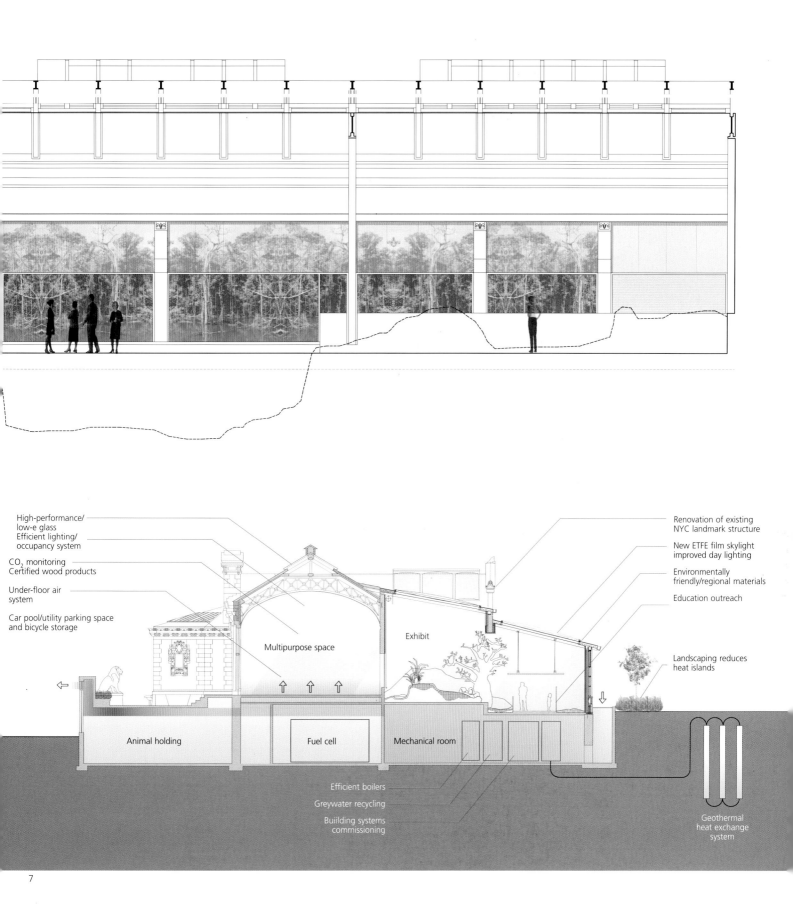

High-performance/
low-e glass
Efficient lighting/
occupancy system

CO₂ monitoring
Certified wood products

Under-floor air
system

Car pool/utility parking space
and bicycle storage

Multipurpose space

Exhibit

Renovation of existing
NYC landmark structure

New ETFE film skylight
improved day lighting

Environmentally
friendly/regional materials

Education outreach

Landscaping reduces
heat islands

Animal holding

Fuel cell

Mechanical room

Efficient boilers

Greywater recycling

Buiilding systems
commissioning

Geothermal
heat exchange
system

7

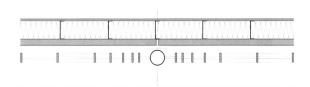

8

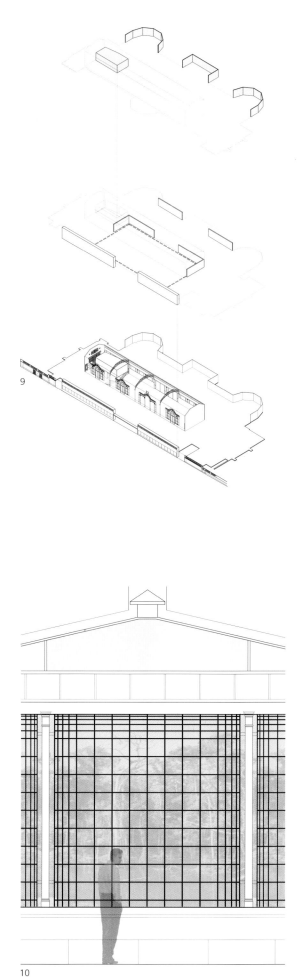

9

10

11

12

13

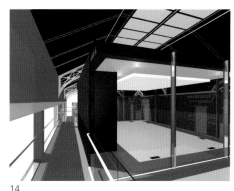

14

15

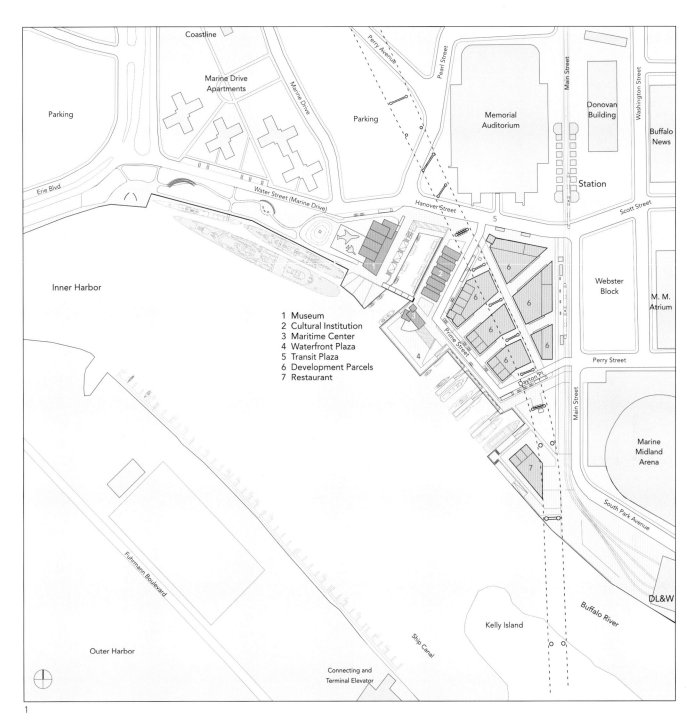

1 Museum
2 Cultural Institution
3 Maritime Center
4 Waterfront Plaza
5 Transit Plaza
6 Development Parcels
7 Restaurant

1

2

Buffalo, New York
Client: Empire State Development Corporation
Completion: 2000

# Buffalo Inner Harbor Master Plan and Naval Museum

1  Master plan
2  Redeveloped waterfront
3  Existing conditions
4  Figure/ground study
5  Model: redeveloped waterfront

3

4

5

The urban design master plan for Buffalo's Inner Harbor, completed for the Empire State Development Corporation, defines new harbor and waterfront amenities at the location of the site of the historic western terminus of the Erie Canal. Located between waterfront parks, Buffalo's light rail line, and the recently completed sports arena—home of the Buffalo Sabres—this new waterfront destination will stimulate local economic development and provide an accessible downtown maritime destination along the Lake Erie shoreline.

The team crafted a finger-like development plan that would leave room for pedestrian views and paths to the waterfront, which is cut off from the city by an elevated highway. The site configuration design, inspired by the Inner Harbor's history and its waterfront orientation, restores the link between land and water. To further enliven the

waterfront, the plan creates docks along a revitalized canal slip, open spaces, and a naval museum. The effort unifies disparate parts of the disused waterfront in order to create a cohesive, attractive recreation and leisure destination.

The plan plays a significant role in the economic revival of the surrounding region. As a focus and anchor for activity in downtown Buffalo, it complements area-wide attractions and defines the region as an international tourist destination. A continuous waterfront esplanade connects Memorial Park, the new naval museum, canal slip, waterfront plaza, and south basin to the existing arena. The plan is aimed at restoring active maritime uses to the Inner Harbor, re-establishing connections between downtown streets, and clarifying circulation patterns along the Buffalo River. The scheme creates three maritime basins to serve the naval museum,

transient boaters, and commercial tour boat operators, restoring a vibrant maritime life to the waterfront.

The siting of the new museum solidifies a connection between the new development below and the existing memorials above, leading visitors through an exterior yard, and exhibit ships in the water. The design of the building expresses its function on the exterior, with a large glass-enclosed public lobby facing the active canal slip. The main black-box exhibition area, separated from the public hall by a clerestory-lit intermediate zone, features the main exhibits. The diffuse daylight creates a sense of orientation for visitors within the large black-box space. Seating for a café as well as outdoor exhibits would lend the museum a distinctive indoor/outdoor character, which will further people the newly refurbished waterfront.

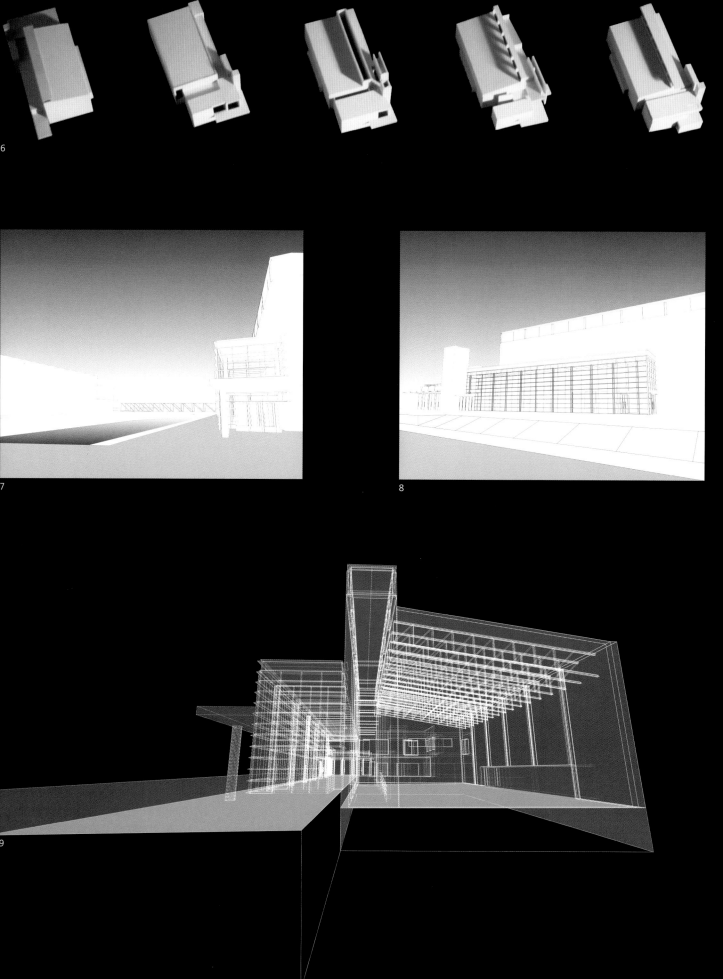

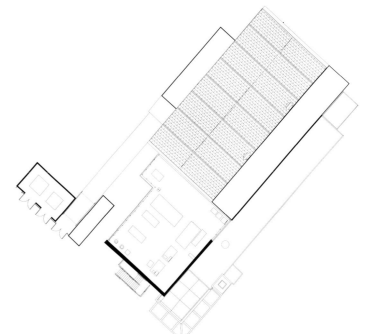

12

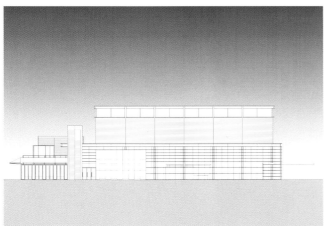

10

13

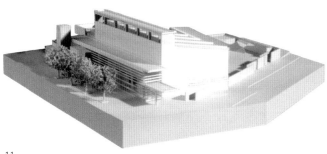

11

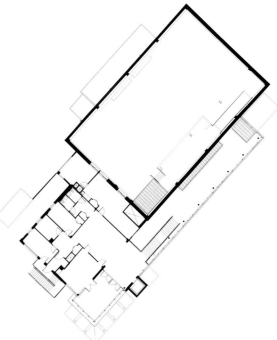

14

1

1   Competition scheme
2   Site plan

# Clinton Green Mixed-Use Project

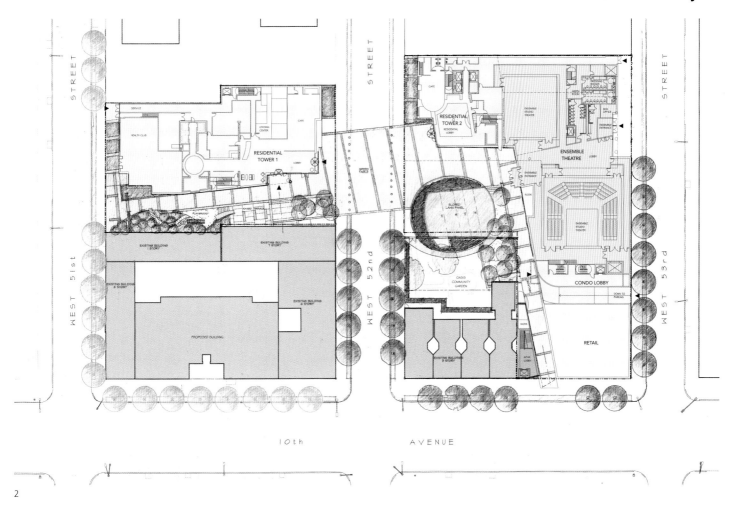

2

In the Clinton neighborhood of Manhattan's West Side, Fox & Fowle Architects has designed a new assemblage of buildings that accommodate residential, cultural, and commercial uses. The concept for the multi-block parcel resulted from a desire to enhance the existing city fabric and create compelling public space. Through carefully scaled massing and the material palette, the buildings are rooted in the Clinton neighborhood. The approach involved keeping the east side of the parcel low-scale to respond to the five-story street wall of Tenth Avenue. High-rise elements were pushed to the west. A network of urban green space is the connective tissue that links the various elements of the project together as well as tying the project into the greater context.

Beginning in the project's competition stage, the design team looked for ways to enhance the synergy of uses through public space, seeking opportunities for the theaters and retail areas to energize and support the residential uses and vice versa. The design features a tent-like covered piazza, which was envisioned as a kind of "mixing bowl" serving many uses. As the project advanced, this idea transformed into a network of pedestrian passages, culminating in a central green space. The passages are activated by patrons of the theaters and retail spaces, apartment building and loft residents, in addition to those using the central green as a destination. The green incorporates a sloped grassy area for relaxing and outdoor performances.

A horizontal layering of function was deemed most effective; public space, theaters, and retail are near or at street level and the residential elements are above. The two 300-unit apartment towers rise above a base inhabited by two separate theater companies, the Ensemble Studio Theater and the Intar Hispanic American Arts Center. Three stories of loft-like apartments are located immediately above these performance spaces. The residential towers are planned to be 24 stories high. Apartments on the upper floors overlook the public open space and take advantage of views to the river and of the midtown Manhattan skyline. Contrasting materials and harmonious geometries give the pair of towers a sense of speaking to each other, while remaining discrete structures with a common language.

This project is expected to begin construction in early 2005 and is expected to earn LEED certification from the U.S. Green Building Council.

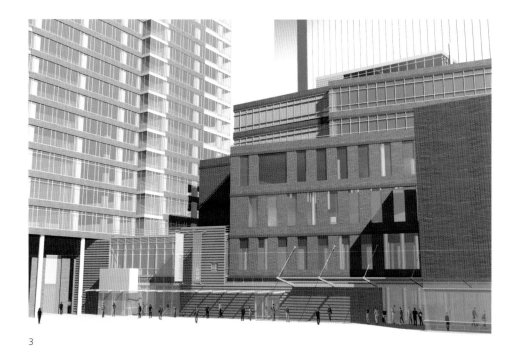

3

3,4,5   Street-level view: cultural complex
    6   Plans: tower floors
    7   Final design

4

5

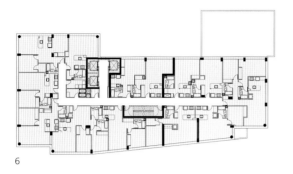

6

7

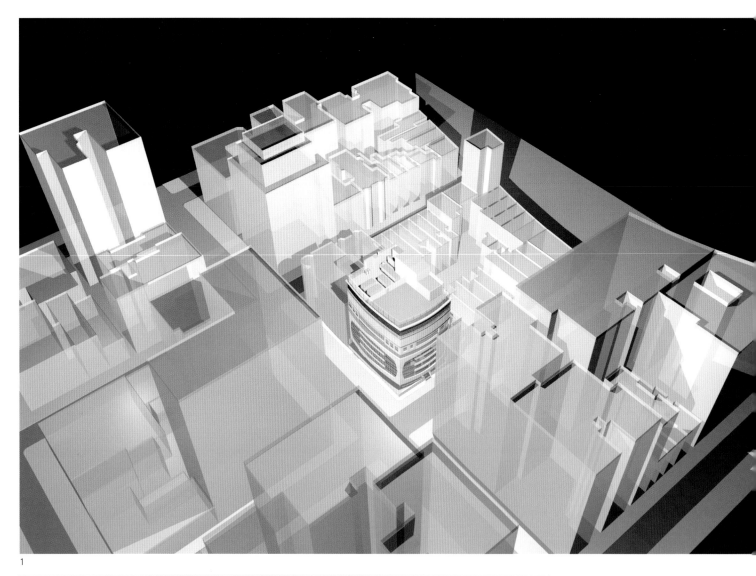

1

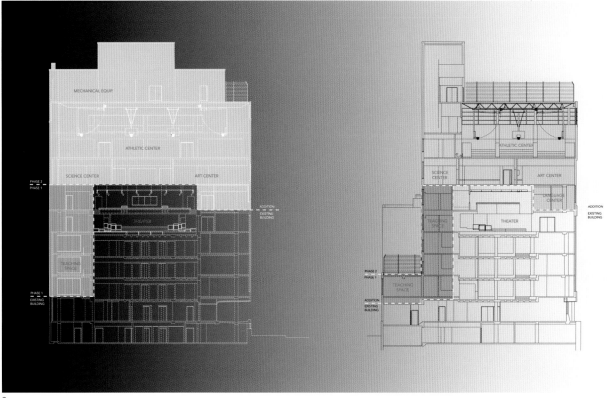

2

3

New York City (Manhattan)
Client: The Calhoun School
Completion: 2004

# The Calhoun School Expansion

1   School expansion in context
2   Sections
3   Existing conditions
4   Elevation

4

The Calhoun School Expansion will add four stories and a mezzanine level to the existing five-story 1973 concrete and travertine building, as well as filling in the building footprint, to add 30,500 square feet. The decision to expand both vertically and horizontally created a number of formal and programmatic challenges. When completed, the Calhoun School will contain a 234-seat, three-quarter-round flexible performing arts space, a high school level gym, new general teaching spaces for the lower, middle, and upper schools, and specialized teaching spaces for science, art, theater, music, dance, and language. In addition, a new vertical core will be integrated into the existing and new floors to maximize the efficiency of the new teaching spaces.

The project goal, aligned with the school's mission, was to "see the learning" happening. This has an impact on how the school relates to the street and the neighborhood as well as on the activity within the building. Externally, this is expressed in the building's use of large windows for all teaching spaces. Internally, the open plan of the existing building, which is a direct expression of the school's teaching philosophy and tradition, and a representation of the prevailing typology articulation of the 1970s era, is reinforced with the placement of the new core. The open classroom ethos of that decade has been refined to allow a variety of flexible teaching and learning environments.

In designing the character of the new spaces, Fox & Fowle Architects sought to heighten the fluidity of circulation between the existing and new, by use of ramps, low partitions and "commons," thereby emphasizing the communal aspects of each floor and/or teaching activity. The challenge for the design team was to retain the identity and character of the light and airy curvilinear form of the original structure. By separating the new top with bands of glass and stucco, layers appear to hover above and not overbear the remaining base. Metal accents are applied to the base and integrated with the new top to visually interconnect the forms and enrich the composition of the base.

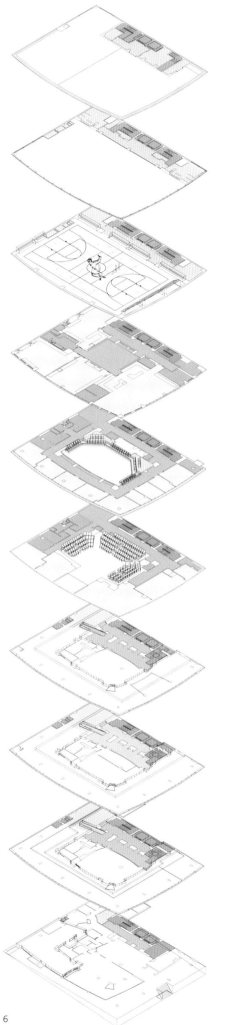

5 Performing arts space
6 Stacked plans
7–11 Construction photographs

7

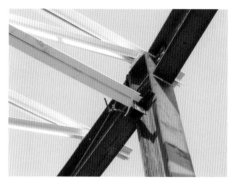

8

9

10

6

11

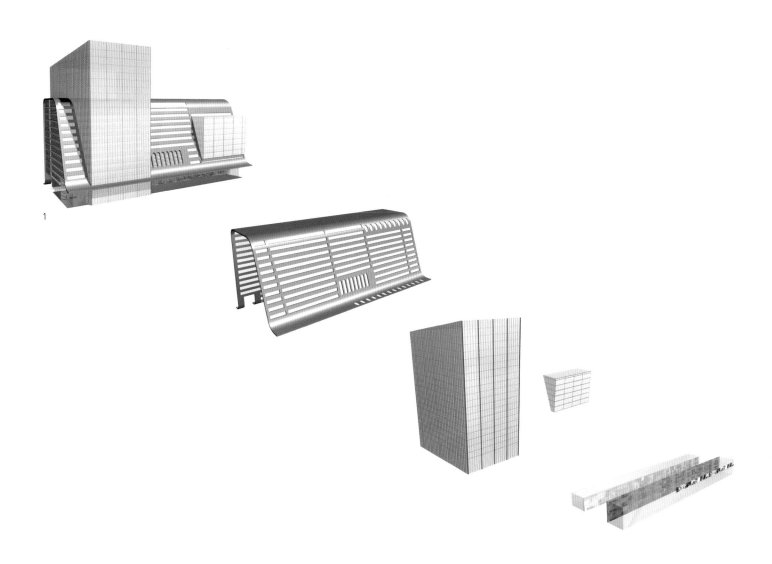

1

2

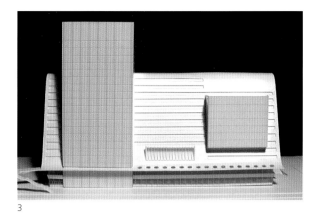

3

Beijing, China
Client: Beijing Jingmai Development Co. Ltd
Completion: 2005

# Ditan Sports Tower

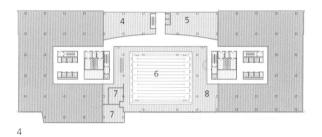

4

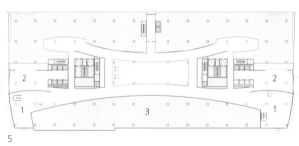

5

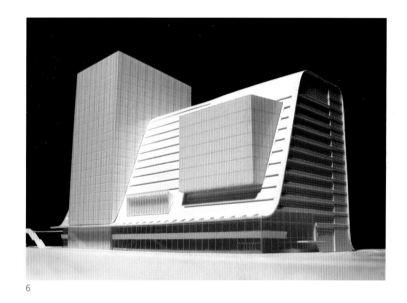

6

1 Retail entrance
2 Office lobby
3 Special store
4 Steam room
5 Gym
6 Swimming pool
7 Lockers
8 Bar/Café

The Ditan Sports Tower for a private developer includes offices, retail, and a government-sponsored swim club and fitness center. The project is located along a major north/south avenue within the second ring road in Beijing, adjacent to some Olympic venues and near the entrance to the gate to Ditan Park (temple of earth), which was an Imperial religious site.

The initial challenge was an existing, stepped-down zoning envelope, created with deference to this important gate nearby. The original zoned massing was very awkward and lacked unity. The inventive solution the team created includes the east/west bar, a folded zinc-clad "blanket" that is animated by fenestration. The edge of this form is the canopy for two floors of retail along the western street, addressing and animating the thoroughfare, and dealing with a failure at street level of much recent architecture in Asia. The health club swimming pool is articulated by a large window at the fourth and fifth floors.

This bar also intersects with an 18-story, glass double-curtainwall volume. The contrast between the rectilinear glass volume and the curving metal volume is striking. The taller structure seems to have emerged through the east/west bar, giving it a sense of energy and vibrancy. The blanket bar was also a design solution to help unite the pieces of the two towers and health club with a strong identity. The double-skin walls of the towers with sandwiched louvers will help control heat build-up on the western side.

1 Building components
2 Model
3 Model
4 Plan: fourth floor
5 Plan: ground floor
6 Model

65

1

2

Seoul, South Korea
Client: Dongbu Insurance
Completion: 2005

# Dongbu Headquarters

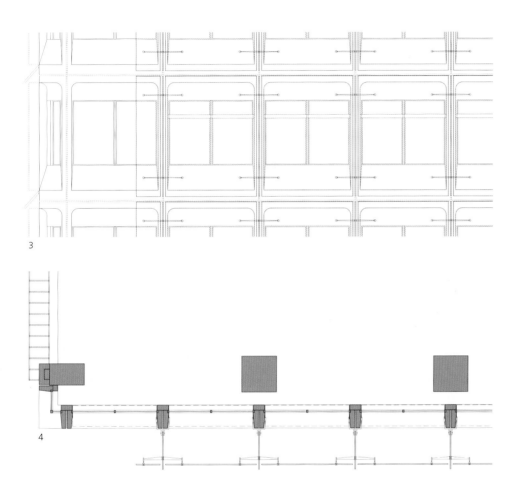

3

4

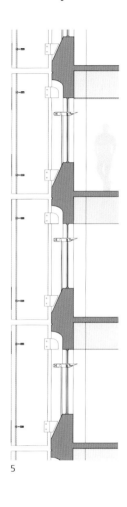

5

Fox & Fowle Architects won a competition for the renovation of the Dongbu Headquarters in Seoul. The building is in the Cho-Dong area and was initially completed in the 1970s; it has been modified multiple times over the years. Fox & Fowle Architects' design transforms the building to reflect the modernity and dynamism of the company, Dongbu Insurance.

The idea was to create a face with depth and mutability. Words and patterns on the glass change as the daylight and artificial light change, this brings a sense of lightness and dynamism to the structure. At night, soft lighting will further animate the structure. The pin-point pattern of fiber-optic lights gradually becomes denser towards the top. Transparency is a strong message here; the second glass skin is a new wrapper on the old

building, but the old building is still visible. The new skins reorder the proportions of the building, and will be detailed with sophistication. The entry sequence and public spaces are designed with as much through-transparency as possible. Portions of the floor are removed between ground floor, the cellar, and the second floor to allow for views, daylight penetration and more vertical proportions.

Utilizing a sheer covering of glazed curtainwall, the work encompasses a new, all-glass, second envelope on the north and south façades that extends up to form a new building top. The owner was expecting to have to rip the façade off of the building; this design keeps the original as one layer in a multi-layered composition. This reuse works on a number of levels: it capitalizes on the embodied energy of the initial skin, it

adds complexity to the composition, and it is an imaginative demonstration of how to reuse a modern building component. The outer skin acts as a thermal buffer, which will reduce loads on the building during extreme temperatures (common in the region). The outer skin is not completely sealed; gaps are left between the glazing units to prevent overheating of the buffer cavity. The design for the re-cladding of the building is conceived to allow the majority of the building occupants to remain in place during construction. The project also involves replacing the east and west façades and a dramatic reconfiguration of the ground floor and second floor. The construction of a new vaulted penthouse creates a new building crown visible from the east and west and through the new north and south façades.

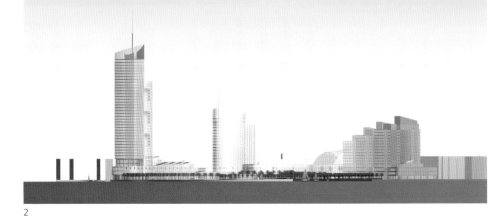

1 Promenade
2 Elevation
3 Aerial view
4 Galleria
5 Location map
6 Master plan

2

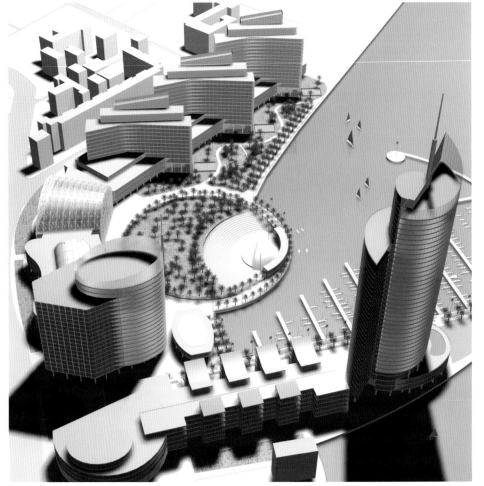

1

3

4

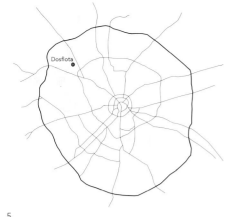

Moscow, Russia
Client: U.S. CapitalInvest Bancorp
Completion: 2004

5

# Dosflota Multipurpose Complex

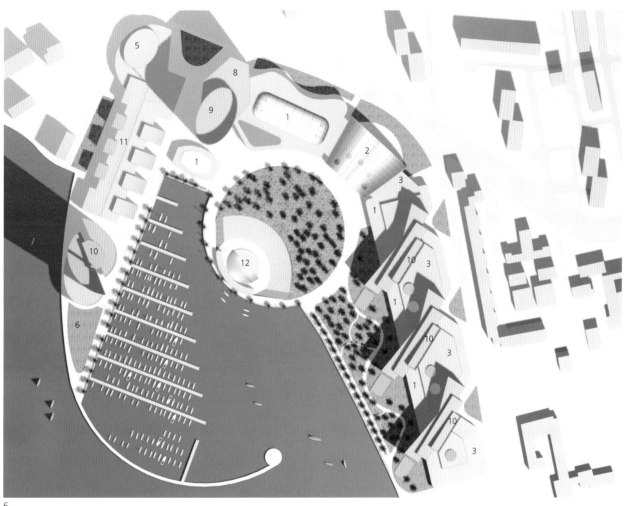

1   Sports Structure
2   Winter Gardens/
     entrance
3   Retail/recreational
4   Yacht Club
5   Health Club
6   Restaurant/bar
7   Shopping Center
8   Hotel
9   Office Tower
10  Residential
11  Residential/
     townhouse
12  Amphitheater

6

The Dosflota Multipurpose Complex, commissioned by U.S. CapitalInvest Bancorp, is planned to be a residential, recreational, and commercial development in the northwestern part of Moscow, on the western bank of the Khimkinskoye Vodokhranilische.

The master plan sets the stage for a center of recreation, retail, and entertainment to be used by residents of the development, those staying in the hotels and working in the offices, and also those visiting from around the region. The goal was to effectively utilize the shoreline and harbor in ways that strengthen the existing urban and social fabric of the district.

Sports facilities underpin the development. Pairing sports with each of the other components is intended to produce a wide range of recreational activities (fitness-based activities, competitive team and individual sports, and leisure games). The promenade, marina, yacht club, and amphitheater are the extension of the sports recreational program. The promenade is the "green necklace" of landscaping that connects the complex to the water's edge. The harbor marina offers secure and protected moorings for 270 light recreational vessels and pleasure craft. The yacht club includes a school, restaurant, museum, fitness center, parking, and storage.

The apartment building is anticipated to target primarily young urban professionals. There will be high-rise and mid-rise buildings as well as low-rise townhouse-style homes. The high-rise apartments will be housed in the complex's signature tower. Hotel and corporate offices will be housed in another tower; the formal dialogue between the two towers will set the aesthetic tone for the development.

The backbone of the development will be the Galleria, a three-story center for retail, commercial, entertainment, and recreational uses. This structure will run the length of the development. At the center, a winter garden will be a multifunction gathering space and centerpiece with views of the marina and amphitheater outside.

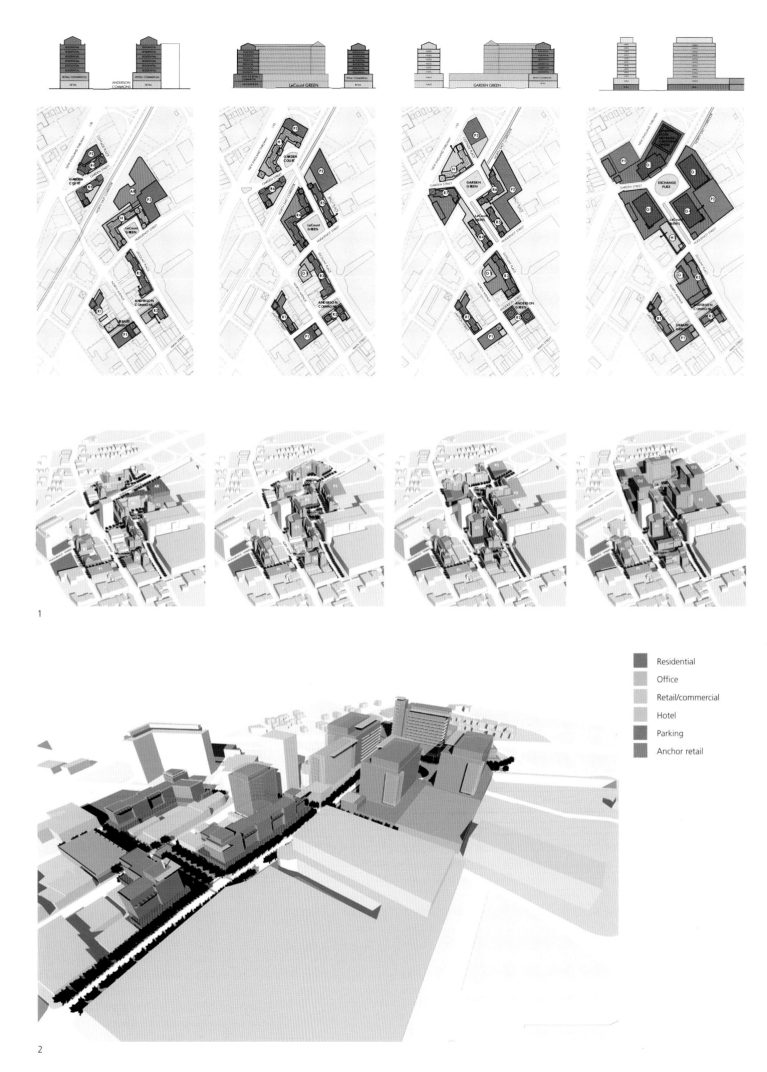

Residential

Office

Retail/commercial

Hotel

Parking

Anchor retail

1

2

New Rochelle, New York
Client: City of New Rochelle
Completion: 2003

# Downtown New Rochelle Master Plan

1   Four redevelopment options
2   Exchange Place scheme
3   Library Green

3

Fox & Fowle Architects has been working with the City of New Rochelle for a decade on planning and urban design projects, including streetscape improvement programs, neighborhood revitalization, and the relocation and expansion of the library plaza as the centerpiece for cultural and residential activity in the downtown. The purpose of the recent effort is to assess the redevelopment potential of eight designated areas in the City's downtown and to identify a public/private partnership strategy for their redevelopment, revitalization and/or retention.

Four options have been developed utilizing differing groups of soft sites. The options range from a minimum development scenario to a maximum development scenario. The Minimum Intervention scheme proposes strategic public sector intervention to support the continued revitalization of downtown New Rochelle, by building upon the recent success of New Roc City and Avalon on the Sound developments. The

purpose of this scheme is to reinforce the core of downtown New Rochelle.

Connective Links proposes strategic intervention in the established blocks between Lawton Street and LeCount Place, from Huguenot Street and Main Street, while proposing a direct link to the north where the railroad tracks are bridged to provide a significant link between the core downtown and upper North Avenue. This scheme offers a more cohesive vision for downtown, by reconnecting it to the northern study parcels.

Public Greens proposes a large open space, Garden Green, to serve as a focus for the new development, while providing a clear link between the downtown and the area north of the railroad tracks. Garden Green would be linked to downtown by an extension of LeCount Place. The extension, LeCount Mews, would be a promenade lined with residential structures and would be the key link between the downtown/

New Roc City and the new residential and hotel development centered on Garden Green. Strategic redevelopment would occur between Lawton Street and LeCount Place, from Huguenot Street to Main Street, to strengthen the pedestrian experience on LeCount Place and to enhance the connection between New Roc City and the library.

The Exchange Place scheme builds upon the development plan described for Garden Green, and proposes more ambitious development with a focus on office use. The open space and mews described in the Public Greens option are used in Exchange Place to support the creation of a downtown office campus. The office campus would have direct access to the I-95 highway and would be easily accessible from the Intermodal Transportation Center. A large open green space, called Exchange Place, would be located over the railroad tracks, and would act as a catalyst for office and retail development surrounding this green, and potentially a conference center.

71

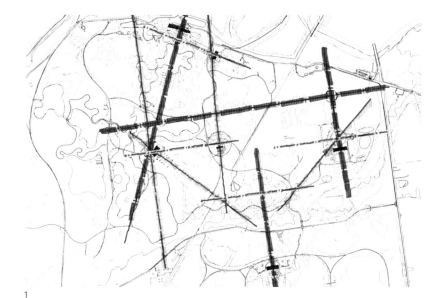

1  Site axis
2  Strategic linkages
3  Spatial and landscape connections
4  Farm barn
5  Farm barn—siteplan
6,7 Existing conditions
8  Ecological environment
9  Existing conditions—aerial view

1

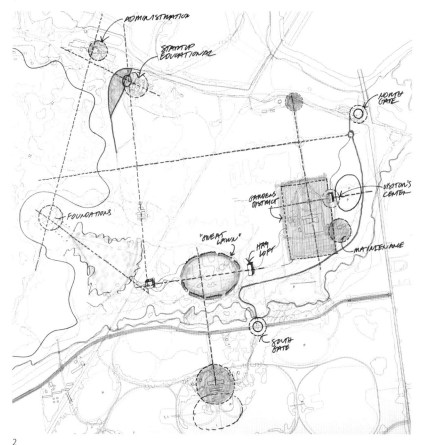

2

4

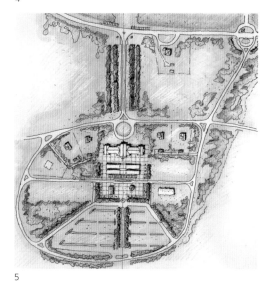

5

Gardens Center Precinct

Reinforce clarity of central open space

Clear trees to create view corridor

Farm Barn

3

6

7

Somerville, New Jersey
Client: Duke Farms Foundation, The Conservation Fund
Completion: 2002

# Duke Farms Master Plan

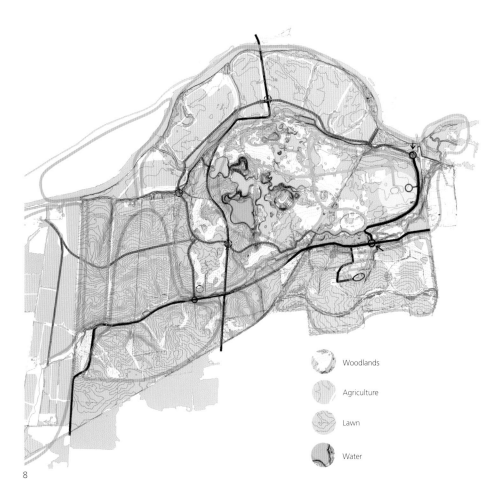

Woodlands

Agriculture

Lawn

Water

8

9

Duke Farms, a 2,700-acre estate near Somerville, New Jersey, developed by J.B. Duke from 1893 – 1905, provides an extraordinary record of the evolution and manipulation of land and water over the course of a century. From interventions incorporating existing features like rivers, brooks, and topographical features, to wholesale creation of a new landscape, Duke's schemes reveal attitudes about man's relationship to the natural world. Doris Duke enhanced the property by purchasing small farms along the western boundary and creating noteworthy display gardens representing the internationalism that was an important aspect of mid 20th-century thought. The Duke Charitable Foundation asked Fox & Fowle Architects to evaluate the uses, facilities, circulation, site issues, and environmentally responsible approaches and techniques in order to realize the vision of an educational facility for the public that uses the natural and cultural resources of the property to interpret human interactions with the land. The design team also implemented the first renovation

of the master plan: the renovation and expansion of the Garden Visitor Center to accommodate the first step of expanded public visitation.

Fox & Fowle Architects analyzed the circulation, open space, and facility implications and precedents for translating the use and maintenance of the property for the enjoyment of a select few to the instruction and enjoyment of many. In the context of suburban sprawl, this transformation of the site use was defined as an opportunity to create a model that is in harmony with the environment. Holistic thinking structured the physical, spatial, and formal approach to the landscape and the reuse of existing buildings and the addition of new facilities. The resultant guiding principles for the phased implementation of the transformational plan outlined parameters of preservation, compatibility, sustainability, connectivity, legibility, enhancement, and access.

The source book proposed ways to maintain the contrasting character of the estate's two worlds:

the farms to west and the more picturesque core. The adaptive reuse of key structures was explored: the coach barn as education center, the farm barn as main visitors' center, the main residence as administrative center, the expanded garden visitors' center as an interim visitors' center, the relocation of service functions to the perimeter, and the enhancement of existing "outdoor rooms" and view corridors. The plan would establish a porous perimeter with trail and open space system for public access; maintain and enhance a parkway aesthetic of sequential visual incidents revealed by movement; create a perimeter system for parking, services, and gates to curtail vehicular traffic from the core; enhance clear, distinctive precincts that are comprehensible; clarify central open space in order to visually link the significant structures; provide renovated buildings in each site precinct to serve as "magnets" for the pedestrian activity in that precinct; and maintain the residential tradition of the small buildings on the estate. Each step of the transformation would follow sustainable guidelines.

2

3

New York City (Manhattan)
Client: Durst-Strong Family
Completion: 2002

# Durst-Strong Apartment

4

The joining of two apartments created a 3,320-square-foot living space in this pre-war landmarked apartment building. The clients were seeking a simple elegant home that would accommodate their shifting needs. The design reinterprets the residence's original characteristics, while adding modern elements to create a graceful, contemporary look.

Due to the deteriorated condition of the existing apartments, a complete demolition was required. New electrical, plumbing, and HVAC systems were installed. The residence's 22 existing windows were replaced with modern, energy-efficient, custom wood windows

Cabinetry and sliding partitions in place of walls allow the characteristics of an open living space to mutate; intimate spaces can be created as required. Glass was introduced, both in the cabinetry and sliding partitions, to enhance the connections between the spaces. The combination of rich wood with streamlined detailing makes the open kitchen warm and inviting. Materials and colors were selected to evoke a unique feeling for each room and to create an overall sense of calm.

5

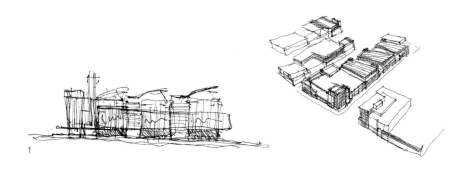

1

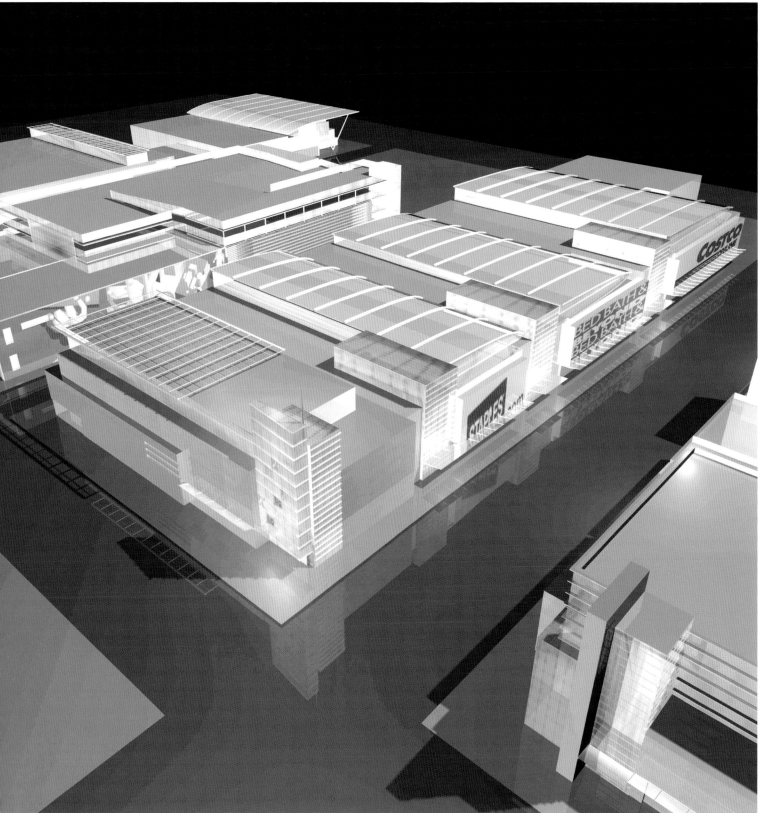

2

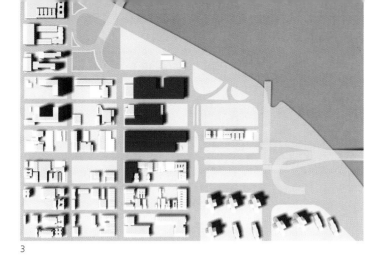

3

New York City (Manhattan)
Client: withheld at client's request
Submitted: 2001

# East 125th Street Corridor Study

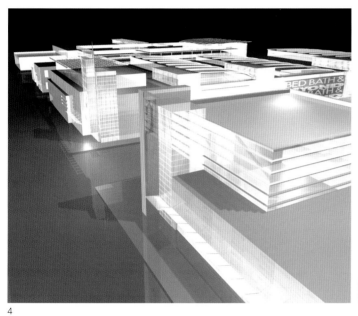

4

5

1  Concept sketches
2  125th Street view
3  Site plan
4  Third Avenue view
5  Integrated signage

This study examined the possibility of a new, million-square-foot commercial development on six sites in East Harlem, a dense urban area with renewed commercial development potential. The architectural challenge for the project was to create responsible, contributory, big box retail in a dense city neighborhood. The development includes a variety of retail and other commercial uses and the project team experimented with a wide range of adjacencies, shared entries, and other strategies to determine the best composition of uses and forms.

The design adopts a modulated scale to maintain a street level presence and not overwhelm the

surrounding low-rise context. Both the program of the project and its architectural resolution aim to integrate the development into the community. The study envisioned a low-rise complex with lightly arcing rooftops—a graceful, contemporary take on infill commercial development. The southeastern piece assumes a shell form, gesturing toward the river's edge. The integration of supergraphic art adds vibrancy to large walls in a formalized take on an inner city tradition.

To build flexibility into the main retail tenant spaces, the plan for the structure incorporates a single mid-block entry to allow access by multiple tenants to upper floors. Community services and

a public technology center are integrated into one of the two other mixed-use buildings, sharing the space with local retail shops. The parking garage contains four full floors of space, plus roof parking, so that parking pressure on the surrounding community is kept to a minimum. A two-story commercial building will accommodate distribution and loading/unloading for a major express mail carrier. Part of this study also included a detailed plan for working with the residents from adjacent neighborhoods, many of whom, in addition to concerns about parking, had concerns about light levels, truck traffic, noise levels, and the integration of significant retail signage into the neighborhood.

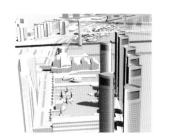

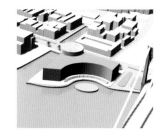
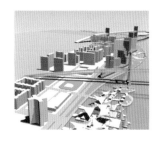

1

New York City (Manhattan)
Client: NYC Economic Development Corporation
Submitted: 2003

# East River Planning Study Proposal

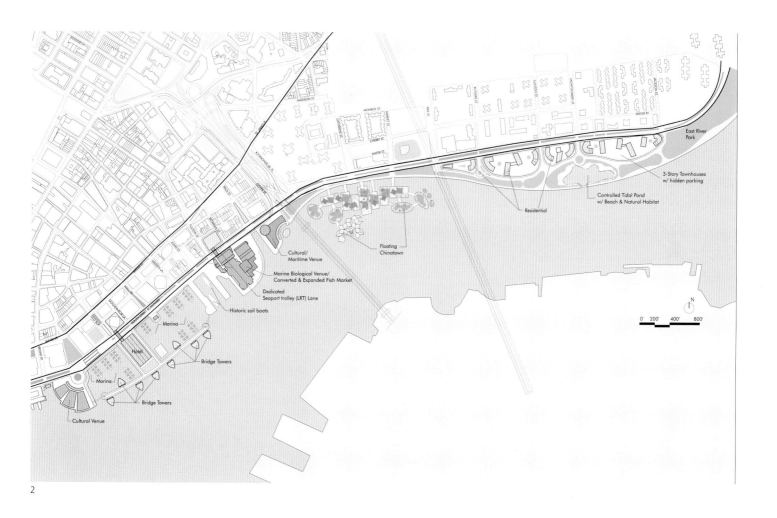

East River
Park

3-Story Townhouses
w/ hidden parking

Controlled Tidal Pond
w/ Beach & Natural Habitat

Residential

Floating
Chinatown

Cultural/
Maritime Venue

Marine Biological Venue/
Converted & Expanded Fish Market

Dedicated
Seaport trolley (LRT) Lane

Historic sail boats

Marina

Hotel

Bridge Towers

Marina

Bridge Towers

Cultural Venue

0'   200'   400'   800'

2

Fox & Fowle Architects was invited by the New York City Economic Development Corporation and the City Planning Department to participate in a competition for the redevelopment of the East River Waterfront in Manhattan. The team effort began with the recognition that a mile of waterfront will take several decades to develop and that the plan must therefore change in response to phasing, economic, political, and other conditions that do not remain consistent over time. The plan defines short-term opportunities that could provide a framework for long-term growth and change.

The approach is threefold: focus on key places along the waterfront where important linkages inland should be made; target those locations where early successes are possible; upon completion, establish a new world-class waterfront district for the city. The strategy is to quickly provide a range of new waterfront activities and venues by utilizing floating structures and selective permanent structures that would be free of lengthy permitting and land assembly difficulties. At the same time, linear improvements along the water's edge, including streetscape, local transit, and viaduct enhancement will be instituted.

The scheme identifies a series of focal points. The Bridge Tower district would be a nexus of active waterfront uses, cultural amenities, and residential towers. The Seaport District, north of the towers, would redefine the festival marketplace seaport into a cultural nexus celebrating the city's maritime roots. Floating Chinatown would pull the neighborhood to the water's edge and onto bridges, floating restaurants, and light structures. East Riverside Park would be the redevelopment of the underutilized pier facility to become a diverse residential community with parks and open spaces. River Edge is designed to transform the physical connection between land and water (a condition that defines all components of this plan). The East River Waterfront here would become a diverse mix of recreational, residential, cultural, and commercial uses to mirror the activity of the city. Neighborhoods would be drawn to the water's edge.

1 Atelier housing
2 Gateway green
3 Community theater/center/meeting hall
4 Northwest aerial view
5 Plan
6 Stormwater management
7 Building blocks
8 Layering of uses

1

2

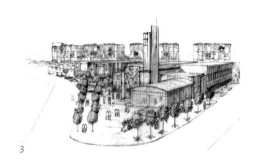

3

## THE CRESCENT: BATH INSIDE OUT

Parti recognizes natural organization of the site:

Rail tracks distinguish the civic and commercial core to the south from significant stand of woodlands to the north;

Crescent of atelier housing forms a datum that defines edge;

Atelier housing is sheathed in a living bris soleil and forms a green / living backdrop to downtown Gloucester;

Civic spaces and uses anchor each end of the crescent - Gateway Green to the west and the Community Theater / Center / Meeting Hall to the east reinforce the civic side of the community;

Mews lined with rowhouses extend south;

Restored woodlands and man-made wetlands support bio  -diversity;

Urban agriculture is an integral part of natural systems;

Man made and natural systems are joined with fingers that extend though the living green spine formed by the atelier housing;

Mix of mutually supportive uses is layered horizontally with superimposed layers of Nature; Civic, Retail, Commercial, and Housing .

### CONTAINER FIT-OUT BUSINESS

In early phases containers are modified on-  site in existing industrial buildings;

As container business is established and grows facilities expand off- site;

Headquarters and showroom remain at Gateway Green.

### GATEWAY BUSINESSES

Ground floor food co  -op and retail;

Upper floors accommodate businesses that outgrow the atelier shop houses;

Constructed from containers designed for "long life / lose fit" to adapt to changing needs.

### GATEWAY GREEN: ECONOMIC & SOCIAL FOCUS

Gateway to downtown;

Community landmark and meeting place;

Location for farmer  is market;

Bus stops are located around the green to encourage commuters to frequent retailers.

### MIXED USE FUTURE

Live / work housing reflects the traditional self resilience of Gloucester  is residents;

The layering of natural systems reflects Gloucester's history of reliance on natural resources (the sea);

The weaving of uses - retail, live / work housing, two-family row houses, and retail uses supports the unique nature of the Gloucester community .

### APARTMENT MODULE

Laundry Module

Bathroom Module

Kitchen Module

### RECYCLED HOUSING

Because of the trade deficit there are over 1 million surplus shipping containers in the northeast which can be easily transported to Gloucester from MASSPORT  ;

Recycling shipping containers will create a market for a surplus product;

Containers are shipped from port by rail;

Containers can be stacked up to 8 high;

Fit-out would create an incubator business in Gloucester;

Residents would customize duplex lofts;

Set back terraces provide outdoor space;

Through floor units are accessed from single loaded corridors;

A living Bris Soleil of bamboo wraps the south facade sheltering south facing terraces;

Shipping containers mirror Gloucester's traditional relationship with the sea.

### LIVING BRISE SOLEIL

Living bamboo screens south facing terraces and lofts providing natural cooling;

Container framework supports planters at all  floors;

Bamboo is available locally from New England Bamboo in Rockport, MA .

### ZIPCARS

Residents reserve the use of shared vehicles;

Environmental benefits /reduced on site parking;

Economic benefits by reducing transportation costs for residents

25% of parking is reserved for ZIP cars.

### POROUS PAVING

Rainwater can penetrate and recharge ground water;

Reduces volume of storm water run-  off and discharge of pollutants.

### ATELIER HOUSING

Live / work housing with ground floor shop houses;

Flexible housing units adjust to accommodate a variety of households and businesses;

Rooftop hot houses support urban agriculture with the social benefits of a community garden.

### COMMUNITY THEATER / CENTER / MEETING HALL

Link to Civic and Business Core;

Social focus for residents and community .

### URBAN AGRICULTURE:

Urban agriculture will reduce dependency on distant food sources, reduce the cost of food; foster social interaction; and reduce the nutrient cycle.

Urban Agriculture reconnects residents to natural systems;

Provide the environmental benefits of a green roof with the social benefits of a community garden;

Rooftop hot houses will provide a significant portion of resident's food needs and create business.

### INTEGRATED COMMUNITY SPACES

Family amenities include a playground and outdoor space at each floor of the atelier housing;

Playgrounds in the sky are staggered horizontally and vertically .

### SHORTENED NUTRIENT CYCLE

Urban agriculture produces food on site;

Human waste is processed in anaerobic tanks;

Methane is extracted as a fuel;

Compost is transferred to the roof gardens;

Waste is distributed to man-made wetlands;

Restored woodlands treat remaining waste;

Transpiration pulls moisture from the leaves;

Moisture falls as precipitation on the gardens

Ground water is recharged;

The nutrient cycle is complete.

### NATURAL SYSTEMS RESTORATION

Restore Natural Systems and Habitat;

Restored woodlands will be integral part of the nutrient cycle by filtrating water through soil aeration and recharging the ground water;

Natural habitat supports the diversification of plant and animal life;

Man-made wetlands complement restored woodlands;

Landscaped fingers will reach through the community and out into the natural systems.

### INTEGRATED RECREATION FACILITIES

Active recreation facilities are integrated with restored woodlands and man-made wetlands;

Nature trails and paths wind through wood lands and wetlands for passive recreation.

### ENVIRONMENTAL LEARNING CENTER

Charter High School will use the man-made wetlands, restored woodlands, and urban agriculture as a living laboratory .

### TOWNHOUSE MEWS

Mews reach out to the community

Row houses bridge the scale of the atelier units and the existing residential areas;

Recycled shipping containers are utilized for economical construction;

Two-family duplex housing provides the social benefits of home ownership and the economic benefits of affordable rental housing;

Ground floor simplex units provide housing for the elderly .

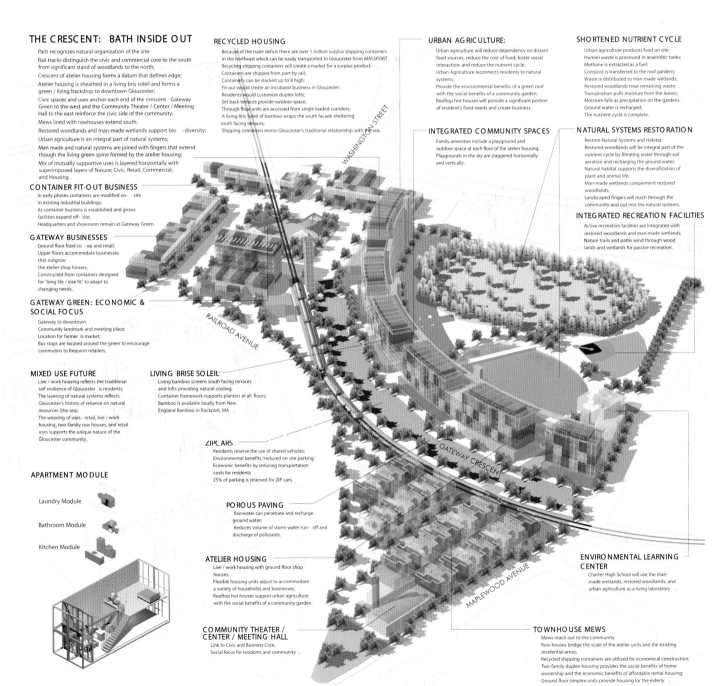

WASHINGTON STREET

RAILROAD AVENUE

GATEWAY CRESCENT

MAPLEWOOD AVENUE

4

# Density Competition: Gloucester Green

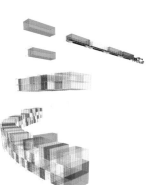

5

1 Gateway Crescent
2 Duplex apartments
3 Fifth-floor playground and community terrace
4 Seventh-floor playground and community terrace
5 Third-floor playground and community terrace
6 Townhouse duplex over simplex units
7 Rail station

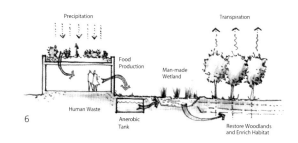

6

**BUILDING BLOCKS**

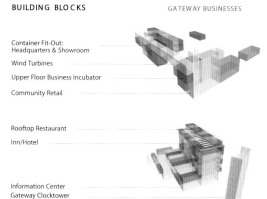

7

Container Fit-Out: Headquarters & Showroom

Wind Turbines

Upper Floor Business Incubator

Community Retail

Rooftop Restaurant

Inn/Hotel

Information Center Gateway Clocktower

**GATEWAY BUSINESSES**

**ATELIER HOUSING**

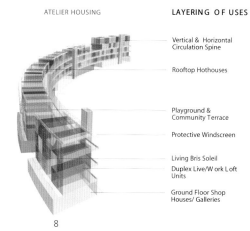

8

**LAYERING OF USES**

Vertical & Horizontal Circulation Spine

Rooftop Hothouses

Playground & Community Terrace

Protective Windscreen

Living Bris Soleil

Duplex Live/Work Loft Units

Ground Floor Shop Houses/ Galleries

Fox & Fowle Architects won a Boston Society of Architects' density competition with a plan for Gloucester, Massachusetts. Gloucester Green is based on an idea expressed in an equation: density = environmental + social + economic carrying capacity. Building on Gloucester's maritime heritage, the plan explores the reutilization of shipping containers as building blocks for development; consolidates development to protect existing woodlands and open space; and proposes a live-work neighborhood. Natural systems are woven throughout to support a sustainable community.

Borrowing from John Wood II's famous Royal Crescent in Bath, the plan for a 17-acre site at the railroad station in Gloucester, Massachusetts recognizes the natural organization of the site and incorporates atelier housing—created from recycled shipping containers—in an arc following the tracks. Constructed from containers designed for long life and loose fit to adapt to changing needs, the atelier spine is sheathed in a living

brise-soleil, establishing a green backdrop to the city. Additionally, the design knits together both the man-made and the natural. Fingers extend through the arc, while layers of mutually supportive uses—natural, civic, retail, office, and housing—are horizontally superimposed for a totally integrated community.

The plan embraces an environmental consciousness for the site that preserves existing woodlands and open space, restores the site's natural systems and incorporates urban agriculture. Additionally, restored woodlands and man-made wetlands support bio-diversity. The plan also incorporates an environmental learning center which will use the man-made wetlands, restored woodlands, and urban agriculture as a living laboratory. To reduce dependency on automobiles, the plan incorporates ZIP cars, for which 25 percent of parking is reserved. Residents reserve the use of shared vehicles, which has an environmental benefit of reducing the requirement for on-site parking and has an

economic benefit of reducing transportation costs for residents.

Anchored by civic spaces at each end, these nodes of communal activity are gateways to the city and its civic core as well as links between a new Gloucester Green and the surrounding neighborhoods. At the western end of the site, the parcel is reconfigured to create a gateway green as a town square to mark the entry into the downtown from Washington Street and to establish a focus for a farmer's market and commercial activities. A ground floor food co-op and retail uses are provided with upper floors designed to accommodate businesses that outgrow the atelier shop houses. A visitors' center and a hotel are also planned, and bus stops are located around the Green, to encourage commuters to frequent retailers in the locality. To the southwest, a community center/theater/hall fronts a civic space that links to the nearby public buildings. The plan also incorporates both passive and active recreation.

1

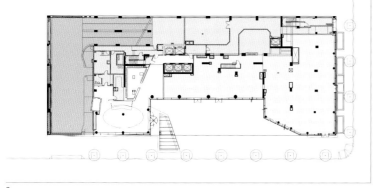

2

New York City (Manhattan)
Client: The Durst Organization, Rose Associates
Completion: 2005

# The Helena

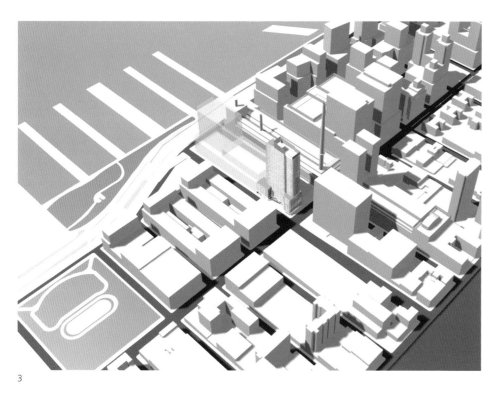

3

4

The mixed-use development planned for Manhattan's West 57th Street will transform this industrial block into a commercially viable mix of office, retail, and showroom spaces. The project area is highly visible and is a key element in the planning context of New York's West Side.

Fox & Fowle Architects' re-massing and re-zoning of the block—which involved an extensive public review process—calls for two towers at the east and west ends of the site (one office, at Twelfth Avenue, and one residential, at Eleventh Avenue). The low-rise mid-block site will house retail spaces, showrooms, and parking. The exploration for the master plan for this parcel included intensive study about streetwalls, setbacks, and building heights. Streetscape improvements will include new sidewalks and street plantings.

The Helena, a 38-story apartment building, is the first active parcel of the West 57th Street development. It will accommodate 597 studio, one-, and two-bedroom units, most with Hudson River views. The design is a reinvention of the classic New York residential typology: floor-to-ceiling glass, wrap-around windows, and column-free spaces. Concrete construction is updated with the addition of metal slab caps, improving thermal performance and lending a modern look. The building's form is devised from the interlocking and varied composition of key elements—building mass, fenestration, balconies—to create a series of volumes seen as individual, slender structures. Green technologies such as a blackwater filtration plant, photovoltaics, and efficient air handling systems are being incorporated. There are also plans for alternative-fuel vehicle hook-ups, $CO_2$ monitors, and other environmentally responsible measures. The design team has submitted the project for the U.S. Green Building Council's LEED rating system and expects a rating at the gold level.

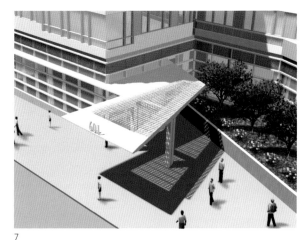

5   Rendering
6   Entry
7   Entry: aerial view
8   3D model of one-bedroom apartment
9   Plan: typical tower floor
10  Sustainable components

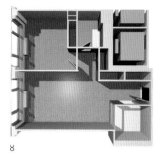

8

9

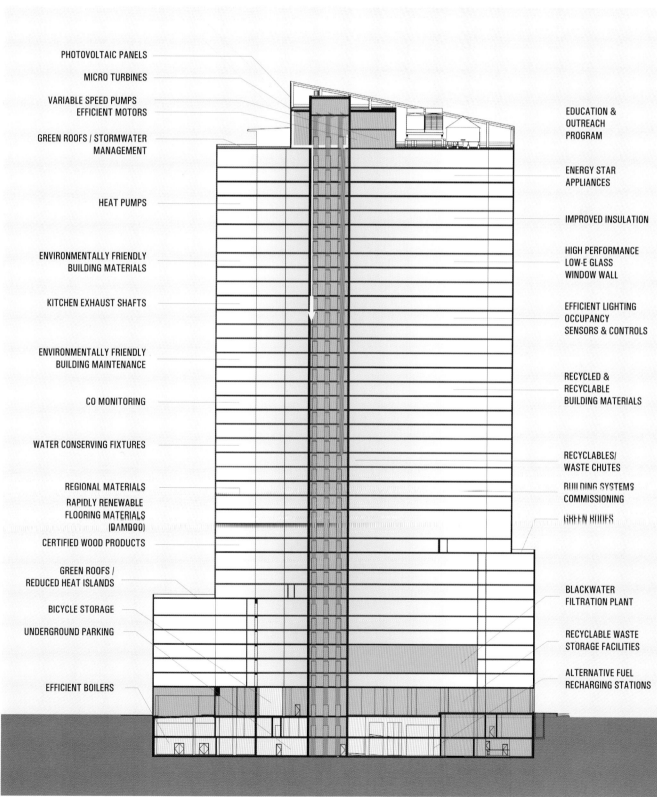

PHOTOVOLTAIC PANELS

MICRO TURBINES

VARIABLE SPEED PUMPS
EFFICIENT MOTORS

GREEN ROOFS / STORMWATER
MANAGEMENT

HEAT PUMPS

ENVIRONMENTALLY FRIENDLY
BUILDING MATERIALS

KITCHEN EXHAUST SHAFTS

ENVIRONMENTALLY FRIENDLY
BUILDING MAINTENANCE

CO MONITORING

WATER CONSERVING FIXTURES

REGIONAL MATERIALS

RAPIDLY RENEWABLE
FLOORING MATERIALS
(BAMBOO)

CERTIFIED WOOD PRODUCTS

GREEN ROOFS /
REDUCED HEAT ISLANDS

BICYCLE STORAGE

UNDERGROUND PARKING

EFFICIENT BOILERS

EDUCATION &
OUTREACH
PROGRAM

ENERGY STAR
APPLIANCES

IMPROVED INSULATION

HIGH PERFORMANCE
LOW-E GLASS
WINDOW WALL

EFFICIENT LIGHTING
OCCUPANCY
SENSORS & CONTROLS

RECYCLED &
RECYCLABLE
BUILDING MATERIALS

RECYCLABLES/
WASTE CHUTES

BUILDING SYSTEMS
COMMISSIONING

GREEN ROOFS

BLACKWATER
FILTRATION PLANT

RECYCLABLE WASTE
STORAGE FACILITIES

ALTERNATIVE FUEL
RECHARGING STATIONS

10

Opposite
Gallery
2   Sales office
3   Material work room
4   Reception
5   Main entrance

New York City (Manhattan)
Client: Herman Miller
Completion: 1996

# Herman Miller Showroom

2                                3

4

5

This 20,000-square-foot showroom is located in the renovated midtown office building that is also home to Barney's new flagship store. The leading furniture manufacturer was looking to respond to the evolving requirements and perceptions of its clients by creating a "learning center" that would serve corporate customers and the architecture and design community. This was an exciting opportunity to work with the Herman Miller research into workplace issues and to further the firm's own exploration into intelligent application of technology. Herman Miller envisioned an environment supportive of what the company calls its "consultative sales approach," which is an integral part of its corporate culture. The center would also need to be welcoming, user-friendly, and designed so that clients could make effective, efficient use of their time.

The Fox & Fowle Architects team responded with a design solution that turned apparent disadvantages—an oddly shaped floor plate and limited floor-to-floor heights—into strengths. The team separated the showroom from the sales offices and created a gallery spine that links the two areas visually. This multipurpose area is a commodious transition space for those arriving and departing. Sliding floor-to-ceiling graphics panels provide copious display space for Herman Miller sales messages, materials, and product photography.

A conventional acoustic ceiling was avoided with the decision to coordinate main trunk ducts and carefully place lights and sprinklers so that an exposed ceiling was possible, thereby maximizing the existing ceiling height, rather than trimming it away. Ceiling heights range from 8 to 18 inches above building standard. The increased openness is pleasant in its own right but also important in terms of allowing natural light to permeate deep into the space.

1

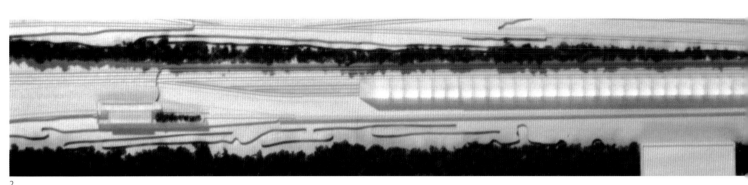

2

3

4

Eastern New Jersey
Client: New Jersey Transit
Completion: 2002

# Hudson Bergen Light Rail Transit System

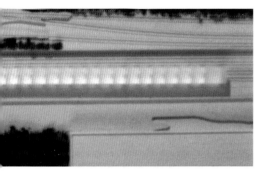

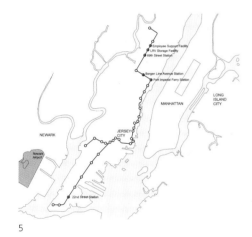

5

6

The Hudson Bergen Light Rail Transit System and its community stations are a strong example of the important connections between transportation infrastructure and architecture. The 12-station extension line will link the urban towns of Eastern New Jersey. Design guidelines were created for the stations so that they would have a consistent look and yet respond to the community context and reinforce local flavor at each site. As primarily outdoor facilities, the stations tend to blend into their urban or natural settings, a goal supported by the work of artists and landscape architects.

This project included preliminary design work for 10 of the 12 stations. The 22nd Street Station in Bayonne reflects the historic nature of its downtown location. Materials and details reflect

both the residential neighborhood to one side and the industrial area on the other. A dialogue was established between the community's landmark buildings and bridges and the rail station. The layout is dictated by ease of movement and the elevator tower creates a visual focus and marker.

At the Port Imperial Ferry Station, cable-supported canopies offer nautical gestures toward the ferry and acknowledge the sweeping views of the river and Manhattan. This project facilitates an eventual move to a final alignment a few hundred feet away.

In an industrial corridor of North Bergen, the 69th Street Station is a lively and secure environment for passengers with a generously lit overpass and

glass block elevator. The design emphasizes the north–south orientation of the station, using a linear pattern and incorporating inscribed poetry into strips of granite to animate the environment.

This project also involved an initial study for the Hoboken Station, which was the first of the stations to be funded and subsequently fully developed as its own project, as well as a conceptual study for the Bergenline Avenue Station, which is now under construction.

1   Port Imperial Ferry Station canopy
2   LRV storage facility
3   69th Street Station
4   Port Imperial Ferry Station elevator tower
5   Plan: Hudson Bergen Light Rail System
6   LRV storage facility

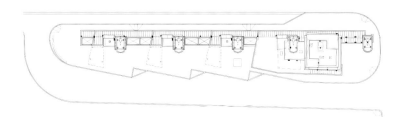

1

2

1    Site plan
2    Entrance and vent shafts
3    Perspective section: core shaft
4    Section: platform level
5    Plaza level

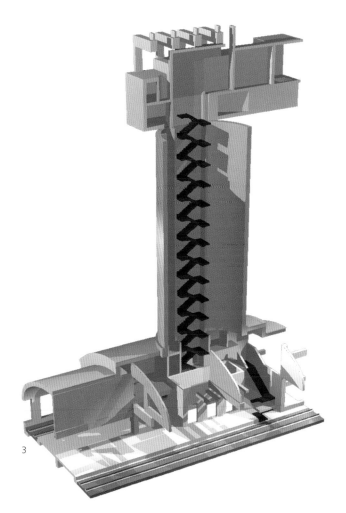

3

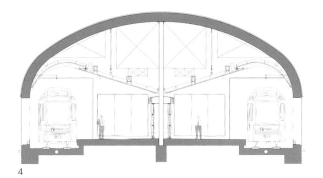

4

# Bergenline Avenue Tunnel Station

5

The Bergenline Avenue Tunnel Station is located in Union City, New Jersey, adjacent to West New York, New Jersey. It will serve as an important intermodal station stop on the Hudson Bergen Light Rail System. The station is unique as, unlike the other light rail stations on this system, it is the only tunnel station, constructed with the platform 160 feet below ground, and an expansive plaza at the street level that forms the public face of the station. The platform will be constructed using an existing train tunnel through the Palisades, which were formed during the Jurassic period. The station will link to other transportation, such as numerous bus lines in the area, in order to provide needed connections for residents in these communities.

The existing context of Union City and West New York is dense and the station plaza's openness will provide a contrast to the existing street edge and form an important open space in the community. At the plaza level, access to the platform below is provided by elevators within a brick and glass headhouse structure, and vent stacks and a sleek glass canopy span the length of the plaza. The vent stacks closest to Bergenline Avenue serve as a clock tower and all of the vent stacks have lighting incorporated both in the top and on one side, opening up to the plaza, that will emit a subtle glow of light during the evening hours. At the end of the plaza, a utility building that houses equipment to run the station stands as a beacon with a glass-enclosed stair tower that marks the end of the station site.

Brick, stone, glass, and metal form the basic palette of the station, which relates to the materials and scale of the adjacent community's existing buildings, and creates a strong civic posture along Bergenline Avenue. It was a key design challenge to respond to the surrounding environment of brick buildings, some of them historic. The team was also challenged to integrate the utilitarian structures, such as ventilation shafts and the utility building itself, at the street level. The vertical shaft containing the elevators acts as a hinge between the street level and the below-grade platform level. At the platform level, the 300-foot-long platform will have a high curved ceiling with some rock of the tunnel partially exposed. A number of artists, including Alison Sky, were employed to incorporate art throughout the platform level; the effort includes two- and three-dimensional works.

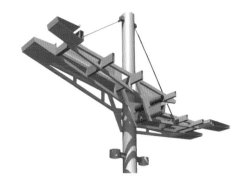

1

2

1   Canopy detail
2&7  Phase 1 in operation
3   Section
4   Model: canopy detail
5   Platforms
6   Site plan

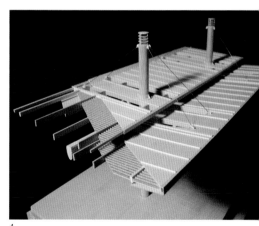

4

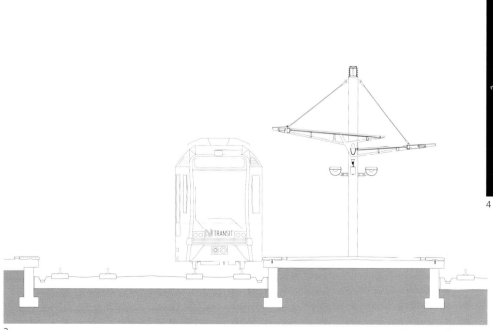

3

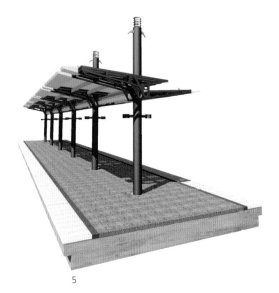

5

Hoboken, New Jersey
Client: New Jersey Transit
Completion: 2002, 2004

# Hoboken Light Rail Station

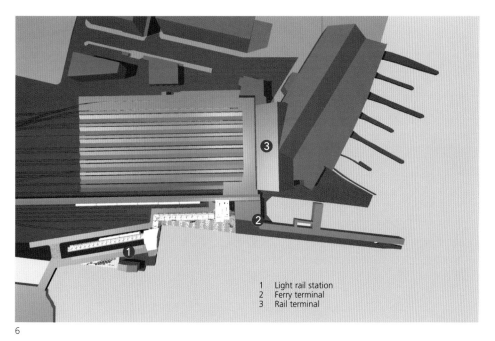

1 Light rail station
2 Ferry terminal
3 Rail terminal

6

7

Fox & Fowle Architects has designed several transit stations for the new Hudson Bergen Light Rail Transit System. The Hoboken Light Rail Station is a new light rail station above the ferry slip between Hoboken and Newport, New Jersey, which provides a link between commuter trains, PATH trains, and ferries, as well as pedestrian access to members of both those communities. This intermodal facility is sited on a central waterfront site in the heart of historic Hoboken. The location of the station on the waterfront encouraged the project team to think about how

to recapture the waterfront for public use, creating public open space and a convenient intermodal connection is a major component of the project.

The project team had to address how to insert a new, transit-oriented structure into the historic context. The team used opposition to create dynamism and balance. The open structure station borrows from the traditional train station vocabulary and makes reference to nautical shapes and forms. But the column and cable-suspension structure is contemporary, providing an aesthetic contrast to

the nearby buildings of historic Hoboken. This contrast was a conscious choice; the project team wanted to celebrate the duality of old and new.

Steel-cabled canopies provide covered access across a bridge to the platforms. Curved glass block windscreens along each platform allow for wind protection for both seating and ticket machines. The design also incorporates works of art into the composition; the elements form a new object within the New Jersey waterfront landscape. The first phase of this project, the platform canopies, is complete.

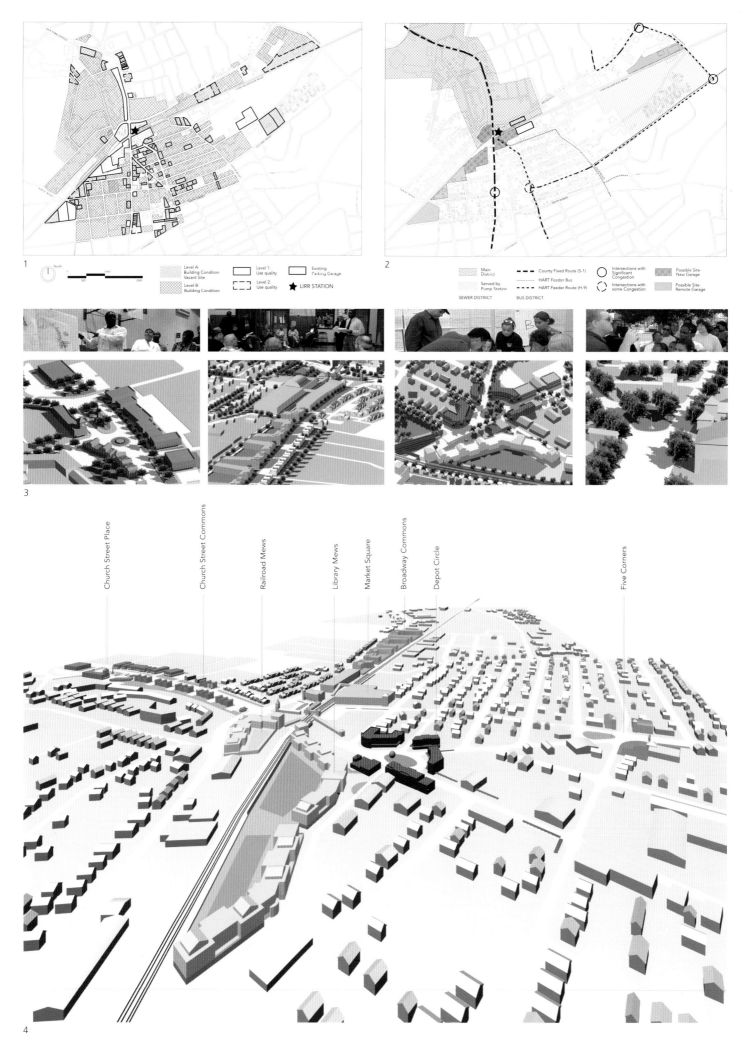

1

2

3

Church Street Place

Church Street Commons

Railroad Mews

Library Mews

Market Square

Broadway Commons

Depot Circle

Five Corners

4

Huntington Station, New York
Client: Vision Huntington
Completion: 2001

# Huntington Station Revitalization Plan

1   Limited retail opportunities at the station
2   Lack of recreation facilities
3   Poor landscaping
4   Station lacks identity
5   Unattractive surface parking
6   Unattractive and uninviting railroad underpass

7   Lack of community identity
8   Lack of focus
9   Poor pedestrian connections
10  Strip retail lacks focus/identity
11  Shortage of rental housing

12  Reinforce existing retail
13  Lack of open space
14  Poor transit connections to station
15  Poor neighborhood connections to station
16  Negative image for community

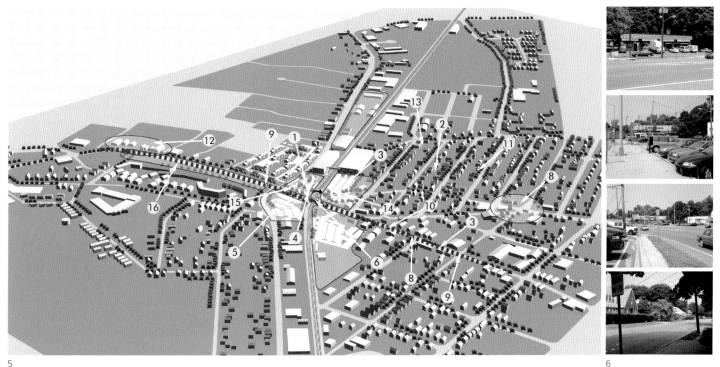

5                                                                                                    6

The Huntington Station Revitalization Plan is an effort to redefine and help shape the development along Route 110 and the station area in the community of Huntington Station, Long Island. The Fox & Fowle Architects team worked to create neighborhood-clustered retail centers and to increase the housing density on sites within walking distance of Long Island Rail Road station. The driving issue was to create opportunities for housing development and new neighborhoods that would take advantage of the existing Long Island Rail Road rail link. Transit-oriented development has proven to be a strong community development catalyst in many areas of the country. It sometimes requires revision of existing zoning, which was also the case in Huntington Station, but the results can be an economically, socially, and environmentally viable mix of uses.

This project was approached with the benefits and opportunities of transit-oriented development in mind, and collaboration with the community was a key aspect of formalizing the plan. A phased workshop process involved dozens of citizens as well as community leaders from the business and government sectors. This process resulted in a framework for redevelopment.

The project defined opportunities and constraints related to the creation of a transit-oriented development plan. It offered planning and implementation strategies for areas perceived as starting points. A wide range of housing types and retail formations was considered in the exploration process for this project.

1   Development opportunities
2   Transportation infrastructure
3   Stakeholder workshops
4   Proposed revitalization plan: aerial view
5   Existing conditions analysis
6   Existing conditions

Shanghai, China
Client: Industrial and Commercial Bank of China
Completion: 2000

# Industrial and Commercial Bank of China Headquarters

2

3

Opposite
    Pudong Avenue view
2   Terrace view
3   Entry plaza

The Industrial and Commercial Bank of China in Shanghai is a new regional headquarters and one of the first new buildings to be designed and built in the city's new economic development zone, the Pudong District. In response to site, orientation, and program, the building is organized into three interlocked slab-like masses, all running parallel to Pudong Avenue. The two frontal masses form the 28-story tower and the low mass toward the rear of the site houses retail banking functions and common spaces such as dining and meeting rooms. At the base of the tower is an elongated banking hall, the featured public space.

Shrouded in glass with protective brise-soleil, and capped with a semi-transparent "parasol" at the penthouse, the south-facing front slab forms a transparent volume that filters light against the solid stone surface of the larger central slab.

Expressed as the armature of the composition, this mass houses the service components of the tower. It is visually energized and accented by a communications tower that is integral to a cubic void at the top mechanical level. Located toward the rear of the site, the seven-story mass containing special functions is pulled away from the tower to create a skylit circulation zone linking entrance lobbies for the tower at both ends. Stairs and ramps connect the tower floors to the specialty function spaces. The primary spaces, the main conference and dining halls, are expressed in a curvilinear volume that counters the curved frontal mass, creates complexity to the composition, and conveys the importance of these functions.

The large linear banking hall is positioned under the frontal mass where its diaphanous horizontal façade expression is juxtaposed against the colossal columns of the piloti. Its architectural development is commensurate with the bank's importance in the Chinese economy. The permeability of the banking hall façade, defined by horizontal stainless steel banding, provides an element of scale and enrichment to the street level experience. At the extreme end of the hall, a large winding stair follows the circumference of the space and leads to the public banking functions on the second floor. A conical skylight marks the center point of the space, counterbalancing the strong columnar expression and flared form at the opposite end. The entry plaza provides an oasis in the center of a bustling street life. The trilogy of traditional Chinese bridges across a reflective pond slows the tempo of the entry experience, affords a chance to observe and enjoy the architecture, and prepares the visitor for the drama of entering the great banking hall.

4

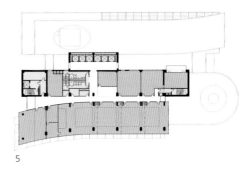

5

6

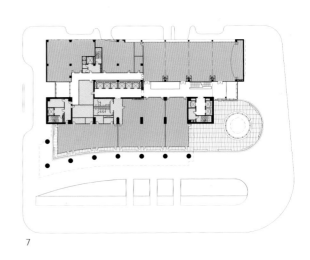

7

8

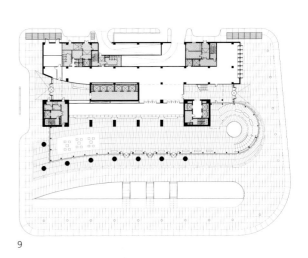

9

10

11

12

13

12&13
Detail: façade
14 Sustainable components
Opposite
Northwest view

AIR FILTRATION

AIR FILTERS
FAN
OUTSIDE AIR
CLEAN AIR TO AIR
HANDLING UNITS

PHOTOVOLTAICS

SUNLIGHT
TRANSFORMER
BUILDING INTEGRATED
PHOTOVOLTAICS
ELECTRICITY TO
BASE BUILDING
POWER

DAYLIGHTING

SUNLIGHT
HIGH PERFORMANCE GLASS
FILTERED LIGHT
REFLECTED HEAT
AND ULTRAVIOLET RAYS
BRIS - SOLEIL

INDOOR ENVIRONMENTAL
QUALITY

DEDICATED DUCT FOR AIR PURGE
DAYLIGHT DIMMING &
OCCUPANCY SENSORS
CO² MONITORS
ENVIRONMENTAL AIR
QUALITY MONITORING
SUNLIGHT
RECYCLABLE WASTE CHUTES
ENVIRONMENTALLY
FRIENDLY MATERIALS &
FURNITURE

14

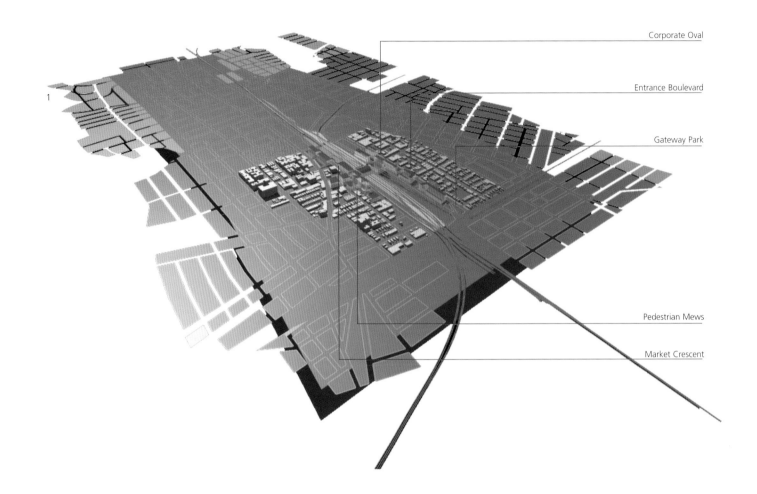

1

Corporate Oval

Entrance Boulevard

Gateway Park

Pedestrian Mews

Market Crescent

2

3

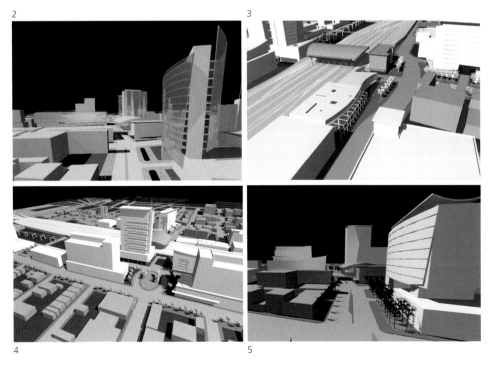

4

5

6

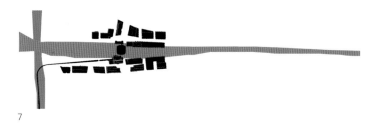

New York City (Queens)
Client: Greater Jamaica Development Corporation/LCOR
Completion: 2000/2005

# Jamaica Transportation Center Master Plan and Office Building

8

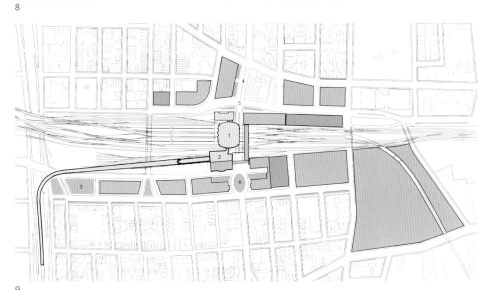

|||| Development Sites

▓ Parking

||| Transit

▓ Open Space

9

With the advent of a new AirTrain link to an existing transportation center in downtown Jamaica, Queens, this comprehensive area-wide master plan outlines a strategy to redefine downtown Jamaica as a commercial business center with an airport-related focus and as a gateway to John F. Kennedy Jr. Airport. The AirTrain will place downtown Jamaica within an eight-minute trip from the airport, closer than any comparable location. The planners aimed to enhance the unique characteristics of the community while helping prepare it for re-emergence as a business center serving the airport nearby. Unlike other airport-related business centers that have developed around major national airports in suburban areas, this is the first time that an existing urban area is being redefined to serve this purpose.

The plan not only defines future building sites but establishes a new gateway into the downtown

area. The urban design strategy is founded on a network of focal places meant to weave together the neighborhoods currently divided by the Long Island Rail Road viaduct. It also strengthens the pedestrian realm at the transportation center by creating new public open spaces and establishing new linkages to surrounding commercial and institutional areas. In response to market opportunities, the development program offers a mix of land uses, (including hotels, office buildings and residential buildings), while maintaining and strengthening existing convenience retail around the transit hub.

The approach has gone beyond identification of development sites and sought to establish key linkages between the new terminal and the existing downtown by a series of open spaces. These provide a focus for redevelopment, connections to the community, and a pleasing setting for transportation upgrades. This plan

strengthens commercial districts and buffers residential areas by clarifying zoning and enhancing streetscapes with appropriate landscape and design features. The definition of progressive architectural elements, coupled with sensitive and traditional connections to the existing urban fabric, is intended to link Jamaica's past and future.

The firm is designing the first new office building in the area as an anchor for the site. This new building furthers the notion of new energy and creates a linkage between the areas to the north and south of the viaduct by enlivening the street level with a retail arm that extends under the viaduct. Canopy structures project from the first story to divert attention away from the massive viaduct. The building materials respond to the site conditions with an opaque terra cotta façade at the rail side and a more transparent glass face to the south. As the first new development in the area, the design stands firm in its catalytic role.

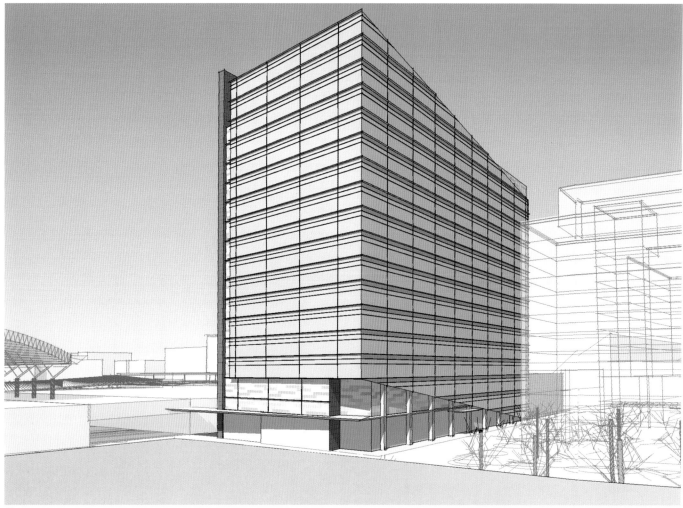

10

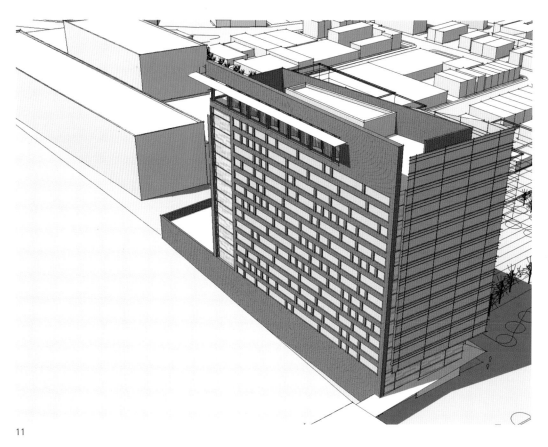

11

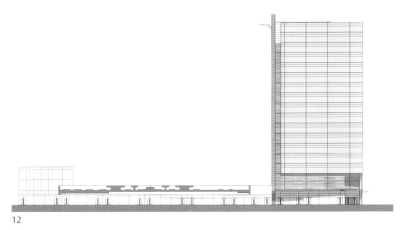

12

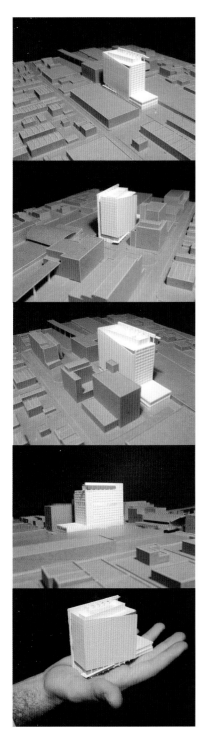

13

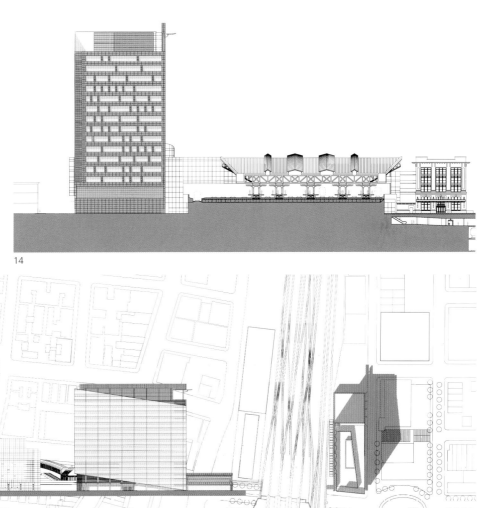

14

15

10&11   Office building: renderings
12&14   Office building: elevation
   13   Office building: study models
   15   Office building: site plan and elevation

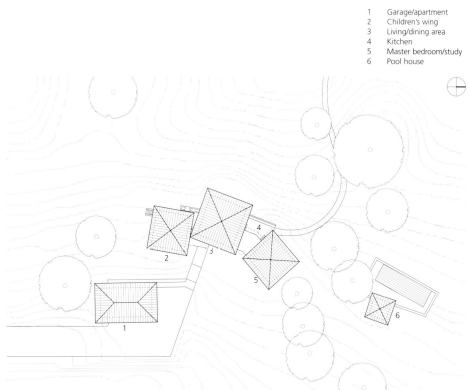

1　Garage/apartment
2　Children's wing
3　Living/dining area
4　Kitchen
5　Master bedroom/study
6　Pool house

1

2

3

4

Washington, Connecticut
Client: Labadie Family
Completion: 1998

# Labadie House

5

A rural, hilly, and heavily wooded site in Connecticut provided the sylvan setting for a house for a family of four. The Fox & Fowle Architects design team spent time at the site and talked at length with the family about how the house would be used and how it should relate to its surroundings. Inspired by a bungalow aesthetic, the designers created a contemporary dwelling that fits comfortably into its context.

The resulting solution is a trio of pavilions that follow the contour of the land. These buildings, plus the swimming pool and bathhouse, and a garage and apartment, nestle into the sloping topography, leaving much of the woods, the pond, and remnants of an old quarry on the site undisturbed. These low profile, single-story buildings house the master bedroom wing,

a children's bedroom wing, and a central wing for the kitchen, living, and dining areas. The kitchen is the link between the dining and master bedroom units and relates closely to an outdoor terrace. Each pavilion has a unique orientation to the outdoors, varying from intimate bucolic settings to long-range views of the hilly terrain beyond.

The house is approached from above, so the roofs were particularly important in this project. They have a slight pitch and are clad in copper, and the center of the pavilion is accented with four chimneys. The roof of the central building has been lifted; it appears to hover above the supporting frame and interior elements. A glass clerestory runs all the way around this pavilion, letting in light, providing a higher ceiling than the bedroom wings, and lending a graceful note

that helps distinguish these more public spaces from the two bedroom structures. Interior walls in this pavilion do not meet the ceiling, adding to the sense of lightness and airiness.

Inside and out, this dwelling is imbued with an honest expression of materials. Cladding is stucco with horizontal wood detailing. Stone piers and a stone pool surround, as well as a fireplace and hearth inside are local fieldstone and shale (some from the former quarry on site). Furniture and specially crafted elements by Jim Schreiber, combined with brightly colored textured plaster walls, lend the interior a vibrant, warm, and clean look simple enough to pair effectively with the dramatic views of surrounding valleys and forests.

6

7

8

9

10

11

6 Entry
7 Corridor
8 Detail: façade
9 Guest room
10 Living room from entry
11 Living/dining area

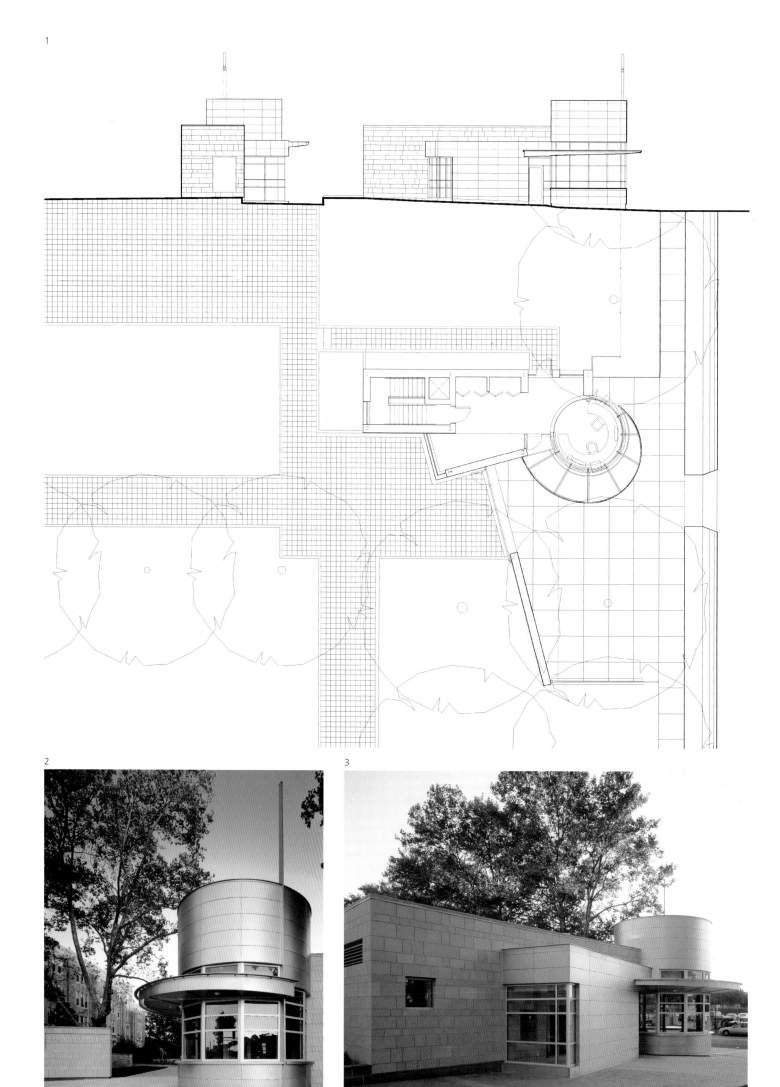

1

2

3

New York City (Bronx)
Client: City University of New York
Completion: 2003

# Lehman College Communication Center

5

The new Communication Center, located on the western edge of the campus, is the new front door for Lehman College. The building's function is a central command center for campus security.

The simple function of this building informed the pure, geometric idea. At most points, the campus is rigidly separated from the adjacent neighborhood by an iron fence. This building is an antidote to that uninviting character. A freestanding entry wall and gate pull back from the edge and break the boundary of public and private, creating a gracious entry. The nautilus-shaped structure curls out with a welcoming gesture from within the newly created plaza. Fenestration provides a 360-degree view, giving security personnel a full view of this portion of the campus while conveying a sense of openness to approaching visitors.

The building is composed of three juxtaposed objects and a spiraling canopy, physically transitioning students and visitors to and through the new campus gate. Stainless steel panels and golden limestone harmonize with existing collegiate Gothic granite, and modern steel and glass buildings nearby. The form is the product of the function, context, and a vision of the relationship between the campus and the community. Many of the security elements are below grade, connected to the campus tunnel system. For a campus with previous conflicts with the adjacent neighborhood, the new building is a welcome, mitigating gesture.

1  Elevation with site plan
2  West view
3  Northeast view
4  Concept sketch
5  North view

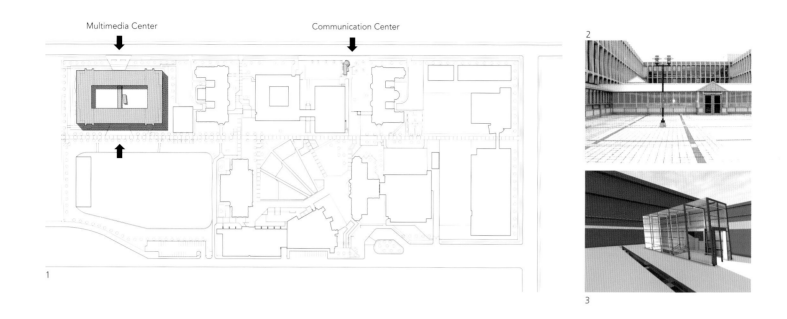

Multimedia Center                        Communication Center

1

2

3

4

New York City (Bronx)
Client: City University of New York
Completion: 2005

# Lehman College Multimedia Center

5

1 Site plan
2 Existing conditions
3 Glass beacon entrance
4 Section perspective
5 Main circulation space
6 Plan: plaza level
7 Plan: basement level
8 Plan: cellar level

6

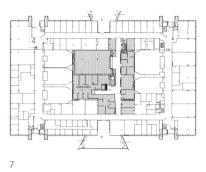

7

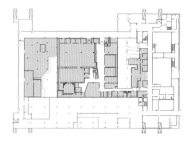

8

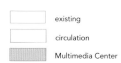

existing

circulation

Multimedia Center

This new high-tech center will serve as one of CUNY's premier multimedia facilities and help create the backbone for expanding journalism and communications programs on the Lehman College campus. The center is to be housed in the basement of the existing Carman Hall, and will include a video studio, audio studio, control rooms, edit rooms, and other administrative and technical spaces. The center had access to 10,000 square feet of space below the courtyard of Carman Hall. With a ceiling height of 23 feet, the designers were able to carve out 20,000 square feet of usable space, including a two-story-height studio space.

The challenge was to create comfortable, engaging space below grade. The key to the design team's vision was to provide a direct link to the main entry level of Carman Hall and the existing exterior courtyard, connection to the public realm, and a visible face for the new facility. The design team invented a kind of underground "valley," traversed by a circulation bridge, within the existing sub-grade structure. The result is a gorge-like space lit by a great lantern at its center. The glass entry piece in the center of the courtyard invites light down into the stairwell (the core circulation for the sub-grade space). The entry serves as the center's attractor, collecting people to its door and to the space below.

The main program elements include the two-story studio and a two-story office curtainwall that slips through linear openings along the main circulation space. The building's existing circular corridors are bisected by additional circulation that creates a viable link from one side of the building to the other. A suspended circulation bridge helps maintain acoustical privacy, while windows into the studios convey a sense of openness and activity. The technology-oriented mission drove material selections; stainless steel and glass are predominant in the simple, clean vocabulary.

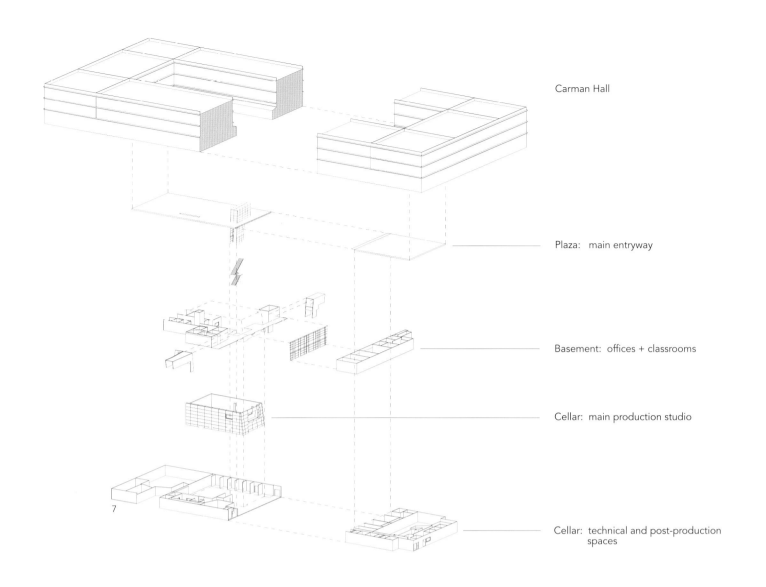

Carman Hall

Plaza: main entryway

Basement: offices + classrooms

Cellar: main production studio

Cellar: technical and post-production spaces

7

8

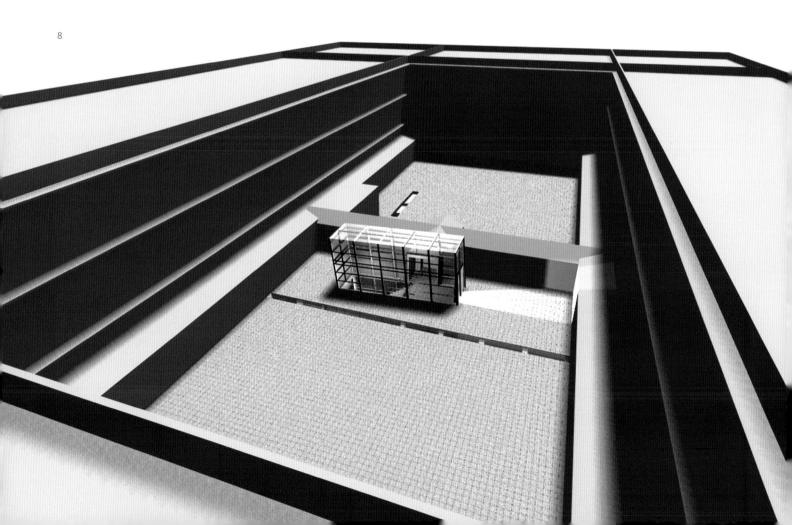

9

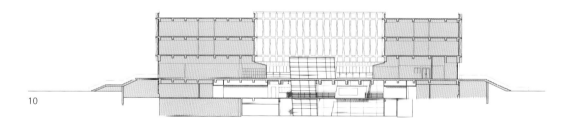

10

7   Exploded axonometric
8   Glass beacon entrance in existing
     courtyard
9   Main catwalk corridor
10  Section: through Carman Hall

1   Rendering
2   Site plan
3   Plan: typical residential floor
4   Interior axonometric
5   Double-height living area
6   Study models

Office Space

Residential

STAGE II
STAGE I

Residential

Commercial

Office Space

2

Moscow, Russia
Client: Konti Construction
Completion: 2006

# Marshal Zhukov Mixed-Use Complex

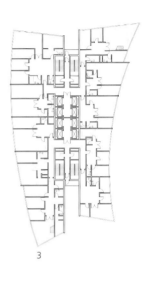

3

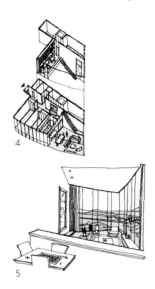

4

5

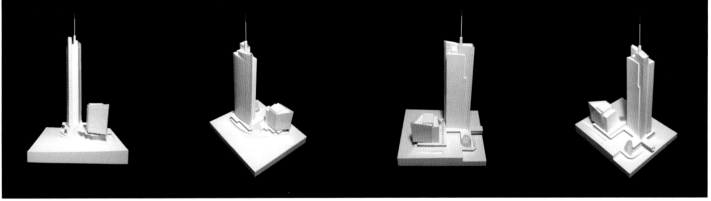

6

The City of Moscow has planned an ambitious "New Ring" of major high-rise developments. These landmark complexes will be mixed-use, with two-thirds residential units, the balance being offices and retail, entertainment and leisure venues. The 330,000-square-meter Marshal Zhukov complex is one of the first in the program and is located at a "gateway" to the suburbs. As such, it has been designed to serve as a prototype in terms of design quality and construction methodology.

The building represents a new type for the region; its architecture is light and airy, in direct contrast to the historic and pseudo-historic masonry towers that currently dominate the skyline. The project will raise the bar on

compelling interior planning, access to light and air, building performance, and efficient and effective construction methods.

The complex is made up of two primary buildings. A lower, prism-shaped volume will be offices; the tall curving slab will be apartments. The formal aspects of the tall element are in part a response to stringent safety considerations. A composition of convex and concave volumes creates many corners and "prows," providing opportunities for introducing light and air into the apartments and maximizing views of Moscow and the lake-dotted landscape to the northwest. At the corners, the living rooms are double height. The concave shapes create a sense of entry to the site

and complex, and the convex forms respond to the Moscow River, which runs parallel to the building.

This project addresses an issue that is frequently overlooked in contemporary development in Moscow: the public realm. At ground level, a winter garden will provide year-round gathering and event space intended to capitalize on the density of the project and the mixes of residential and commercial uses, which includes restaurants and a spa on the lower levels. This winter garden overlooks the river and serves as the hub between pedestrian "bridge" connections and between the various elements of the building and parking facilities.

1

2

3

4

5

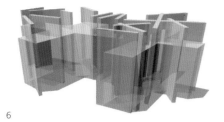

New York City (Manhattan)
Sponsor: Max Protetch Gallery
Submitted: 2002

# Max Protetch Gallery: A New World Trade Center Gallery Show

7

As participants in the New World Trade Center ideas exhibition at the Max Protetch Gallery in New York City, Fox & Fowle Architects created a "layered construction" that represents one approach to the reconstruction effort. The proposal involved burying West Street and topping it with a park, leaving the footprint of the towers vacant as hallowed ground, and creating a mixed-use project and a new transportation hub within the new density reasserting itself.

Creating a vision for this site involves thinking about invention and reinvention in a layered way; the blend of infrastructure, transportation, and architecture is one that Fox & Fowle Architects deals with often. The complexity was both familiar and inspiring to the Fox & Fowle Architects team.

The team also recognized the need to let urban design take the lead in this proposal, and many aspects of the firm's proposal have in whole or in part been acknowledged as important aspects of the urban design strategy that is now shaping the district.

This proposal answers the obligation to build an exemplar precinct, an urban fragment that embodies the highest aspirations for the future of the city. This precinct, unlike its predecessor, is connected to both the irrational downtown and rational uptown grids. It is linked to the balance of the city and the region beyond a new transportation hub—a Grand Central Station for downtown. It serves, by virtue of a new grade-level park above a buried West Street, as a connector

between the 19th-century western city edge and Battery Park City. As the surrounding city rushes in to fill the chasm created by the terrorist attacks, the twin footprints of the towers are left as voids, as hallowed ground. They exist in uneasy balance as places of silence within the new, vibrant, dense city pattern.

1   Aerial view
2   Figure/ground study
3   Green space
4   Detail
5   South aerial view
6   Concept model
7   West aerial view

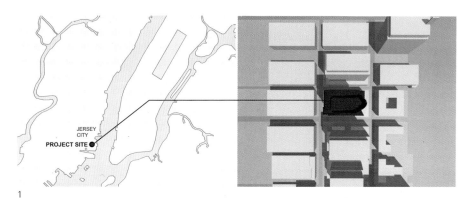

1 Location map
2 Model: aerial view
3 Plan: typical tower floor
4 Plan: second floor
5 Plan: ground floor
6 Model: east view

JERSEY CITY
PROJECT SITE

1

2

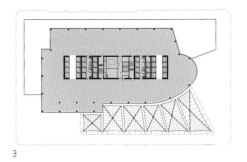

3

# Merrill Lynch Headquarters

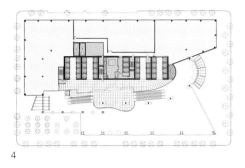

4

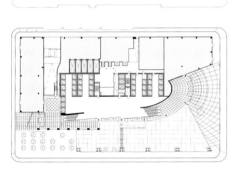

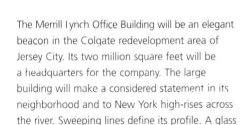

5

6

The Merrill Lynch Office Building will be an elegant beacon in the Colgate redevelopment area of Jersey City. Its two million square feet will be a headquarters for the company. The large building will make a considered statement in its neighborhood and to New York high-rises across the river. Sweeping lines define its profile. A glass signature element is nestled between shorter masonry masses, giving this building a lighter aesthetic than its more angular and predominantly masonry neighbors.

The team imagined the tower as a composition of multiple masses. A soaring bull nose transitions into a gracefully curving volume that is the heart of the composition. Clad in mirrored glass, with a slight horizontal banding, the form appears to be carved away from a larger organic volume. The deeper the carving becomes, the smoother and more monolithic the surfaces get. The all-glass

tectonic atrium at the base will allow volumes to read through to the street level where the public can experience the building under weather protection. The primary entry will be sited directly at the base of the bull nose where a fan-shaped canopy reaches out to receive pedestrian traffic. The buttressing elements of the base will be clad in stone to respond to the existing masonry and stone context. The tall, curvilinear element will be reflective glass to lend a sense of solidity by day and allow it to glow at night. The sweeping, rounded line of the tall element gives the tower a sense of grace and slender height that belies its significant square footage.

The seven-story public winter garden at the base of the building was not originally part of the program; this is a gesture that Fox & Fowle Architects has had success with in other communities. Placing public open space at the base of a large tower is

an important aspect of making the project a contributing part of its neighborhood. In this case, the developing nature of the neighborhood makes this particularly important. It will be a year-round amenity for the public and Merrill Lynch employees; it also enhances the environment of the offices that overlook it.

Office floors are being planned to optimize natural light and take advantage of impressive views. The design team is exploring the use of light shelves and other techniques to draw light deep into the floor plate. The company's interest in providing a healthy workplace has also led to research into ways to ensure quality indoor air, as well as a displacement air system (under-floor air) to boost efficiency and personal-preference adjustment. Lighting systems will also be selected to provide the greatest efficiency and utility and the building's skin will include integrated photovoltaic panels.

121

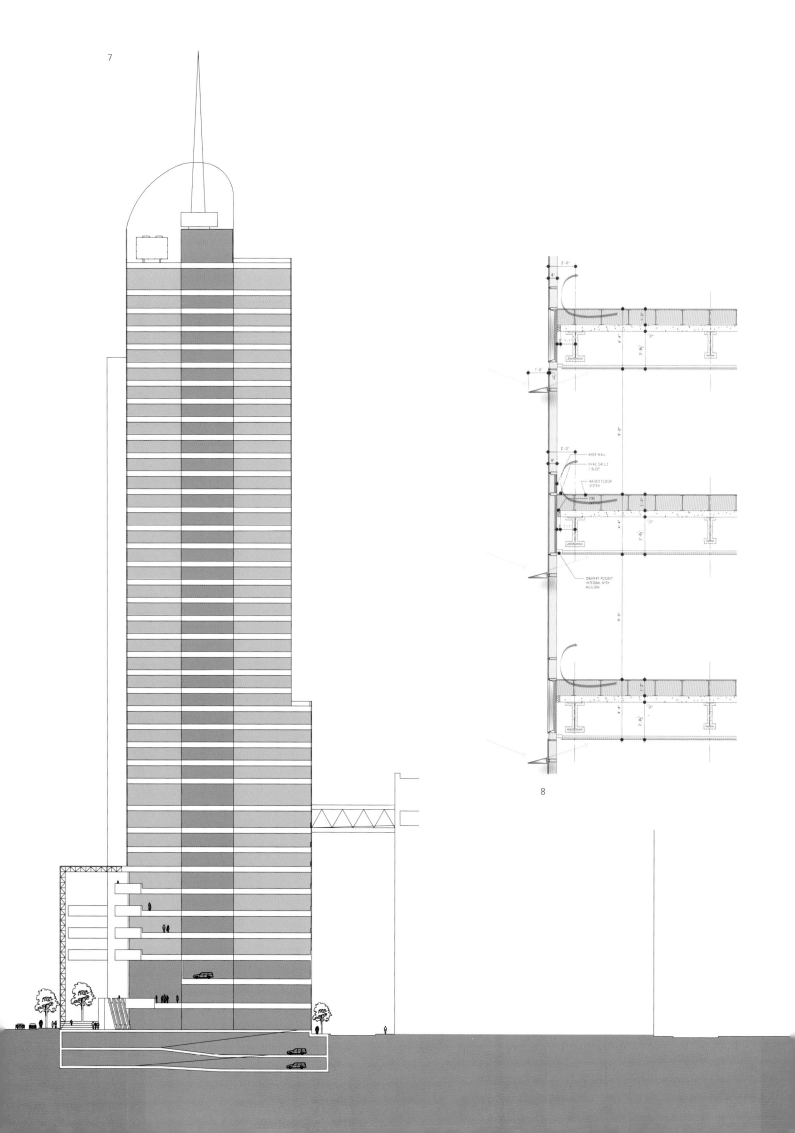

8

KNEE WALL

HVAC GRILLE
/ SLOT

RAISED FLOOR
SYSTEM

FIRE

DRAPERY POCKET
INTEGRAL WITH
MULLION

9

10

11

1

2

1  East view
2  Model detail:
   commercial development
3  Zoning plan
4  Location map

New York City (Queens)
Client: The Arete Group, Louis Dreyfus
Completion: 2000/2006

# Midtown East Development Plan and Office Building

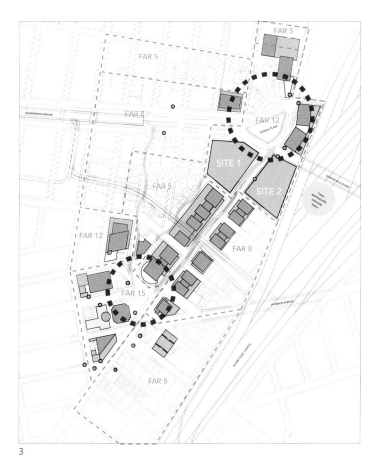

3

4

The impetus for the Midtown East Development Plan was a private developer's interest in promoting development on privately owned parcels surrounding a major transportation hub in Long Island City, Queens, directly east of Midtown Manhattan. As part of the process of defining development strategies for a specific site, the plan was created to influence public officials to move forward with the rezoning of this area and to spur private investment. The plan, developed and championed by Fox & Fowle Architects, succeeded in motivating City Planning to adopt an approach to rezoning that advocated maximum densities on sites with direct transit links.

Long Island City has a distinctive mixed-use character that comprises historic residential neighborhoods, widely recognized arts attractions, landmark buildings, open spaces, and industrial buildings and offices. It is a transit hub that channels diverse lines directly to Manhattan. The project involves the redevelopment of the Queens Plaza subway station with links to Queensborough Plaza, the proposed rail connection to LaGuardia Airport, and the proposed Amtrak/LIRR Station at the Sunnyside Yard. In addition, the plan anticipates more than three million square feet of commercial development directly linked to the hub.

The cohesive massing of the proposed development defines a major public space in Queens Plaza. By concentrating development density at either end of the project area and maintaining the existing zoning in between, the plan preserves the scale of Jackson Avenue. As a result, more conversions of industrial buildings for housing and retail will be ensured and new development along Jackson Avenue will be low-scale and akin to the existing scale.

The building forms are being developed as glass crystals, designed to contrast with the heavy industrial warehouse fabric. Creating a coherent streetscape with integrated open space was essential to the plan's vision for the district to establish a recognizable and welcoming sense of place. These open spaces provide a focus for redevelopment, connections to the community, and a pleasing setting for transportation upgrades. The plan was the result of a multi-disciplinary process that involved planners, designers, economists, engineers, and others. The mission behind the plan was to enhance the unique characteristics of the community while helping prepare it for re-emergence as a business center serving the airport nearby.

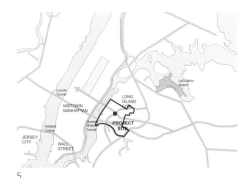

5

6

7

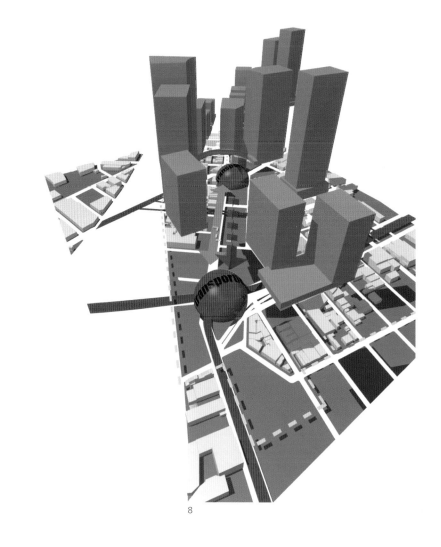

8

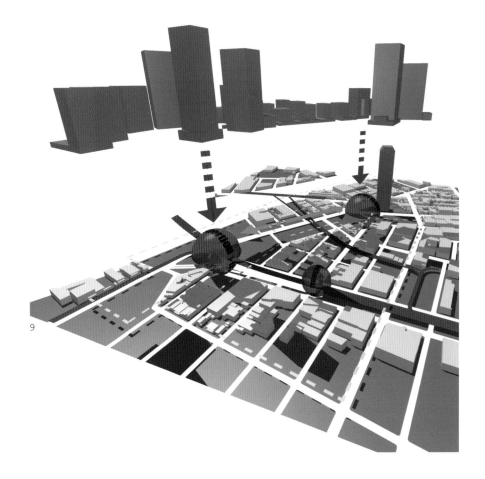

9

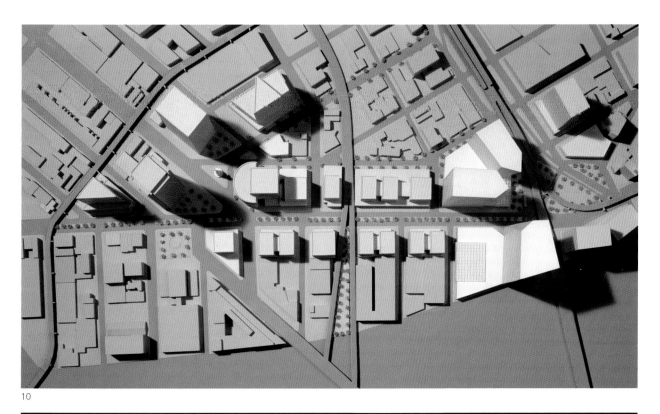

10

11

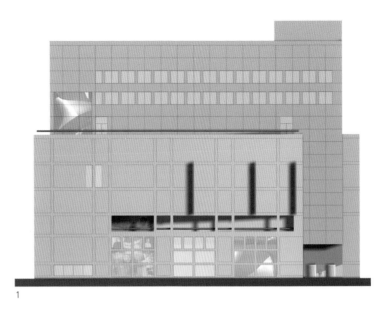

1

2

3

1    Elevation
2&3  Lobby
4    Model: aerial view in context
5    Diagrams: site analysis
6    Diagrams: concept

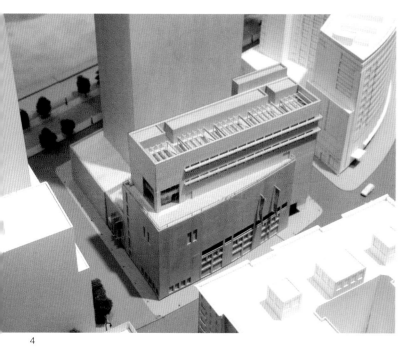

New York City (Manhattan)
Client: Museum of Women
Submitted: 2000

# Museum of Women:
# The Leadership Center Competition

4

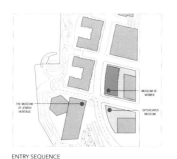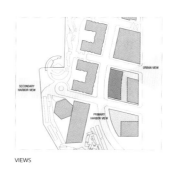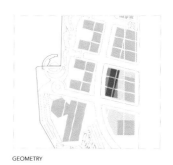

CONTEXT      ENTRY SEQUENCE      VIEWS      GEOMETRY

5

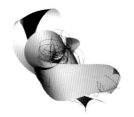

6

The team of Fox & Fowle Architects and Susana Torre of TEAM for Environmental Architecture was a finalist in the competition to design the new Museum of Women: The Leadership Center in lower Manhattan. The Battery Park City design guidelines applied here, and the five finalists were challenged to create a meaningful civic building that would be a multi-use facility featuring women's history and educational programs to promote female leadership.

The building is articulated in two masses, a building within a building. The lower mass responds to the street-level scale and embraces the lighter, more slender mass that rises behind it. The building responds, in form, massing, and materials, to the lower Manhattan neighborhood dominated by masonry structures that follow the street grid. It is, however, far more permeable visually and physically at the street level than most of its neighbors. The Fox & Fowle Architects/TEAM design engaged the dichotomies of interior and exterior and public and private to allow the building to interact with street level activity and permit views from the street deep into the building.

The museum was designed to be experienced from the top down. The path through the galleries is non-hierarchical, and the exhibitions can be traveled in multiple ways. However, at the beginning and end of the museum journey, the visitor experiences a multifaceted, dynamic, double-height space generated by the motions of a dancer. Dance is acknowledged as the earliest art form to welcome female participation. This celebratory space is memorable and beautiful and links the museum-goer's visit to a deeper history of events.

Fox & Fowle Architects' Battery Park City Sustainable Design Guidelines were a starting point for issues of sustainability; the project expanded on these precepts so that the new museum would set a new standard for civic buildings.

129

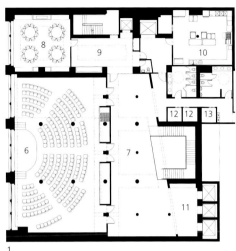

1   Program space
2   Lobby
3   Storage
4   Service entry
5   Security
6   Community and
    Student Center
7   Gallery
8   Executive dining
9   Pre-function
10  Kitchen
11  Elevator lobby

1

2

3

4

5

New York City (Manhattan)
Client: New School University
Completion: 2003

# New School University Arnhold Hall

6

7

This project represents the final phase in the conversion of a large department store for academic use as part of the New School's urban campus. The Arnhold Hall Building houses the Theresa Lang Community and Student Center, a new site for performing and academic arts, the Tishman Gallery which also serves as pre-function space, the Dorothy H. Hirshon Suite, administration offices, and student program areas. The lobby serves as one of the primary front doors of the campus. The project team used light, both natural and artificial, and the counterpoint of curved and angled wall planes to create a dynamic, yet cohesive sequence of spaces reflective of the University's unique character.

The passage from the street to one's arrival in the Cultural Center is marked by a sequence of light, a metaphor for the illumination of education. Natural light frames the double-height entrance. A backlit glass panel glows above the opposite wall of the entry vestibule. Deeper into the space, a floor-to-ceiling wall of glass, illuminated with light pipes, dramatically frames the open stair to the second floor gallery. Within the center, the space, with its angled ceiling and minimally detailed framing wood walls, is focused on the natural light of the existing double-hung windows along the street wall.

By bringing a sense of movement from outside to inside, the design team emphasized the central

importance of the school to the neighborhood as a place of community and connection.

A strong, curved plane takes the visitor into the lobby on the first floor. An east–west diagonal plane counters it, marking a new "zone" as the visitor moves up to the second-floor cultural center. There, the angled wall, in a strong, deep gray, has an established presence and solidity. A sequential ceiling plan contributes to the spatial differentiation. Existing columns also provide a progression and rhythm; every other column rises to an articulated capital. The space reads simply but has great discipline. The elements work together, including the Sol LeWitt wall drawings, visible from both floors, which provide a sense of unity to the two areas.

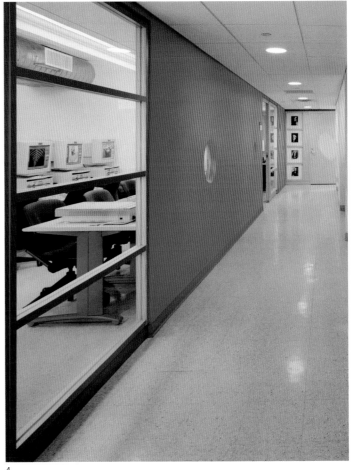

1 Plan: ninth floor
2 Plan: eighth floor
3 Media Lab
4 Classrooms
5 Programming diagram
6 Information desk

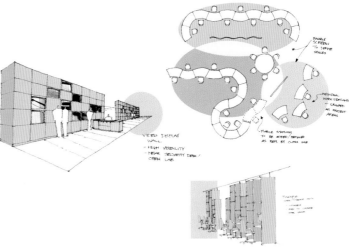

5

New York City (Manhattan)
Client: New School University
Completion: 1999

# New School University Knowledge Union

6

Fox & Fowle Architects has completed a series of projects for the New School University in New York, part of the institution's long-term effort to renovate and unify its multi-building campus throughout Greenwich Village. The first was a new two-level technology center built in two phases on the eighth and ninth floors of Arnhold Hall, a former department store. The Knowledge Union is seen by the institution as an important symbol of its commitment to and leadership in the use and teaching of electronic technology. It is intended to showcase the technology of the school and will eventually become the heart of wider technological capability dispersed throughout the campus.

The 12,000-square-foot multimedia facility includes classrooms equipped for computer, video, and sound presentation for computer graphics instruction; digital video and audio editing labs; computer stations, and an equipment center and faculty resource center. The Knowledge Union Lounge offers a place for ad hoc gatherings, a stage for connections between students, faculty, and visitors. An open stair links the two floors.

Future flexibility was an important consideration in this project, from both a spatial and technological point of view. The Fox & Fowle Architects team created a variety of spaces to address this issue. Large open areas are flexibly arranged and ancillary smaller spaces provide much-needed acoustic privacy for the teaching and execution of multimedia production.

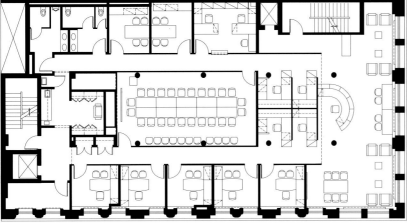

1

3

4

# New School University
# Robert J. Milano Graduate School

5

The Robert J. Milano Graduate School of Management and Urban Policy renovation is one of several projects that Fox & Fowle Architects has completed for New School University. The Robert J. Milano Graduate School needed space to accommodate meeting, research, and faculty offices, and the operation of the school's respected programs, including the Center for New York City Affairs, the Community Development Research Center, the Health Policy Research Center, and the Milano Nonprofit Management Knowledge Hub.

The school's new home was created on five floors of a 1900s loft building with entrances on Fifth Avenue and 13th Street and was named Fanton Hall. The school was designed to promote communication and collaboration among staff, faculty, and students. This mission defined the logic of the plan: open or group spaces framed by offices, interior window walls bringing exterior light to the interior, integration of different space types with the existing building's window spacing and structural framework.

Unstructured meeting areas provide a public, open feel on each floor and also help tie the floors together as parts of one space. These spaces are located at the building's most open corner and benefit from dual exposure to natural light. Interior spaces are divided by walls of etched glass. These semi-transparent panels bring natural light into the building, rather than leaving it the domain of the windowed spaces at the periphery. Some existing elements, such as cast-iron columns, were left exposed. These contrast with the rectangular grid of the interior glazing and the panels of perforated metal, elements of the palette of contemporary details. The regularity of the plan is enriched by a range of material textures and colors, an array of contemporary lighting fixtures, and careful treatment of natural light.

1　Plan: eighth floor
2　Fanton Hall
3　Faculty office
4　Reception area
5　Conference room

1

2

1　Building and topographical integration
2　Model: aerial view
3　Vehicular and pedestrian circulation
4　Program elements and organization

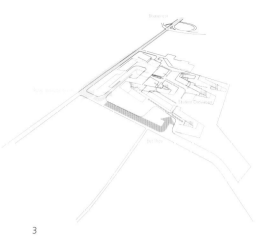

Perth Amboy, New Jersey
Client: New Jersey School Design Competition
Submitted: 2003

# Perth Amboy Public High School Competition

3

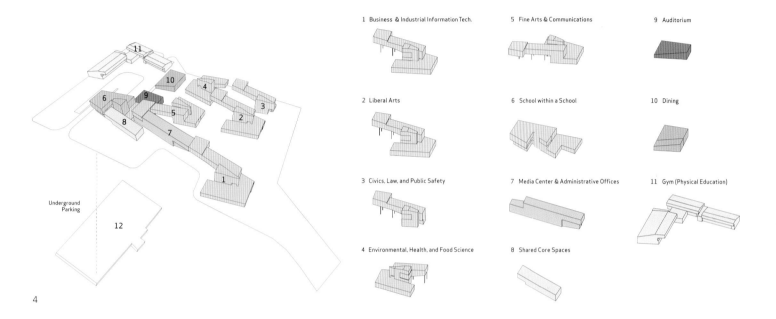

1  Business & Industrial Information Tech.

2  Liberal Arts

3  Civics, Law, and Public Safety

4  Environmental, Health, and Food Science

5  Fine Arts & Communications

6  School within a School

7  Media Center & Administrative Offices

8  Shared Core Spaces

9  Auditorium

10  Dining

11  Gym (Physical Education)

Underground Parking

12

4

Fox & Fowle Architects' concept for the new Perth Amboy High School was selected as one of four finalists from nearly 200 entries. The competition organizers hoped to elicit potent new ideas about the future of education, especially in New Jersey's economically troubled cities. The site for the school is in the midst of a residential neighborhood in Perth Amboy, a formerly thriving, but now ailing, industrial port.

The approach to the design of the new high school centers on an alternative perception of the meaning and method of education—one that provides an arena for the students of the city to discover and explore their own self-awareness through an amalgam of experience and personal evolution. The majority of Perth Amboy's students are in the midst of efforts to find their own function and identity in a society that often seeks to assimilate and erase rather than acknowledge and treasure. To properly serve the unique needs

of these students, the high school itself must encourage cultural multiplicity and allow for the creation of novel identities within our changing culture. It must configure a social construction that advances heterogeneity while advocating a coherent, participatory education.

The solution for the site maximizes the identity of each academy by creating a community of discrete units. A permeable, accessible campus emerges, dispersed across the site, acknowledging its extents and variation. Through this externalization, the students can witness what is happening around the campus and can also be seen, promoting a self-awareness and overall consciousness of the school community. Informed by the existing topography and circulation patterns, the interwoven configuration makes multiple uses of the ground, not just as a fixture underfoot, but also as an inhabitable dimension and overhead shelter. Green roofs are part of an integrated

sustainable network and environmental teaching tool. The angular, expansive nature of the site plan compels students to walk outside, promoting health and interaction among the student population. Spaces shared with the public community are focused toward the more active, public boulevard. Buses carrying students enter at a more internalized entrance toward the quieter, academically-focused western sector.

Each academy is composed of four elements, the nucleus of which is the Instructional Commons, a roofless, glass-enclosed box that serves as an identifying marker for each of the five academic cells. Each academy is anchored with a concrete shelf that rises from the ground and terminates in fixed nodes. Composed with modular construction pieces, the formation allows for extreme flexibility and encourages additive expansion and further connection.

5

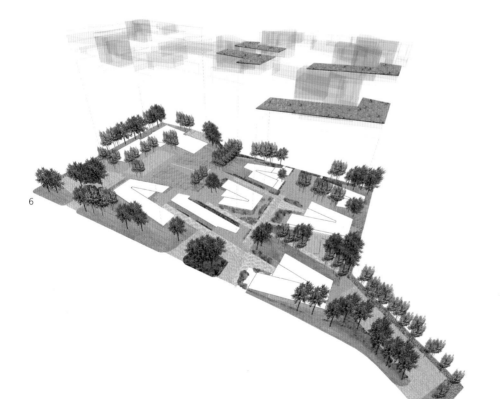

6

5    Academic green
6    Landscape/building design
7    Section/elevation
8    View to cafeteria
9    Sustainable components

7

## Topographical Integration

**Solar Roof**
South facing Photo voltaic array on roof offsets peak cooling loads during summer months.

**Building Orientation**
Site Specific orientation of major building elements to maximize energy efficiency and natural light.

**Vegetated Roof**
Multiple benefits gained by delaying stormwater runoff, reduced heat gain and attenuating sound.

**Skylights**
Strategically introduce natural light to improve quality of underground spaces.

**Ecological Site + Water Management**
Permeable paving diverts stormwater and allows precipitation to recharge groundwater.

**Retention Pond**
Located at lowest point on site to collect recycled and diverted stormwater.

**Geothermal Heat Pump**
Geothermal heat exchange between HVAC system and earth or a pond-water heat sink.

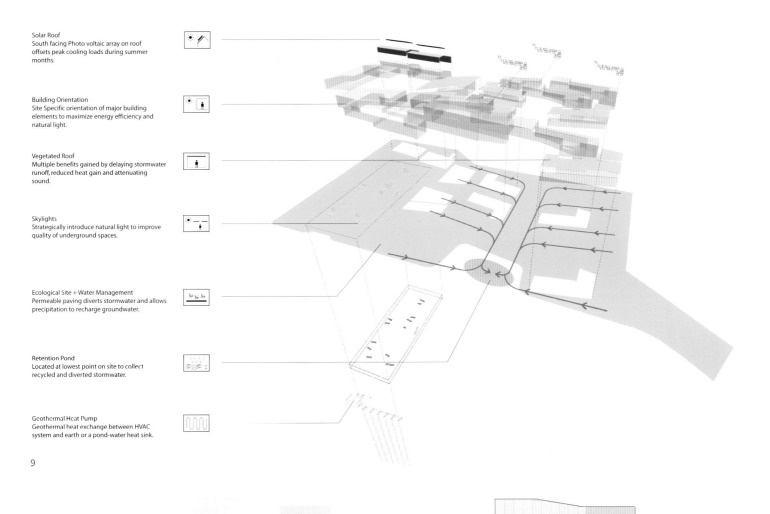

10

Expandability

Steel Structure

Terracotta Skin & Atrium

11

12

10 Model: campus entry
11 Design elements
12 Academy entrance

13 Model: aerial view
14 Academy program components
15 Instructional commons

13

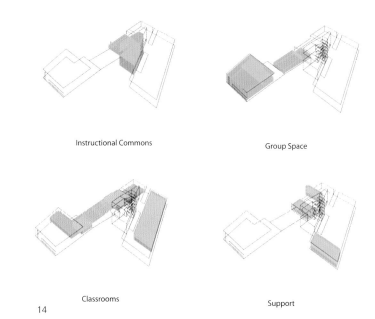

Instructional Commons

Group Space

Classrooms

Support

14

15

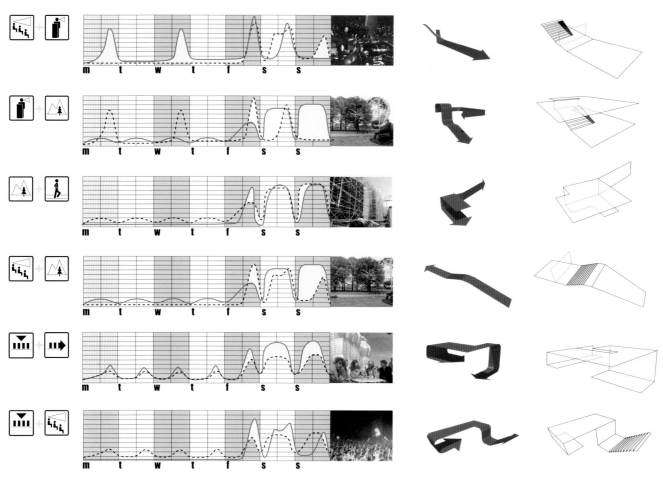

1

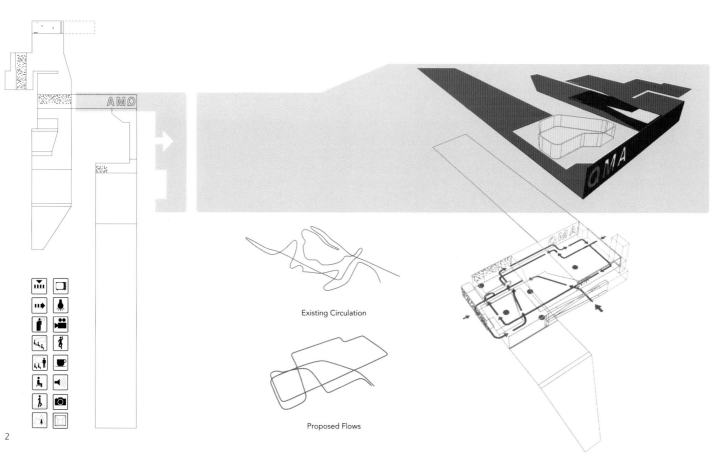

Existing Circulation

Proposed Flows

2

142

New York City (Queens)
Client: New York City Department of Design and Construction
Submitted: 2001

# Queens Museum of Art Competition

3

4

The Fox & Fowle Architects design for the Queens Museum of Art competition addressed the diverse population of the surrounding neighborhood as one of the central issues. The site is a former World's Fair venue in Flushing Meadows Corona Park, which is bisected by the major thoroughfare of Grand Central Parkway.

The team took the living museum idea literally. Visitors are visible as the living force within. The design exposes the building's skeleton and wraps it in a new skin, a gesture that would transform the old museum and prepare it for a new life as a "living" cultural center, representative of its diverse neighborhood. The new "wrapper" becomes the building shape; it is a continuous surface. Public spaces of the museum look or open onto outdoor spaces; when weather permits, the building can be opened up almost completely. This play between façade and form stemmed from the team's desire to put the whole building on display.

A series of filters defines the paths along which people move through the program spaces and the interstitial spaces between them. This blurring of boundaries between gallery, workshop, and gathering space inspires a fluid environment with programmatic flexibility for display of a wide range of artistic presentation. The team wanted to create a series of spaces that could be continuously experienced and yet feel discrete from one another. The idea was that the architecture would not compete with its contents but instead be a backdrop to the visitors' interaction with art, technology, event, and each other. The Fox & Fowle Architects team sees this design as an unfolding story. The designers envisioned the museum as a celebration of evolution from past to present and a stage for transition from present to future. Here, the traditional museum is being challenged and reinvented to include ideas about how people experience the museum itself and how they respond to its contents. This is an interactive museum; people are part of the show.

1   Diagram: programming and events
2   Diagram: pedestrian circulation
3   Plan
4   Diagram: components

143

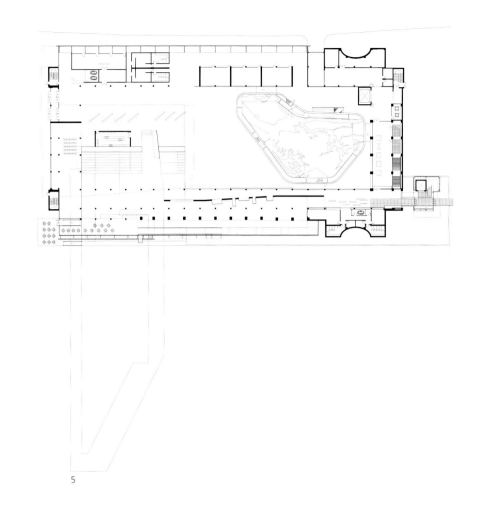

5

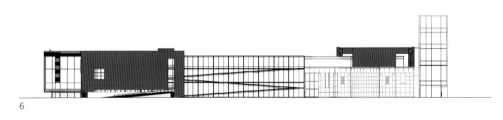

6

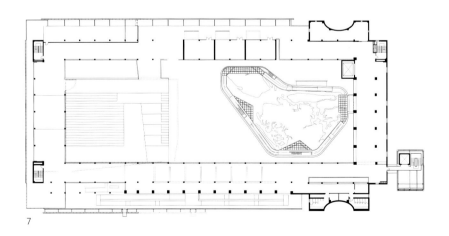

7

8

5   Plan: ground floor
6   Elevation
7   Plan: lower floor
8   Outdoor theater
9   Model

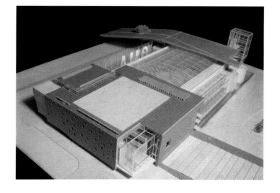

9

10

11

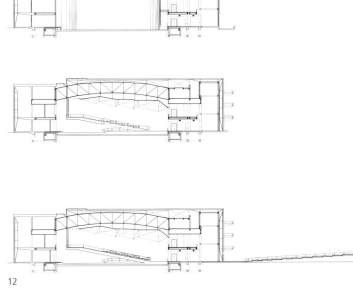

12

10&11   Multipurpose space
12   Sections
13   Workshops
14   Detail: gallery wall
15   Exterior signage

13

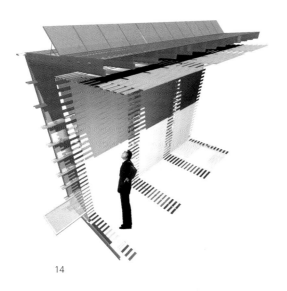

14

15

1

2

New York City (Queens)
Client: City University of New York
Completion: 2006

# Queensborough Community College
# Holocaust Resource Center and Archives

3

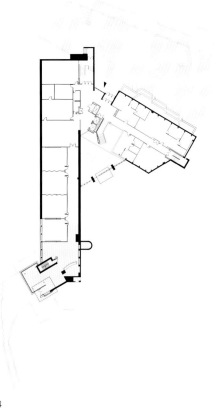

4

5

Located at a prominent spot on the Queensborough Community College campus, a pavilion addition and interior renovation has been designed to house the Holocaust Resource Center and Archives. The new building—the first project to result from the master plan—will be fully integrated with the first floor of the original facility, in a seamless design that will highlight the unique features of both structures. With this expansion, the center will be better equipped to teach the legacy of the Holocaust and 20th-century Jewish history to a broad student population.

The scheme includes two glass-framed cubes, a simple, pure lantern form conceived as a symbol of hope. One cube will support the program's requirement for a reception and exhibition space. The second, smaller cube carves out the entry into the lobby through the existing masonry wall. The interior of the existing building's first floor wing was entirely reorganized to meet the center's needs for flexible exhibition spaces, a new library and efficient and effective administration space. The outdoor plaza will create a destination within the campus for introspection and contemplation.

The metal and glass design responds to the natural topography and location on the property. A new entrance establishes and renews an identity for the 30-year-old building, reinforcing the link between students and the educational programs.

The solution responds to the current patterns of campus pedestrian circulation for the placement and orientation of the glass addition, the ramp entry sequence, and the outdoor plaza to expand and enhance visual and physical relationships.

1   Pavilion addition
2   Detail
3   Site plan
4   Plan: ground floor
5   Model

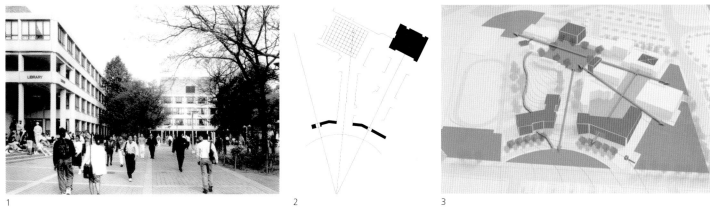

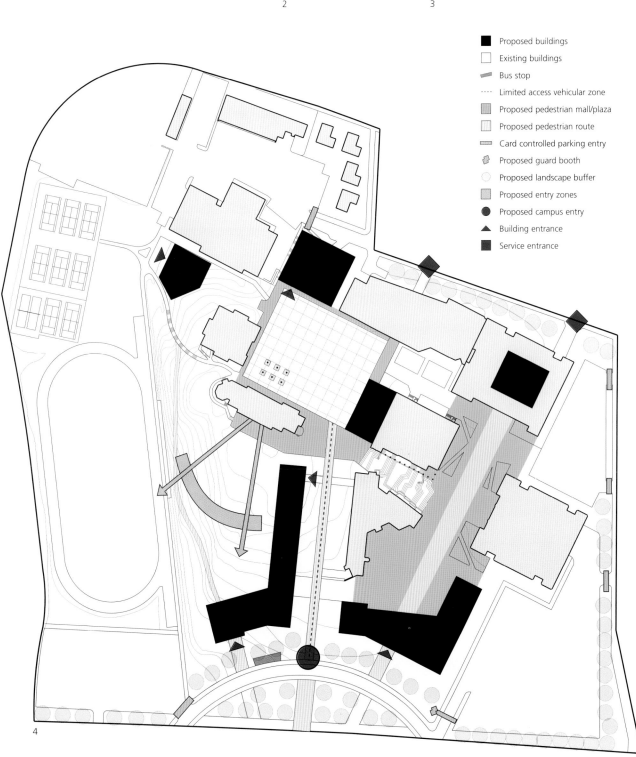

**Proposed buildings**

☐ Existing buildings

⬌ Bus stop

····· Limited access vehicular zone

▦ Proposed pedestrian mall/plaza

▦ Proposed pedestrian route

▭ Card controlled parking entry

🛡 Proposed guard booth

○ Proposed landscape buffer

▦ Proposed entry zones

● Proposed campus entry

▲ Building entrance

■ Service entrance

1

2

3

4

New York City (Queens)
Client: City University of New York
Completion: 1999

# Queensborough Community College Master Plan

5

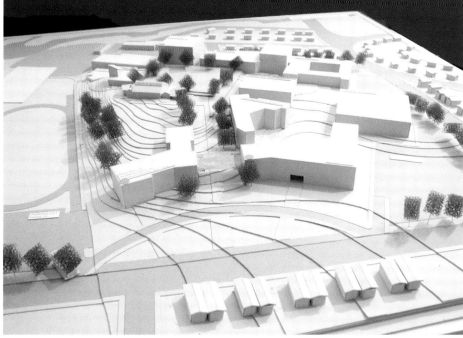

1 Existing conditions
2 Diagram: access
3 Diagram: circulation
4 Master plan
5 Existing conditions
6 Model: master plan

6

The community college is located on a 34-acre knoll in a residential part of the Bayside neighborhood of Queens. This school was established in 1958 as a part of the City University of New York system. Today, the expanding curriculum and outdated facilities at Queensborough Community College has forced the institution's leaders to engage in a thorough re-evaluation of transportation and circulation issues, space and program requirements, buildings and site conditions, and evolving faculty and student demands.

The Fox & Fowle Architects' master plan strengthens the existing axes to improve campus pedestrian circulation while enhancing physical and programmatic ties to the surrounding community. A series of courtyards were designed to encourage movement to various destinations throughout the campus. Administration spaces are consolidated in a single building to allow redistribution of classrooms through the campus. This also allows students to access all administration needs in one location. Advanced class and laboratory requirements and relocation of demolished temporary structures will be accommodated in new structures.

The plan exploits the location of existing buildings and open spaces, responds to campus topography, and removes obsolete structures. It also adds new buildings and creates campus boundaries with strong visual identity and a clear hierarchy of entry points. A series of versatile quadrangles each have a distinct character, which is defined by topography and bordering building uses. Plan goals also include facilitating pedestrian and vehicular circulation throughout the campus with clearly defined paths and mechanical conveyances where necessary to eliminate barriers. Tree-lined parking and service areas are suggested at the campus periphery, accessible to both streets and college buildings, acting as a buffer for campus quadrangles and walkways. The plan also recommends establishing opportunities for signage and for the materials and scale of architectural and landscaping elements to enhance campus cohesion.

1

2

3

4

5

Rochester, New York
Client: Bausch & Lomb, Excellus Blue Cross
Blue Shield, City of Rochester

# Rochester Revitalization

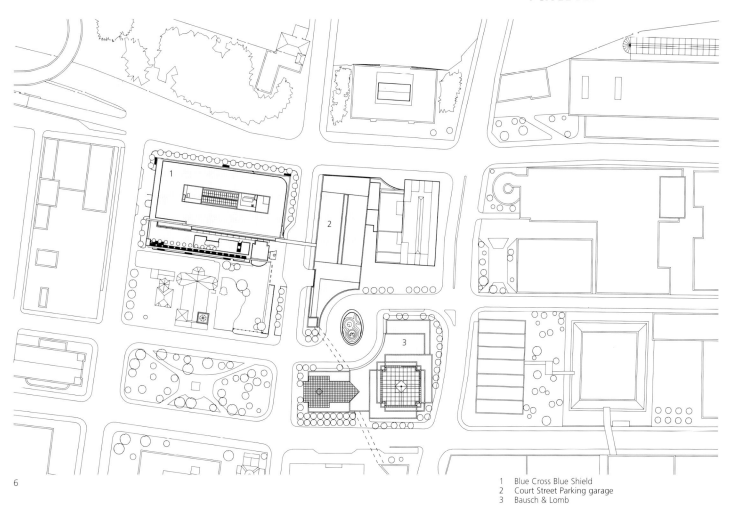

6

1 Blue Cross Blue Shield
2 Court Street Parking garage
3 Bausch & Lomb

Over a period of several years, Fox & Fowle Architects designed a group of buildings—two headquarters buildings and a city-owned parking garage—in downtown Rochester, New York. They became part of the revitalization of the historic but long-neglected part of town. Clustered around Washington Square Park, a landmark space designed by Frederick Law Olmsted, the buildings integrate themselves into the fabric of the neighborhood while at the same time bringing contemporary freshness and aesthetic diversity to the mix. Broad thinking resulted in a rerouting of the street pattern to create a new sense of place.

The Bausch & Lomb World Headquarters building is a 20-story granite-clad tower that gives distinction to the small city's skyline and is the centerpiece of the revitalized area. The building core is at a 45-degree axis to the prevailing

geometry to maximize exposure to the urban plaza. Light red granite cladding complements the surrounding urban palette, while the stainless steel gabled roof contrasts sharply with the flat roofs of the neighboring towers. An inviting glass and steel winter garden is a year-round urban park for this northern city; visited by hundreds of people each day, the winter garden has become a cherished oasis, the civic centerpoint of the area's redevelopment. The roofscape references the office tower's roofline as well as churches nearby. At the lower level, the city's Skywalk Tunnel System extends to connect to midtown, the public library, a parking garage, and the neighboring corporate headquarters.

The Finger Lakes Blue Cross Blue Shield building completes the urban assemblage in the historic district. Designed to emphasize energy efficiency,

flexibility, and workspace quality, the six-story glass and brick building acknowledges its historic context as well as issues of daylighting, acoustics, indoor air quality, and ergonomics to enhance employee health, job satisfaction, and productivity.

These projects became catalysts for urban renewal through a combination of Fox & Fowle Architects' vision and the concerted effort of private, public, and planning and design interests. The private investment was recognized as an opportunity by the city, county, and other entities. The New York State Urban Development organization and the Historical Society provided critical support and the city funded the critically important parking garage, as well as a major addition to the public library, and pedestrian bridges and tunnels linking all three of these projects to each other and to the existing downtown skyway system.

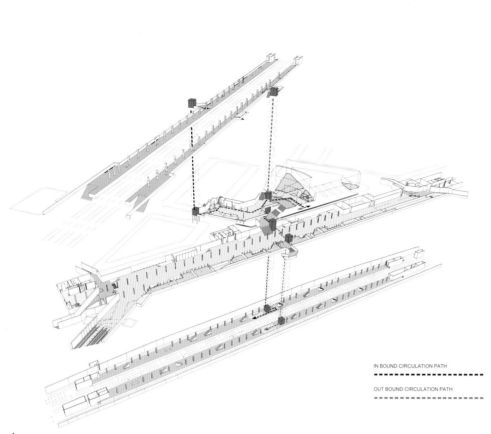

IN BOUND CIRCULATION PATH

OUT BOUND CIRCULATION PATH

1

3

1    Exploded axonometric
2    Rendering: main entrance
3    Existing conditions
4    Model
5    Plan: site and roof

2

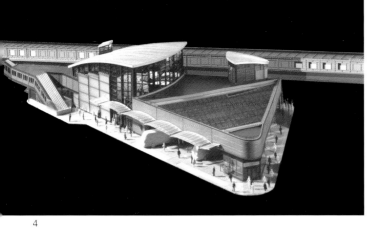

New York City (Queens)
Client: MTA New York City Transit
Completion: 2004

# Roosevelt Avenue Intermodal Station

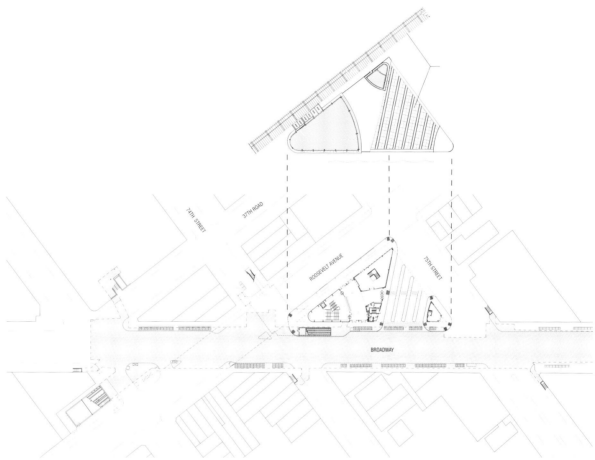

5

The Roosevelt Avenue Intermodal Station serves as an entrance and transfer point between the elevated and subgrade lines, buses to LaGuardia Airport, and other transit lines for the region. The design of the terminal building, conceived by Fox & Fowle Architects in association with Vollmer Associates, provides a modern beacon for the community that is rooted in the historic infrastructure.

The roof arcs up into the shape of a large fan, bringing a graceful line to the utilitarian facility and the industrial materials of the transit system itself. The glazed entry pavilion serves as a civic space. Various glazing techniques—blue-green terra cotta panels, robust steel detailing, and engaging geometry all under the arcing roof— create a compelling space that will serve the neighborhood as identifiable civic space as well as providing services for travelers passing through. The space will be further enlivened by a 60-foot-wide by 15-foot-high clerestory glass mural. The

architects are working closely with artist Tom Patti, who will design and fabricate the piece.

The parabolic structural grid ceiling provides a roomy interior. The iconic hub space is a place that people pass through quickly at various levels. Air conditioning this space seemed questionable to the designers, especially given that it is open to other spaces and is connected to the underground tunnel system. This space functions as a natural chimney; it draws warm air up through the station and vents it out through louvered windows, a low energy means of cooling the mezzanine and platform levels, which are both below grade.

A skylight system allows daylight penetration while incorporating integrated photovoltaics to power below-grade lighting systems. Photovoltaics will also be installed in the elevated platform's roofs in compliance with green guidelines for the entire system authored by Fox & Fowle Architects. The

two-part PV system will generate approximately 65 kilowatts per day, which will sometimes be used on site and at other times be fed back into the power grid.

The design team worked with the various stakeholders involved, to meet and exceed agency standards and to transform this project, which could have been a standard remodel/upgrade with the addition of a utilitarian entry space, into a benchmark project. It is on track to be a model facility in terms of energy efficiency, but also for making an aesthetic statement that is powerful yet responds to a wide range of elements. The community was very involved in this project, which helped bring to light what those who live nearby believed was important in terms of the physical and social nature of the surrounding site. This informed the design process as it became clear that the low-rise neighborhood would benefit from an iconic public form at its transit hub.

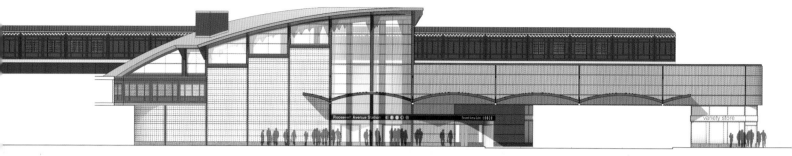

6

7

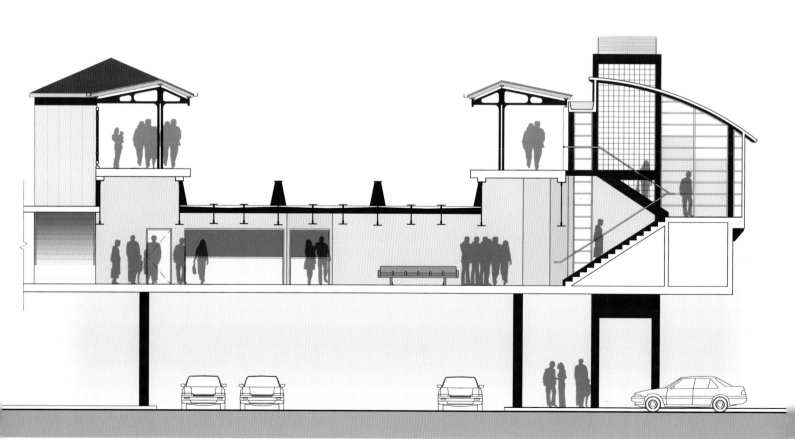

8

9

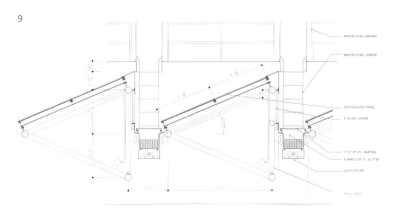

PAINTED STEEL RAILING

PAINTED STEEL LADDER

PHOTOVOLTAIC PANEL

2" ALUM. LOUVER

1 1/2" ST. GRATING

FORMED 3/8" PL. GUTTER

LIGHT FIXTURE

STEEL TUBES

10

3,100 Sq Ft of Building Integrated Photovoltaic Panels
ON SOUTH FACING GLASS SKYLIGHT
With 30% Daylight Penetration
Will Produce +/- 30,000 Kwh Ac Per Year

OPEN GLASS LOUVERS ON ALL SIDES
To Provide Natural Ventilation And Draw
Hot Air From Subway Level

OPEN LOUVERS ON NORTH FACE
To Provide Natural Ventilation

IRT MEZZANINE

BUS DEPOT

COMPRESSED NATURAL GAS (CNG)
Used In Buses

TERRACOTTA CLADDING
Low Embodied Energy;
No V.O.C.s;
Regionally Produced

IND MEZZANINE

STORMWATER RETENTION TANK

CENTRALIZED LIGHTING SOURCE

RECYCLABLE BUILDING MATERIALS
(ALL GLASS & STEEL)

Section through New Subway Station & Bus Terminal

BROADWAY    BROADWAY

11

1

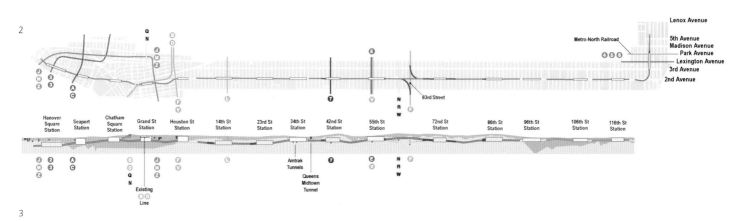

2

Lenox Avenue
5th Avenue
Madison Avenue
Park Avenue
Lexington Avenue
3rd Avenue
2nd Avenue

Metro-North Railroad

63rd Street

| Hanover Square Station | Seaport Station | Chatham Square Station | Grand St Station | Houston St Station | 14th St Station | 23rd St Station | 34th St Station | 42nd St Station | 55th St Station | 72nd St Station | 86th St Station | 96th St Station | 106th St Station | 116th St Station |

Amtrak Tunnels

Queens Midtown Tunnel

Existing Line

3

1   Aerial view: 2nd Avenue
2   Route map
3   Section: tunnel
4   Diagram: system analysis
5   Diagram: programming

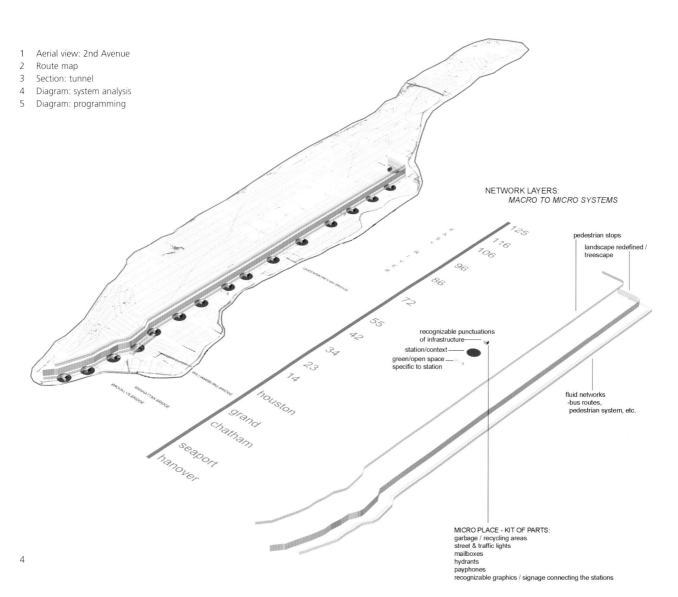

NETWORK LAYERS:
*MACRO TO MICRO SYSTEMS*

pedestrian stops
landscape redefined / treescape

recognizable punctuations
of infrastructure
station/context
green/open space
specific to station

fluid networks
-bus routes,
  pedestrian system, etc.

MICRO PLACE - KIT OF PARTS:
garbage / recycling areas
street & traffic lights
mailboxes
hydrants
payphones
recognizable graphics / signage connecting the stations

4

New York City (Manhattan)
Client: MTA New York City Transit
Completion: 2020

## Second Avenue Subway

ARRIVE    CONNECT    CONTAIN

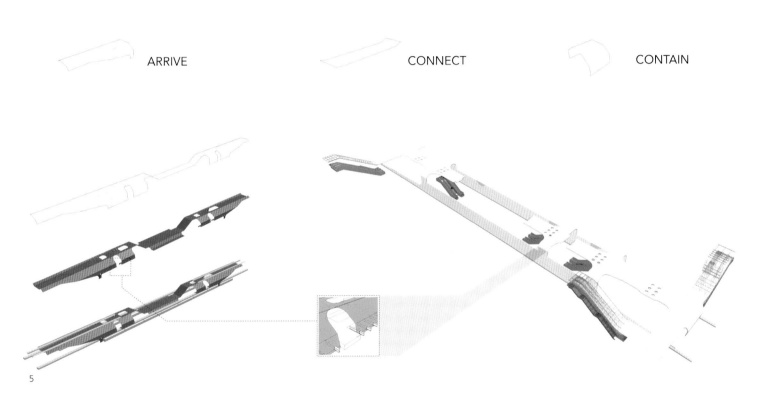

5

The Second Avenue Subway line in New York will run from 125th Street to Whitehall Street, the full length of Manhattan's East Side. The line will ease congestion on the Lexington Avenue line and provide a connection to mass transit for the east side of Manhattan. Fox & Fowle Architects is helping to create this complete new line that will allow the realization of New York City Transit's goals: environmental responsibility, high-performance design, neighborhood integration, and maintainability in the context of creating a system that meets passengers' needs for security, ease, and comfort.

It has been a long-time priority at Fox & Fowle Architects to elevate infrastructure standards with exuberance and attention to design. Much of the Second Avenue Subway work is below grade, but significant planning and conceptual work have

gone into the project at the ground level and below. Fox & Fowle Architects' designers are acutely conscious that people typically have more contact with infrastructure every day than they do with most buildings, beyond those they live and work in. Understanding transportation projects as a journey is important; good design can elevate that experience.

Fox & Fowle Architects is working collaboratively with a large team of engineers led by DMJM+ Harris/Arup, transit officials, and others; in a project office, some 200 people work side by side so that the full benefits of multidisciplinary integration and open communication can be realized. For the Fox & Fowle Architects team, this approach is an extension of how they usually work and it has been invigorating. Part of the role of Fox & Fowle Architects on this project has been to expand the exploration of the program to more fully engage

with the identity of the line above grade and how that intervention occurs in each neighborhood. Part of the team's mission is to reconcile a series of opposing elements: the line must have an identity that is its own, but also fit within the larger system, and it must also be welcoming and inviting, as well as secure and accessible, in each neighborhood.

The final resolutions for the stations will contain significant elements of commonality through universal platform, canopy, and enclosure components. For variability and to create a sense of identity for each of the diverse neighborhoods, each station design will integrate community-responsive art installations. There is a strong sense that the new line has an opportunity to capture the energy and enthusiasm of the city by celebrating the civic realm and providing an exciting experience for tourists and residents alike.

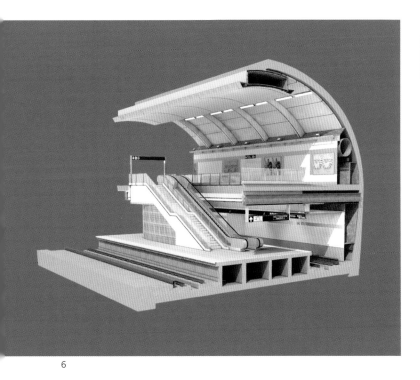

6

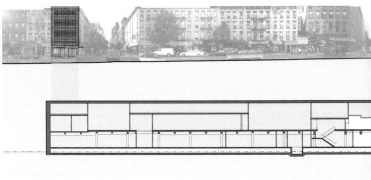

8

6    86th Street station—mezzanine and
     platform levels
7    86th Street station—mezzanine and
     vertical circulation
8    86th Street station—section
9&10   86th Street station—ancillary structures
11   86th Street station—plan: ground level
12,13&14   86th Street station—entrance studies

7

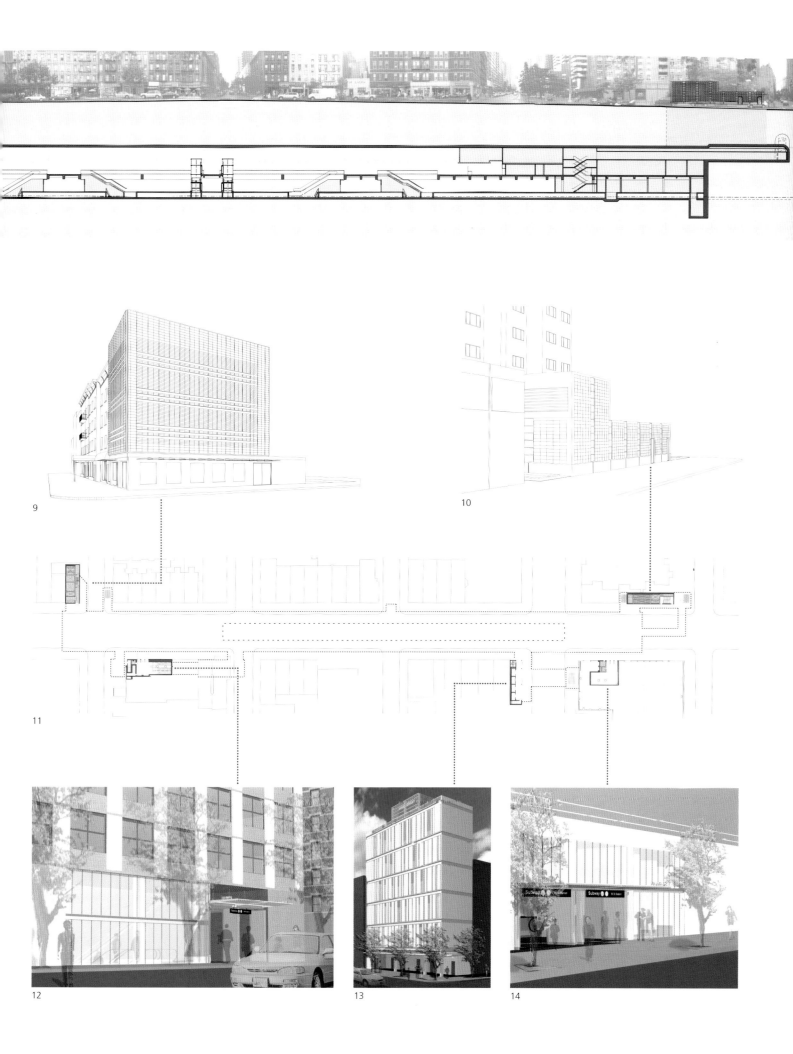

9

10

11

12

13

14

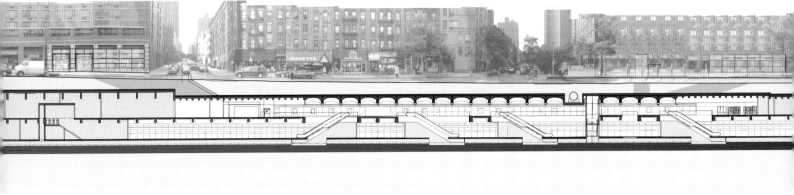

15

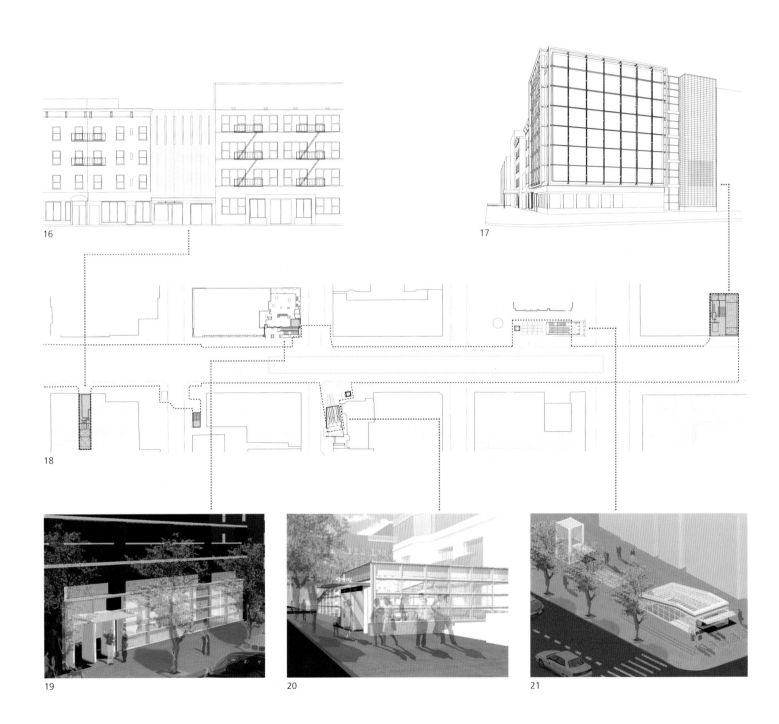

16

17

18

19

20

21

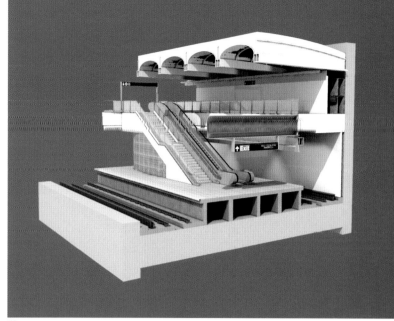

22

23

2

1 Corridor
2 Executive office
3 Conference room/reception area
4 Detail: workstation screen

New York City (Manhattan)
Client: Skanska New York
Completion: 1999

# Skanska New York Offices

3

4

The firm designed a complete renovation of the 11th floor of a pre-war Madison Avenue building for Skanska Construction Company. The project involved working with the client to develop a program, space plan, and several custom-designed elements. Skanska New York had the dual role of client and construction manager, which allowed for a creative purchasing schedule and a compressed construction schedule.

A full-height sandstone block wall marks the entry to the office and creates the construction company atmosphere desired by the client. There is a strong sense of material and attention to craft here and throughout. Aluminum display rails allow artwork in the entry to be changed easily and also lend order to the space. Bold planes of color and simple geometric volumes coordinate the inner office space.

The space plan emphasizes teamwork, which is central to the company's approach to its work. Workstations are made entirely from custom millwork. The stations are set up in clusters of four, each cluster centered on a column. Tables, which are allowed to move about as needed, are adjacent to each group for ad hoc meetings and other requirements. Exterior offices are minimized to allow views to the windows from any position in the office. Partially screened areas were created for privacy within the open office setting. Conference rooms are distributed throughout the space with varying degrees of privacy or openness.

The offices convey the look and feel of the construction industry. Utilitarian materials, such as concrete block, maple, plywood, exposed scaffolding fasteners, and stained concrete flooring, helped carry a rough-hewn-but-professional theme throughout the space. Exposed ceilings, galvanized ductwork, and mill-finish cable trays reinforce the construction aesthetic. Translucent data wiring stretches from cable trays to the top of workstations, providing maximum adaptability. Sustainable building materials were employed where possible. This is achieved through the use of low-embodied energy, rapidly renewable materials, and products such as soy-based particleboard for workstations, corrugated polyester panels as space dividers, bamboo flooring, and rubber floor tile made from recycled tires.

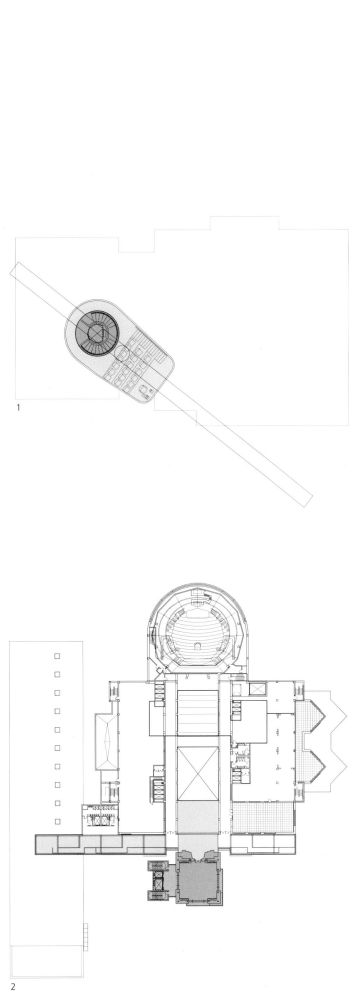

1

2

3

4

5

Jersey City, New Jersey
Client: Liberty Science Center
Completion: 2006

# Skyscraper! @ Liberty Science Center

7

Crane cab

Crane lobby 1
Crane lobby 2

Observation level

Habitat

Form & Function
Tower/stair

Building the building

Underground World
Skyscraper World
Skyline Theater

Tower Gallery

6

1    Plan: roof
2    Plan: tower level
3&4  Model
5    Model: detail
6    Section
7    Photomontage of skyscraper tower

The Liberty Science Center, in Liberty State Park, is mounting a permanent exhibit that will explore the modern skyscraper. It will examine the scientific and technological principles involved in the design and engineering of the structures, as well as the impact they have on local and regional environments and ecosystems. According to the center, "With these buildings a part of our present and future, it is imperative that we learn about how to make them a part of a sustainable society."

Fox & Fowle Architects has designed a transformation of the center's existing observation tower into a "skyscraper under construction," which will house and be the exhibit itself. The tower will be reconfigured and partially demolished to maximize exhibition space. The existing cladding will be removed and replaced with cladding that is part of the new building design and represents the possibilities of contemporary curtainwall systems. A new structure, housing the new stairs and elevators, will be added. It will culminate in a rotating tower-crane cab, up-sized to fit a class of 25 students.

After being contacted by the Port Authority of New York and Jersey, the center expressed interest in installing structural steel from the demolished World Trade Center in part of the exhibit. The center will display a hammer column and one of the 20-ton core columns of the towers and other artifacts retrieved from Ground Zero in the months following the September 11 attacks.

This project has involved consultation with numerous organizations and individuals, including Thornton-Tomasetti Engineers, the Skyscraper Museum, the National Science Foundation, the Port Authority, Columbia University Oral History Project, the National Building Museum, the Council on Tall Buildings and Urban Habitat, and an extensive and esteemed advisory panel. Fox & Fowle Architects has worked hard to provide leadership and momentum for this "industry barn-raising."

10TH FLOOR

9TH FLOOR

8TH FLOOR

7TH FLOOR

6TH FLOOR

5TH FLOOR

4TH FLOOR

3RD FLOOR

2ND FLOOR

1ST FLOOR

AFTER RENOVATION

UPPER SCHOOL

LOWER SCHOOL

MIDDLE SCHOOL

VISUAL ARTS

PERFORMING ARTS

PHYSICAL EDUCATION

ADMINISTRATION

SUPPORT SPACE

1

2

3

1   Master plan
2   1985 addition
3   Detail: addition
4   Lobby
5   Library: study area

# The Spence School

4

5

The Spence School is an independent K–12 girls' school which was founded in 1892 on the Upper East Side of Manhattan. It is housed in a neo-Georgian building designed for Miss Spence and her school in 1929 by John Russell Pope. Since 1980, Fox & Fowle Architects has designed incremental and major changes to this grand building to ensure that the facility continues to meet the evolution of educational requirements. Each modification of the building has maintained the sense of community and intimacy of the original, respecting but not replicating the old. These interventions have helped transform a small boarding school into a 600-student institution that ranks among the top in the country.

Earlier modifications to the building obscured some of its fundamental logic. With each renovation, Fox & Fowle Architects has brought back the inherent clarity and strength of the building's plan through re-establishing or reinforcing the "donut" of circulation around the central elevator core.

The 1985 addition to the original building added 25,000 square feet of new program space. Using similar materials (brick and limestone) and a symmetrical composition, the addition respects the historic character of the older building while updating it with the clean detailing of centralized bays.

The more recent library and media center renovation was a two-step process. The original library and the Lower School library, located in a classroom, occupied one third of the floor. Through the relocation of lockers and offices, the library grew to fill the entire floor. The treasured intimacy of the original library was maintained yet redefined through the careful use of materials, the ceiling treatment, and a new openness of the plan. As in the main renovation, environmentally sensitive measures were implemented, with special attention given to elements that would impact on the quality of the indoor air.

Most recently, with the Lower School moving to another facility, Fox & Fowle Architects developed a new master plan and has begun implementation of a phased renovation that completely reworks the upper four floors of the building. The renovation design was preceded by a comprehensive analysis of existing spaces, the school's current goals, and projections of future needs. The resulting master plan looked beyond defining the uses and character of the gutted spaces. It also planned for optimal uses within the remaining spaces. The design team continued a strategy for creating centers of identity within the school. The restructuring, supported by the careful location of color, lighting, and ceiling articulation, will create a distinct space and identity for the Upper and Middle schools, an expanded science center, a floor devoted to performing arts, a consolidated art center, as well as new general purpose classrooms throughout the building. Functional spaces are grouped and detailed so that identifiable centers of activity occur throughout the school. Each has its own character while it is clearly connected to the whole. A quality of openness and natural light is maximized.

6

7

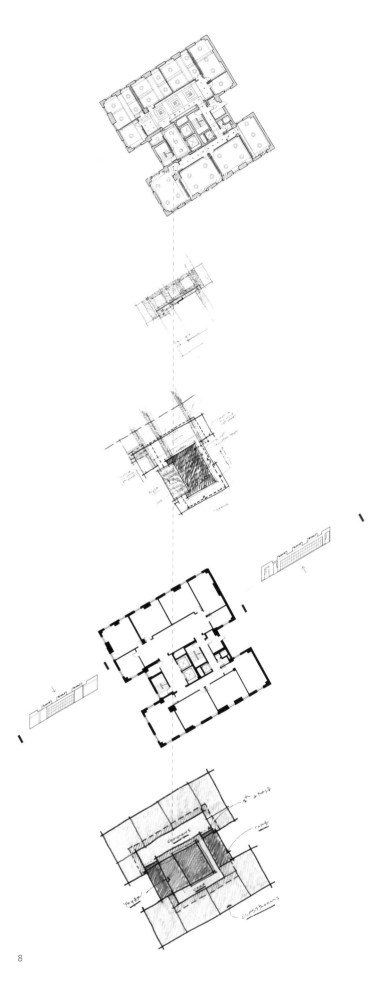

8

9

10

6　Library: lower school section
7　Library: upper and middle school section
8　Diagram: stacked plan
9　Middle school commons area
10　Chemistry room

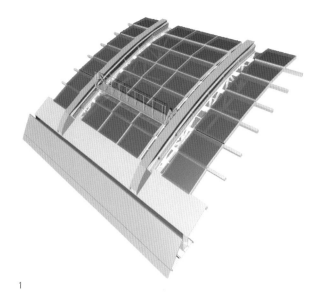

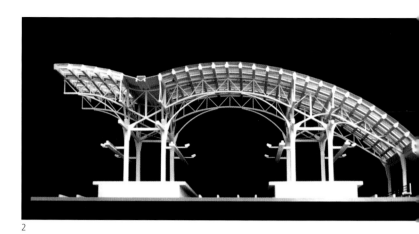

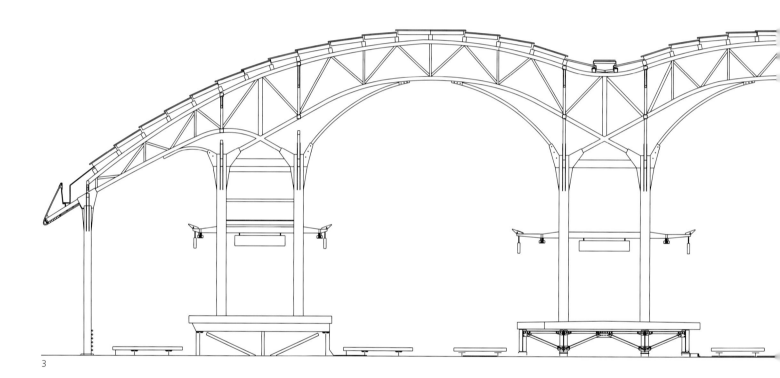

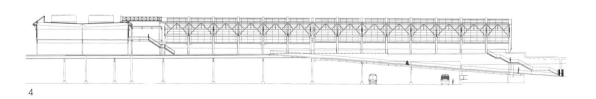

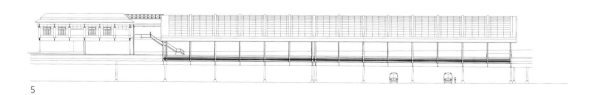

1  Detail: photovoltaic panels
2  Model: canopy
3  Section: canopy
4  Section: looking west
5  Elevation
6  Rendering
7  Existing conditions

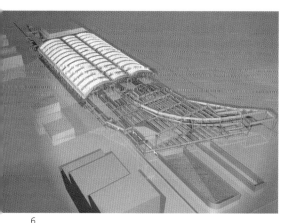

6

7

# Stillwell Avenue Terminal

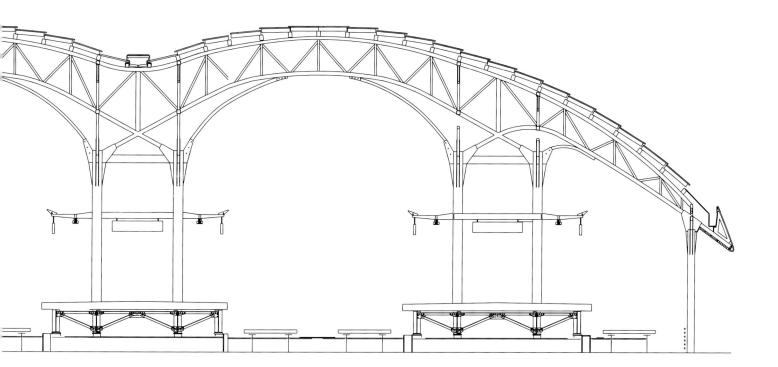

This growing intermodal station in Coney Island serves four lines of the New York City subway system and several commuter bus routes. Some 11,500 people pass through the station each day. The station, originally opened in 1915 as the Brooklyn, Bath & Coney Island Railroad, needed an architectural and structural overhaul to coincide with New York City Transit's need to improve service and other government agencies' efforts to stimulate private and public investment to revitalize the Coney Island area.

Circulation, accessibility, and security were key drivers of the design inquiry behind this conceptual study. The goal was to intensify the

terminal's civic presence in order to help unify surrounding communities. Using the expressive strength of architectural history, the structure is a celebration of the railroad presence aimed at stimulating future development.

The Fox & Fowle Architects' study for the station resulted in a design that would unify the four platforms and various tracks under a soaring glass-and-metal roof structure with laminated photovoltaic (PV) panels that arch from platform to platform. The panels would generate some 200 kilowatts of electricity for the station. A fundamental goal for the project team on this project was to provide a useful and attractive

"transportation shed" that would be economically and environmentally sustainable over the long term. The station's existing terra cotta façade on Surf Avenue will be restored. The overall aesthetic statement is respectful of the past while expressive of current and future transportation technologies.

The chief concern for this project was to create a celebratory civic space; the station has the potential to be revived to its former position as neighborhood hub. Highlighting the expressive and historic role of the transit station as a civic typology offered an opportunity to make Stillwell Avenue Station the centerpiece for a memorable new destination at New York's Coney Island.

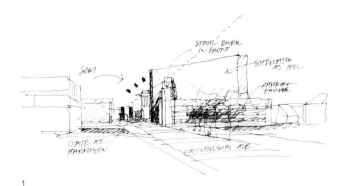

1

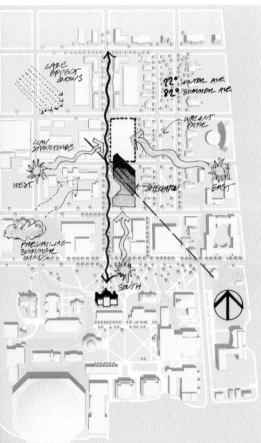

2

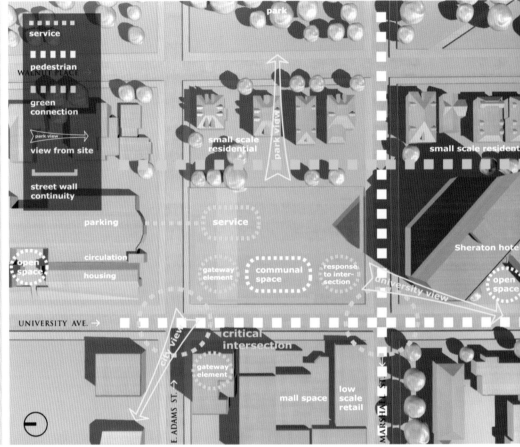

3

1 Context vignette
2 Climate analysis
3 Campus plan response
4 Model: southwest aerial view
5 Model: University Avenue view

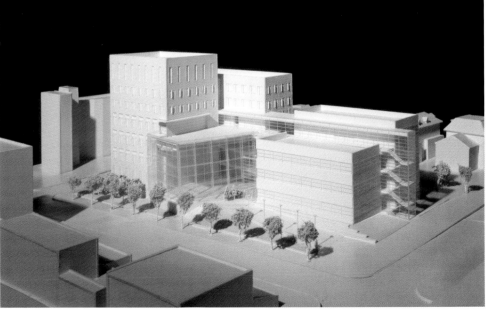

4

Syracuse, New York
Client: Syracuse University
Completion: 2005

# Syracuse University Martin J. Whitman School of Management

5

The Martin J. Whitman School of Management will be one of the first major facilities completed following the university's new Campus Plan. This 165,000-square-foot new building includes classrooms, auditoria, and space for collaborative teaching and learning for the 1,400 students, as well as executive spaces, room for distance learning facilities, and space for theme-based interdisciplinary research.

School leaders see the new facility as an important step toward enhancing its competitive position in the marketplace. For this reason, and because the school serves several categories of students— undergraduates, professional graduate students, and distance learners—issues of identity proved central to this project. The design also supports dedicated space for the stimulation and support for theme-based interdisciplinary research by faculty and students, as well as expanded student services.

The building's context was also a major factor. The building responds to the campus's expansion into the urban neighborhood and will help form a new gateway to the university complex. In terms of the urban neighborhood, the building must deal with the scale of a nearby 11-story hotel and more prevalent one- and two-story residential buildings that make up most of the neighborhood.

The building reads as three interconnected but discrete volumes joined by a central glassy space. A strong, seven-story element is the gateway corner piece and a lower, jewel-like element (the great hall) projects to the street line. The classroom volume is set back to create an entry plaza that engages the street. The great hall, a place for informal assembly and special events, becomes a feature of the street that relates in scale to the low-rise elements on the opposing block. As an all-glass structure, the hall will

animate the building by day and become a glowing beacon at night, bringing vitality and excitement to University Avenue.

An internal, glass-encased "street" runs north–south the full length of the building. This unifies the three different functional expressions. Because the stairs and main horizontal circulation are all within this glass spine, the building will be very animated from the outside by the movement of people, both day and night. School leaders wanted the design to provide distinct spaces for the various school populations so that dedicated gathering spaces within them would promote interaction with those students' peers. A glass commons or great hall presents an identity and face to the campus that will create an ambience of openness and welcoming that this historic campus has traditionally lacked. The project includes numerous green design features that will build on 30 years of campus-wide sustainability initiatives.

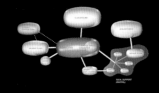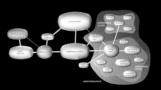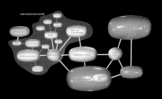

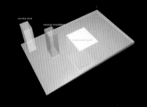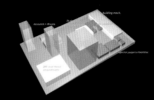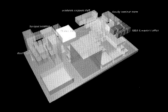

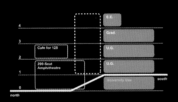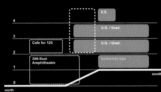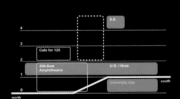

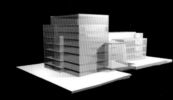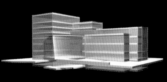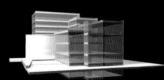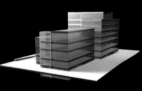

Opposite above
    Programming and massing
Opposite below
    Model: northeast
    aerial view
8   Plan: sixth floor
9   Plan: fourth floor
10  Plan: second floor
11  Plan: first floor

8

9

10

11

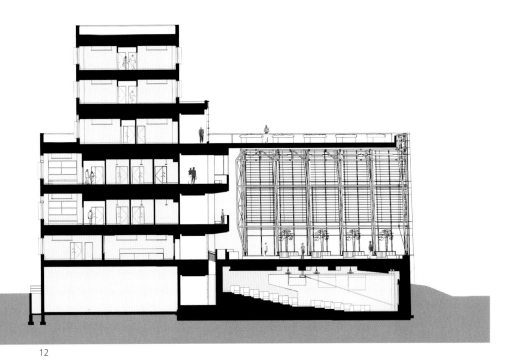

12

13

14

15

16

12 Transverse section through atrium
13 Construction photographs
14 Model: northwest corner view
15 Model: main entrance
16 Model: Atrium
17 Sustainable components

High-efficiency air filtration
High-efficiency pumps and fans
No CFCs
Demand-controlled ventilation

Occupancy sensor control

Efficient building skin

High-albedo roofing

Radiant heating and cooling

Central communicating corridor
Maximum daylight

Restored landscaped areas

Blast furnace slag

Under-floor ventilation

17

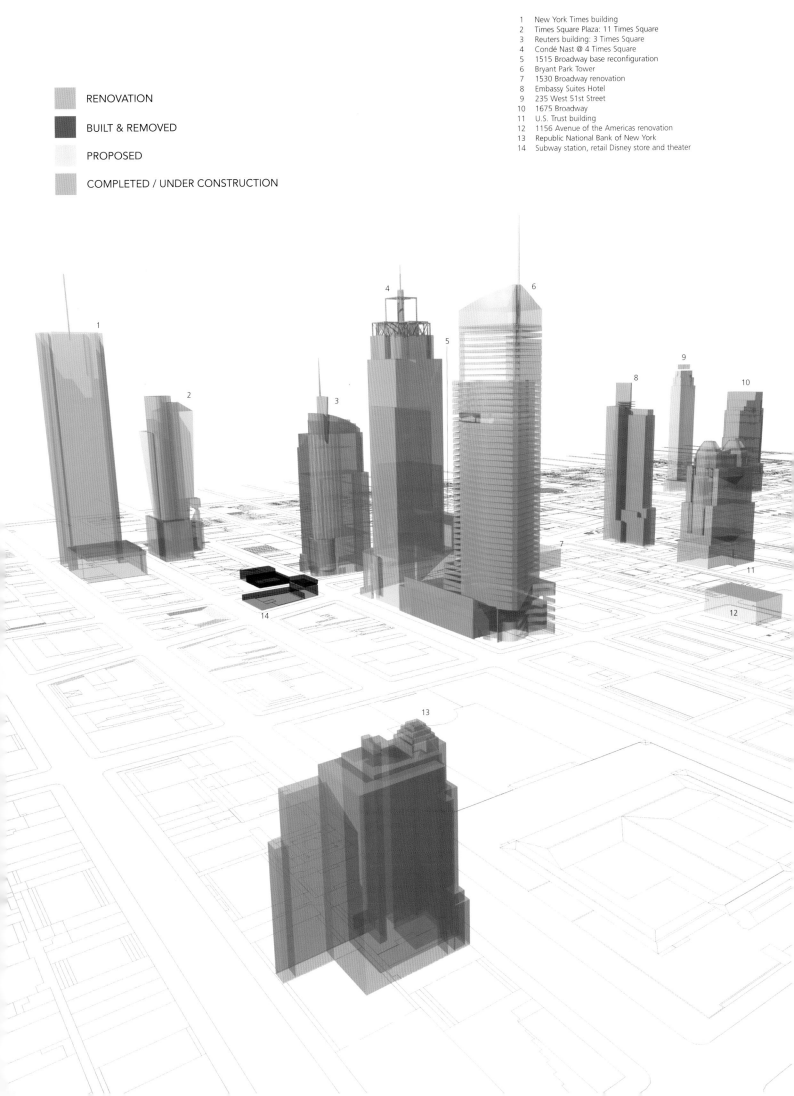

RENOVATION

BUILT & REMOVED

PROPOSED

COMPLETED / UNDER CONSTRUCTION

1   New York Times building
2   Times Square Plaza: 11 Times Square
3   Reuters building: 3 Times Square
4   Condé Nast @ 4 Times Square
5   1515 Broadway base reconfiguration
6   Bryant Park Tower
7   1530 Broadway renovation
8   Embassy Suites Hotel
9   235 West 51st Street
10  1675 Broadway
11  U.S. Trust building
12  1156 Avenue of the Americas renovation
13  Republic National Bank of New York
14  Subway station, retail Disney store and theater

Opposite:
　Rendering: Fox & Fowle projects
2　District plan: Fox & Fowle projects
Following pages:
　Bird's-eye view of Times Square

# TImes Square Buildings

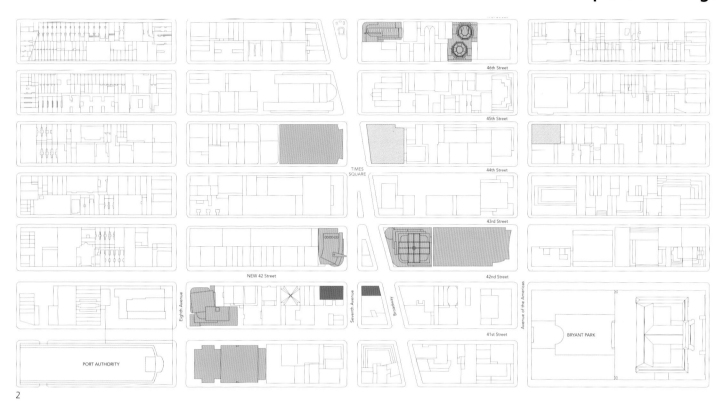

2

In 1982, the City of New York, anxious to preserve Times Square as a world-famous symbol of commercialism and hyperactive nightlife, passed regulations requiring all new buildings to display illuminated signage in specific areas. These regulations were intended to steer memories of Times Square past toward a revitalized future. More than any other architectural firm, Fox & Fowle Architects has been responsible for this transformation. Projects and completed buildings on the diagram show almost 20 years of continuous activity, from small renovations to 50-story skyscrapers. Every ingredient of the neighborhood has been reinvented in various creative ways including themed retail, transit structures and entrances, signage "spectaculars," corporate branding, theaters, hotel, and office space.

The ability of Fox & Fowle Architects' design team to consider massing, context, and signage inventively has driven these projects, and demonstrates that compelling architecture is possible here and that it can be people-friendly. This is in contrast to much of the office architecture from earlier eras in this midtown zone, where the scale was overwhelming, inappropriate, and

determinedly unfriendly to pedestrians. While the firm has had a very significant role in the shaping of this district, it has done so without stamping an identifiable design signature in the neighborhood, which is important to the long-term aesthetic success of this diverse assemblage.

The firm's design for the Embassy Suites Hotel was the first building in the district to be created in accordance with the Times Square signage regulations. Thirty-eight floors of hotel, public, and retail spaces were designed to span over the existing five-story, interior landmarked Palace Theater. The theater received a new marquee and façade as well as restored and expanded interiors. Illuminated, 120-foot-high billboards, characteristic of Times Square, were prominent and mandated features of the new hotel and theater frontage. Fox & Fowle Architects designed the interior spaces to reflect the "culture" of Times Square as well as Embassy Suites' commitment to quality and hospitality.

An earlier project, 1675 Broadway, is a 35-story office building with retail space on the ground floor. The firm designed a new marquee and

façade for the theater in this building. Slender multiple setbacks, individually recessed windows, and an interplay of thermal and polished granite combine to lend the building an elegant verticality. Incorporating the interior-landmarked Broadway Theater, home to many famous musicals, this project was the first to restore the energetic spirit of Times Square in this area, which had been previously dominated by undistinguished commercial structures.

Since that time, the firm has worked on 3 Times Square, 4 Times Square, and 11 Times Square, among others. Each effort involved a creative assessment of the zoning and design guidelines and a melding with the clients' desires and the architectural aspiration to make a valuable addition to the streetscape and the skyline. It was also important that these efforts help spur ancillary development, furthering the district revitalization. In each case, the design teams strived to make the most of the site and energetic context. In the case of 4 Times Square, a tremendous amount of square footage was shoehorned into a building that seems to evolve out of its urban, signage-laden context in a natural way.

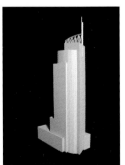

2

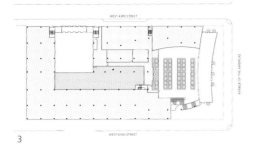

3

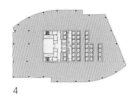

4

New York City (Manhattan)
Client: The Durst Organization
Submitted: 2002

# Bryant Park Tower

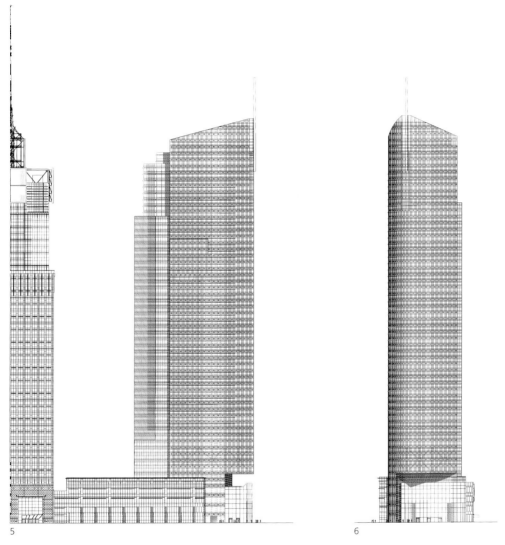

5

6

Fox & Fowle Architects created a conceptual design for a commercial office tower on the Avenue of the Americas between 43rd and 42nd Streets. This linchpin site is an important visual and physical connector between the corporate district around Bryant Park and Times Square. The building would complete the corner of the block (on which 4 Times Square is also located) and fill in a key gap in the neighborhood. The developer sought 1.8 million square feet in total, which resulted in a 47-story tower. The scope included the office and retail core and shell and it included a not-for-profit dance studio and the retention of the landmarked façade of the Henry Miller's Theatre. Larger floors in the lower mass would be designated for trading floor use. The team also analyzed a subway

connection consisting of two stairs from street level to the first cellar and a passage between two stations. A large public space at the project's base would provide an important amenity and give the public access to space on that corner.

The masses interlock at the base, marking the corner as transition, and creating a dramatic overhang projecting from the top of the sixth floor. This element addresses the street, yields a piece of the corner to pedestrians, and lends a human, street-level scale to this large building. The sculptural tower is massed with a delicate touch and soft lines to help minimize the scale of the building and to maximize the light and air available to interior spaces throughout the

floorplate. The sweeping curves, playing off the adjacent buildings' primarily rectilinear profiles and forming a new gateway to the 42nd Street/Times Square business district and tourist/theater venue, would be a graceful presence at the corner of Bryant Park.

The concept was developed with the intention that this would be a state-of-the-art, high performance facility, exceeding current standards for environmental responsibility in high-rise construction. The exploration included under-floor air supply, photovoltaics, fuel cells, co-generation, and various other energy efficiency measures, including efforts to draw daylight deep into the building.

2

Opposite:
    Southwest corner
2   North view
3   Northwest view
4   Northwest tower view

New York City (Manhattan)
Client: The Durst Organization
Completion: 1999

# Condé Nast Building @ 4 Times Square

3

4

The strongest demonstration of Fox & Fowle Architects' leadership in sustainable design was the Condé Nast Building @ 4 Times Square building for the Durst Organization. Completed in 1999, the 48-story, 1.6 million-square-foot tower was the first sustainable skyscraper in the U.S., and one of the only such speculative projects in the world. Fox & Fowle Architects led a large team that included the Rocky Mountain Institute, Natural Resources Defense Council, NYSERDA (New York State Energy Research and Development Authority), Steven Winter Associates, Earth Day New York, Green October, Consolidated Edison, and Kiss + Cathcart, Architects. The project was a model for its integrated process from the start. This challenging but invigorating way of

working is something the firm has championed as the most effective way to achieve optimal systems within the architecture.

The project reflects a relationship of horizontal and vertical elements that takes cues from the early International Style high-rise, Philadelphia's PSFS Building. The Condé Nast building relates to the ephemeral signage and energy of Times Square while maintaining a solidity that engages masonry towers nearby. Signage is celebrated at the tower's base as both an integral part of the architecture and as a series of planes and icons layered over the façades in the Times Square vernacular. The collage effect of multiple planes and expressions at the base is deliberate.

In addition to raising the bar on skyscraper efficiency and effectiveness, the Condé Nast Building @ 4 Times Square is an example of sensitive attention to physical context. Its west and north façades are clad in metal and glass, and literally and figuratively reflect the visual activity of Times Square. The east and south façades are composed of stone and glass and present a refined personality, addressing midtown Manhattan and Bryant Park. The building engages its two divergent contexts, rather than trying to blend them into one. The architects were concerned about the building's bulk overpowering Times Square, which inspired stepped massing and finer-scale articulation on that side.

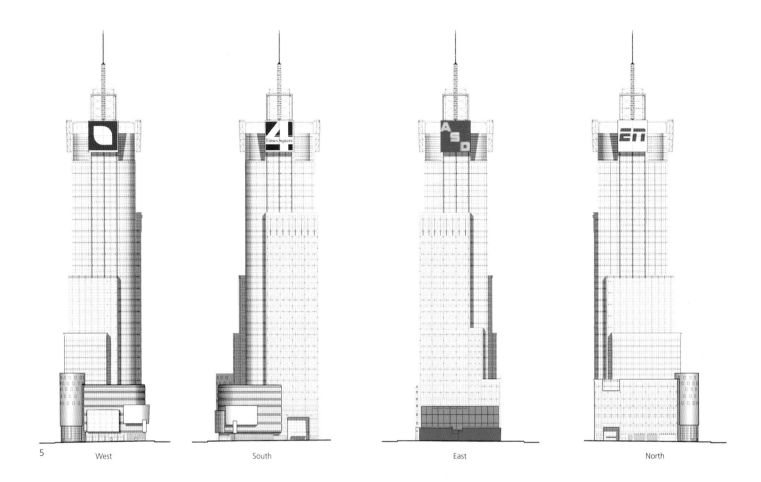

5     West                  South                 East                 North

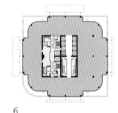

6

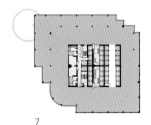

7

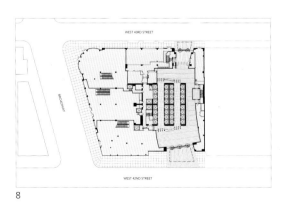

8

The top of the building evolved from a highly efficient hat truss. Topped with a cubic frame to contain a satellite dish farm and a communications tower, the truss takes a German-cross plan form that is marked by 70-foot-square super-sign armatures on each face. This solution allowed for the distinction the designers sought, the superior structural strategy and an unexpected revenue stream for the building owners. As is often the case, the commitment to an integrated process, which can at times be difficult to organize and execute, resulted in a design that achieves much more than one goal.

The team analyzed a large number of on-site energy systems, including wind turbines, fuel cells, gas turbines, thermal storage, and more. Integrated photovoltaics and fuel cells were used for the first time in a building of this type. The photovoltaics, while supplying a small portion of the base building's power, were used primarily for demonstration purposes and to advance the industry to more efficient, large-scale installations. The initial plan called for eight 200-kilowatt fuel cells; two were installed (because of the inability to return excess off-peak energy into the power grid). The project became a catalyst for the U.S. Green Building Council's LEED rating program and set a new national standard for environmentally responsible commercial projects.

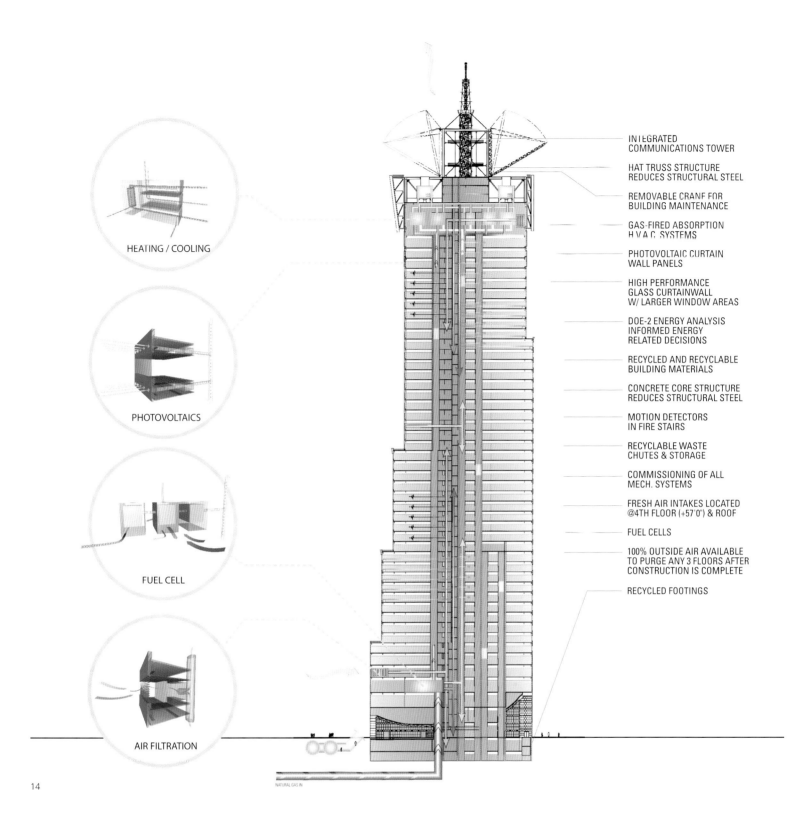

HEATING / COOLING

PHOTOVOLTAICS

FUEL CELL

AIR FILTRATION

INTEGRATED
COMMUNICATIONS TOWER

HAT TRUSS STRUCTURE
REDUCES STRUCTURAL STEEL

REMOVABLE CRANE FOR
BUILDING MAINTENANCE

GAS-FIRED ABSORPTION
H.V.A.C. SYSTEMS

PHOTOVOLTAIC CURTAIN
WALL PANELS

HIGH PERFORMANCE
GLASS CURTAINWALL
W/ LARGER WINDOW AREAS

DOE-2 ENERGY ANALYSIS
INFORMED ENERGY
RELATED DECISIONS

RECYCLED AND RECYCLABLE
BUILDING MATERIALS

CONCRETE CORE STRUCTURE
REDUCES STRUCTURAL STEEL

MOTION DETECTORS
IN FIRE STAIRS

RECYCLABLE WASTE
CHUTES & STORAGE

COMMISSIONING OF ALL
MECH. SYSTEMS

FRESH AIR INTAKES LOCATED
@4TH FLOOR (+57'0") & ROOF

FUEL CELLS

100% OUTSIDE AIR AVAILABLE
TO PURGE ANY 3 FLOORS AFTER
CONSTRUCTION IS COMPLETE

RECYCLED FOOTINGS

14

NATURAL GAS IN

LEGEND

| TENANT SPACE | | HOT WATER | △ | COOLING TOWER | |
| BASE BUILDING | | COLD WATER | △ | ABSORPTION UNITS CHILLER | |
| TOILET ROOMS | | FRESH AIR | △ | FUEL CELL | |
| PARKING & BIKE STORAGE | | ELECTRICITY | △ | AIR FILTER | |
| ELEVATORS | | NATURAL GAS | △ | PUBLIC TRANSPORTATION | |

Opposite:
    42nd Street
14   Sustainable components

15

16

17

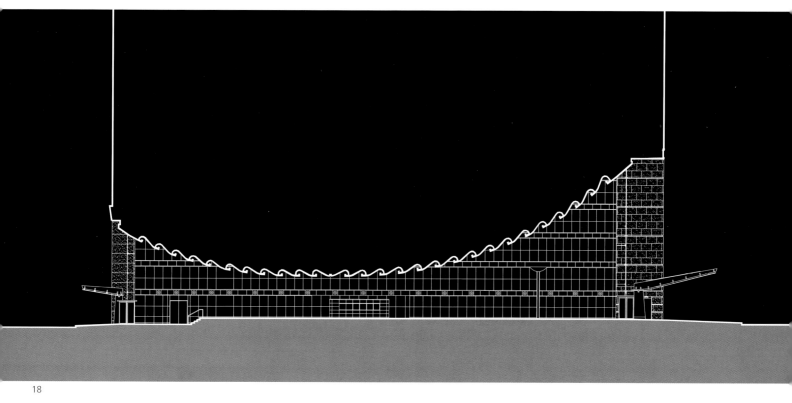

18

19

20

New York City (Manhattan)
Client: *The New York Times* Company, Forest City Ratner Companies
Completion: 2007

1   View: west tower
2   Eighth Avenue lower façade

# *New York Times* Headquarters

2

Fox & Fowle Architects has had the opportunity to partner with Renzo Piano Building Workshop to design what will be a seminal high-rise building. Located on Eighth Avenue between 40th and 41st Streets opposite the Port Authority Bus Terminal, the project falls within the footprint of the 42nd Street Redevelopment Project, the same governing auspices as the Condé Nast Building, the Reuters Building, and 11 Times Square. The tower is part headquarters building for *The New York Times* Company and part speculative development by Forest City Ratner. *The Times* will occupy half of the building's 1.6 million square feet; corporate and retail tenants will fill the remainder.

Renzo Piano's initial vision for the building generated during the international competition is one of lightness, transparency, and mutability. Delicate veils of glazed ceramic tubes float off of a highly transparent all-glass tower. Sometimes

shimmering, sometimes a crisp play of light and shadow, sometimes bathed in colored early morning or late afternoon sun, the building will reflect and amplify the city's atmospheric conditions. In contrast to the diaphanous screens, a network of robust structural steel will be exposed at the four notched corners of the tower.

The building appears to hover above the ground floor, creating a highly vibrant and transparent public realm including entrance lobbies, a *Times* Center auditorium, and shops. At the center is a green courtyard, which brings in light to the large base floor that will house the newsroom and associated spaces and will be visible from each of the three street exposures. Rigorous planning and systems coordination has resulted in a seamless integration of core, skin and interior spaces unprecedented at this scale. The office space for *The New York Times*, designed in

collaboration with Gensler, will echo the spirit of the New York City industrial loft rendered in state-of-the-art technologies: high ceilings; ample natural light; clear expression of structure; open planning; and systems that promote flexibility and occupant comfort.

The ambitious vision involves numerous innovations, such as the use of ceramic as a material for the tubes, architecturally integrated exposed structural steel, a daylight-responsive shading system, intricately detailed steel-and-glass canopies, multilevel interconnecting stairs, under-floor air distribution, an on-site co-generation plant, and acoustic variability between speech and music in the *Times* Center. Fox & Fowle Architects orchestrated an open and energetic process that included consultation with many outside experts, copious research and testing, construction of mock-ups, pre-bid collaboration with subcontractors, and rigorous cost evaluation.

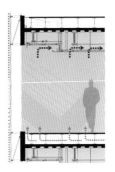
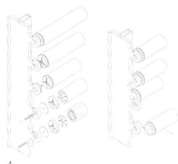

3       4       5       6

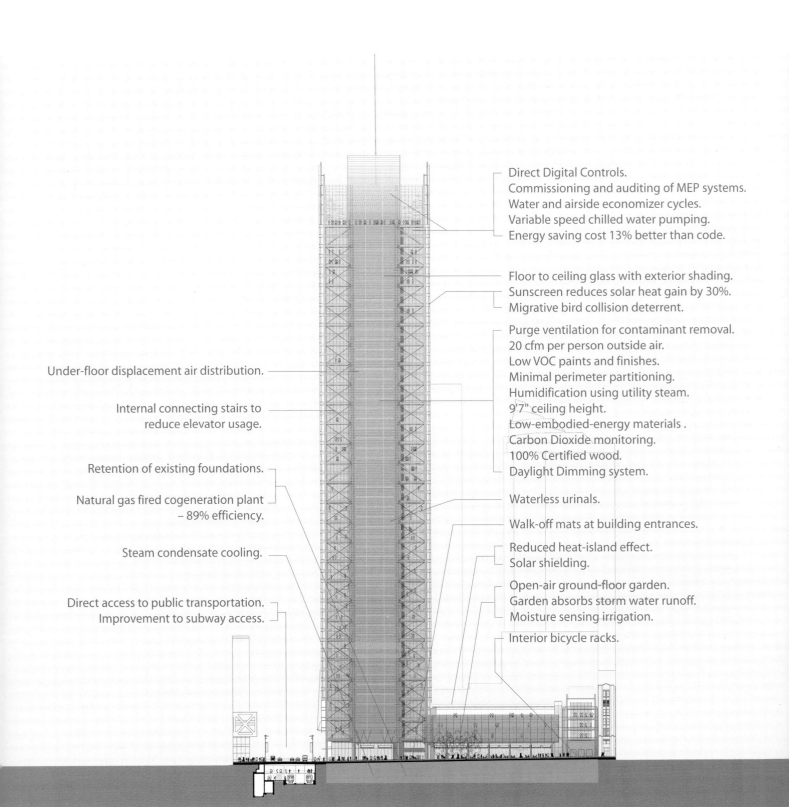

Direct Digital Controls.
Commissioning and auditing of MEP systems.
Water and airside economizer cycles.
Variable speed chilled water pumping.
Energy saving cost 13% better than code.

Floor to ceiling glass with exterior shading.
Sunscreen reduces solar heat gain by 30%.
Migrative bird collision deterrent.

Purge ventilation for contaminant removal.
20 cfm per person outside air.
Low VOC paints and finishes.
Minimal perimeter partitioning.
Humidification using utility steam.
9'7" ceiling height.
Low-embodied-energy materials .
Carbon Dioxide monitoring.
100% Certified wood.
Daylight Dimming system.

Under-floor displacement air distribution.

Internal connecting stairs to
reduce elevator usage.

Retention of existing foundations.

Natural gas fired cogeneration plant
– 89% efficiency.

Steam condensate cooling.

Direct access to public transportation.
Improvement to subway access.

Waterless urinals.

Walk-off mats at building entrances.

Reduced heat-island effect.
Solar shielding.

Open-air ground-floor garden.
Garden absorbs storm water runoff.
Moisture sensing irrigation.

Interior bicycle racks.

7

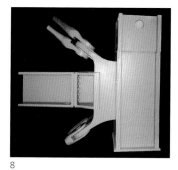

8  9  10  11

3  Diagram: daylighting and under-floor air
4  Exploded axonometric: façade detail
5&6  Mock-up: screen components
7  Sustainable components
8  Mock-up: exterior steel connection
9  Study model
10  8th Avenue entrance
11  Mock-up: interior
12  Plan: roof
13  Plan: typical tower floor with podium roof
14  Plan: ground floor

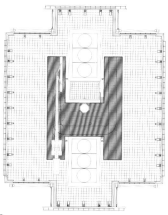

12

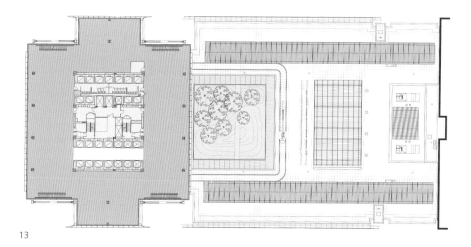

13

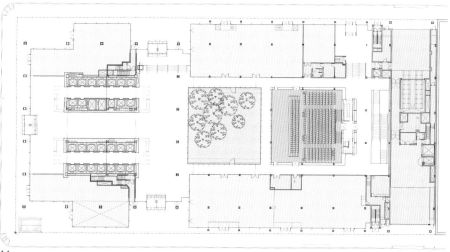

14

New York City (Manhattan)
Client: Rudin Management Company, Reuters America
Completion: 2001

# The Reuters Building

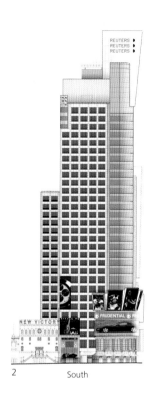 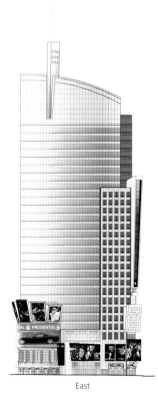 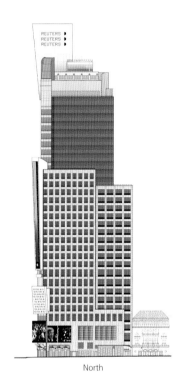 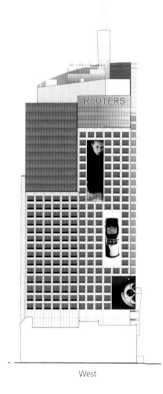

| 2 | South | East | North | West |

The Reuters Building at 3 Times Square is an armature for signage in a neighborhood ruled by a "survival of the loudest" visual aesthetic, with a surprisingly peaceful interior at its core. The building is wrapped at its glass-lobby base in video monitors. From the ninth to the 23rd floor, the wedge-corner element is a giant LED sign, which transmits news of the moment, the Reuters Index. Massing is heavy at the base, where the signage is the most prominent. Signs inside the lobby function as a connector to the immediate physical context and an invitation to people on the street, where there is a pattern of movement that takes the eye to the building's top.

Along the north side of 42nd Street, new, intimately scaled low-rise retail volumes maintain the remarkably well preserved street wall containing the New Victory and Times Square theaters. These volumes are completed with characteristic signage and a highly articulated architectural expression in stone and terra cotta,

reinterpreting nostalgic motifs of the old Times Square. At the corner, a seven-story drum-shaped structure pulls the street wall around the corner toward the north. As its curvilinear façade conjoins with the building, it forms a space that draws the sidewalk in and forms a three-story mid-block lobby. On the northeast corner, a 20-story stone-clad mass rises from the street with a scale and stature appropriate in the context of the Paramount building further to the north, and 1 Times Square to the east. This exposure has a strong Reuters presence from the street to the building's top.

This building was designed with an eye toward the views people would have of it from various distances and angles. There is an episodic and dynamic quality about the differing façades, which is particularly appropriate to Times Square. A key aspect of this project is the transformative sequence between public and private. The entrance lobby evolves from the void created between figural masses and the suspended tower above,

permitting the busy sidewalk to enliven the lobby through an all-glass wall. As one steps through the security system toward the rear of the lobby, there is a four-sided proscenium of light that transitions the ambience from Times Square cacophony to sedate elevator lobbies that appear to be carved from a solid marble building core. To ensure that the Times Square presence is never out of consciousness, the elevators glow with the energy of a concave illuminated glass wall set within a partially mirrored stainless steel enclosure.

The Reuters Building features a covered entrance and connecting stair to the Times Square subway system. A projecting canopy announces the entry with an animated, illuminated subway sign. Designed for maximum visibility within this busy neighborhood, the nine transit lines that converge beneath Times Square are identified at street level by an armature combining wayfinding with the neon vernacular of the area.

3

4

5

6

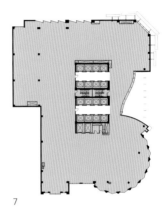
7

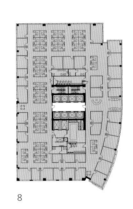
8

9

3 Southeast view
4 Entrance
5 Lobby
6 Plan: ground floor
7 Plan: typical base floor
8 Plan: typical tower plan
9 Detail
10,11&12 Detail: lobby and elevator
13 Sustainable components

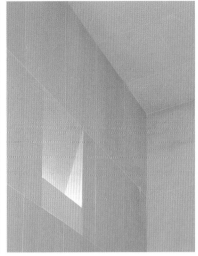

10        11        12

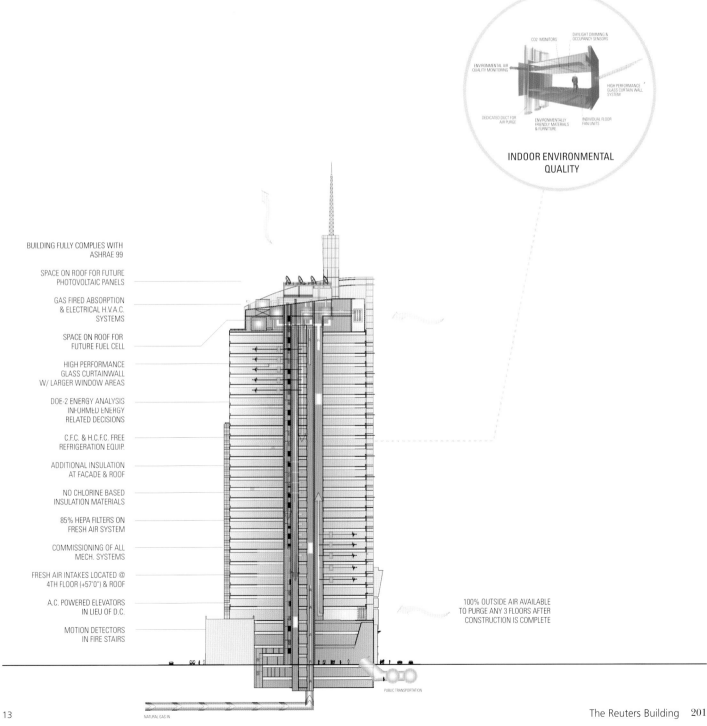

INDOOR ENVIRONMENTAL QUALITY

ENVIRONMENTAL AIR QUALITY MONITORING

CO2 MONITORS

DAYLIGHT DIMMING & OCCUPANCY SENSORS

HIGH PERFORMANCE GLASS CURTAIN WALL SYSTEM

DEDICATED DUCT FOR AIR PURGE

ENVIRONMENTALLY FRIENDLY MATERIALS & FURNITURE

INDIVIDUAL FLOOR FAN UNITS

BUILDING FULLY COMPLIES WITH ASHRAE 99

SPACE ON ROOF FOR FUTURE PHOTOVOLTAIC PANELS

GAS FIRED ABSORPTION & ELECTRICAL H.V.A.C. SYSTEMS

SPACE ON ROOF FOR FUTURE FUEL CELL

HIGH PERFORMANCE GLASS CURTAINWALL W/ LARGER WINDOW AREAS

DOE-2 ENERGY ANALYSIS INFORMED ENERGY RELATED DECISIONS

C.F.C. & H.C.F.C. FREE REFRIGERATION EQUIP.

ADDITIONAL INSULATION AT FACADE & ROOF

NO CHLORINE BASED INSULATION MATERIALS

85% HEPA FILTERS ON FRESH AIR SYSTEM

COMMISSIONING OF ALL MECH. SYSTEMS

FRESH AIR INTAKES LOCATED @ 4TH FLOOR (+57'0") & ROOF

A.C. POWERED ELEVATORS IN LIEU OF D.C.

MOTION DETECTORS IN FIRE STAIRS

100% OUTSIDE AIR AVAILABLE TO PURGE ANY 3 FLOORS AFTER CONSTRUCTION IS COMPLETE

PUBLIC TRANSPORTATION

NATURAL GAS IN

13                           The Reuters Building    201

14

15

14 North view
15 Details
16 42nd Street subway entrance
17 Section: subway entrance

16

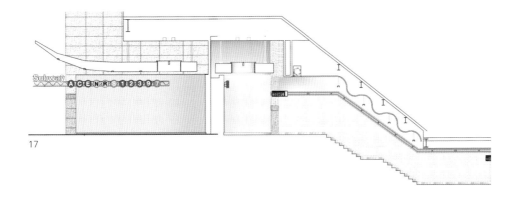

17

New York City (Manhattan)
Client: Milstein Brothers Real Estate
Completion: 2006

# Times Square Plaza

Opposite:
Office building scheme
2    Study model in context

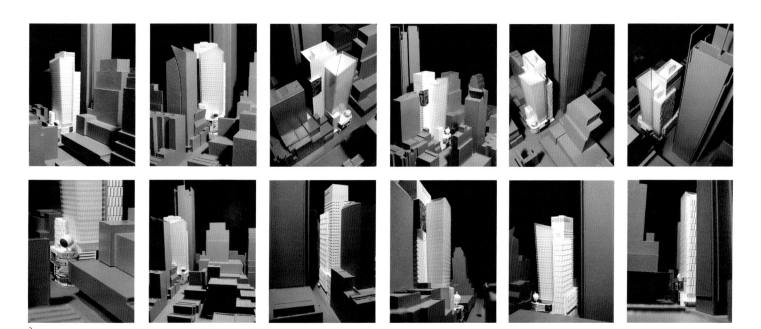

2

The Times Square Plaza project, at 42nd Street and Eighth Avenue in New York, will define the western gateway to the revitalized Times Square business district and entertainment venue and will assume a critical position between its divergent neighbors: the energetic Westin Hotel to the north (Arquitectonica) and the distinguished *New York Times* building (Renzo Piano Building Workshop / Fox & Fowle Architects) to the south.

This project illustrates a view of the city as a dynamic force field. Here, the contrast between strong verticality in the shaft and strong horizontality at the base is important. The building's position at this intersection called for a light-hearted spirit and energetic profile. Extensive computer rendering modeled the experience of pedestrians and people in other buildings to test how the composition would read from various perspectives.

The urban context means that most people who experience the building will do so at a medium scale, which is a condition unique to a dense environment.

Illustrating the inherent challenges of design in a commercial context, two approaches were simultaneously developed: an office building scheme and a residential/hotel scheme. Both utilize a "universal base" treatment allowing for marketing and programming flexibility even during initial phases of construction.

In both schemes, a group of masses is arranged and clad according to both function and exposure; the building reads differently on each side. In the office building scenario, three primary masses make up the high-rise; they will be sheathed in gradated combinations of glass and stainless

steel curtain wall panels. The most dominant volume accentuates the corner site, angling up into an energetic, exaggerated, and rectangular shape that appears to have been stretched tall. Crisp edges further reinforce the corner and the sheer height of this mass. In the residential/hotel scenario, a bent and radiused slab-form clad in semi-reflective glass addresses the corner and is anchored by a stainless steel armature.

The base common to both schemes has super-scale signage (consistent with the district's guidelines) that studs the lower floors, especially at the 42nd Street corner. This is a composition of set pieces; the result is highly volumetric. High performance glazing, copious daylight, energy-efficient systems, and state-of-the-art environmental controls will elevate this project beyond its peers in terms of environmental responsiveness and efficiency.

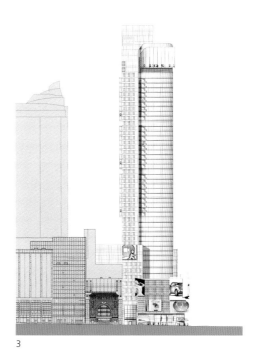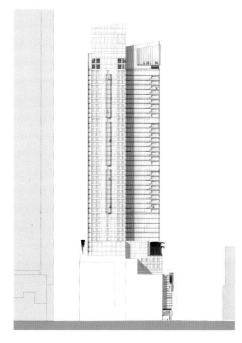

3

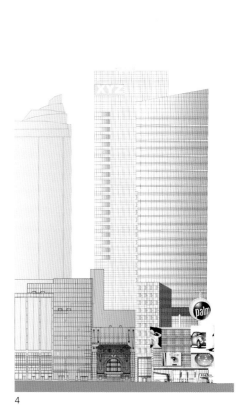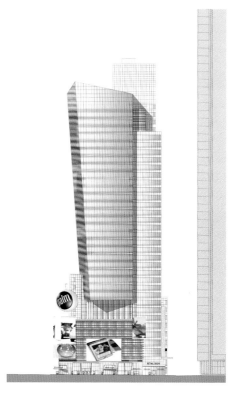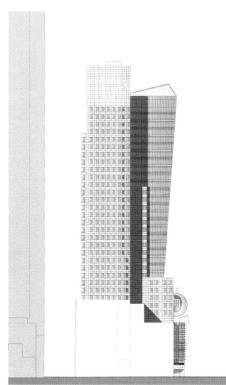

4

3   Elevations: residential/hotel scheme
4   Elevations: office building scheme
Opposite:
    Residential/hotel scheme

1 Street level with preserved
  mosaic signage
2 Section
3 Detail: signage
4 42nd Street façade

1

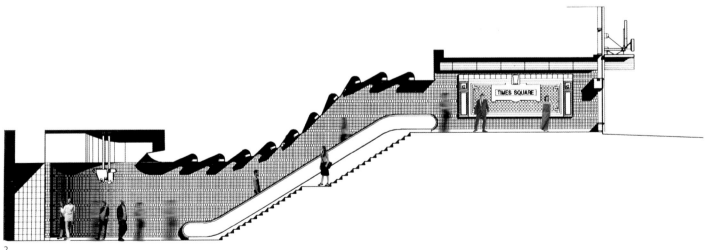

2

New York City (Manhattan)
Client: MTA New York City Transit
Completion: 1998

## Times Square Subway Entrance

4

The Times Square Subway Station for the Metropolitan Transit Authority/New York City Transit serves approximately half a million riders each day. This project's context is rich and multi-layered. It includes the visual cacophony of today's Times Square and the theatrical history of the district. The Fox & Fowle Architects team utilized standard Transit Authority components and well-chosen custom elements to capture the exuberance and energy of the "Crossroads of the World."

The project was conceived as an extension of the active streetscape. The movement is carried from the exterior to the interior: the undulating canopy outside becomes the ceiling inside. A sculpted ceiling with cove lighting continues the dynamic to the tracks below. On the track level, a curved lighting and sign element, suggesting an old Broadway marquee, becomes the focal point of the station, orienting the rider and directing them to the 11 lines the station serves.

The team was challenged to create a distinctive design and Times Square statement using Transit Authority standard lamps, materials, and other components. On the first floor, the team pendant-mounted a standard linear fixture within the undulating ceiling, giving the light more vibrancy and sparkle. The concourse level marquee was inventively created using standard linear fluorescent lights in an unusual faceted pattern. The original station mosaic was relocated from a less used area of the platform, restored, and mounted on the first floor at entry level.

The neon and the sequential "chaser" lights of the exterior canopy became an identifier for Times Square and reflected the team's careful calculation for defining the "special moments" of the project. This custom focal point of the project has become the new standard for all Times Square subway projects. The structure has been razed to make way for a new development. It will be rebuilt in its original form, a testament to its success as a major gateway to and identifier of the subway system.

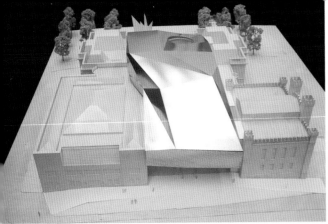

1

2

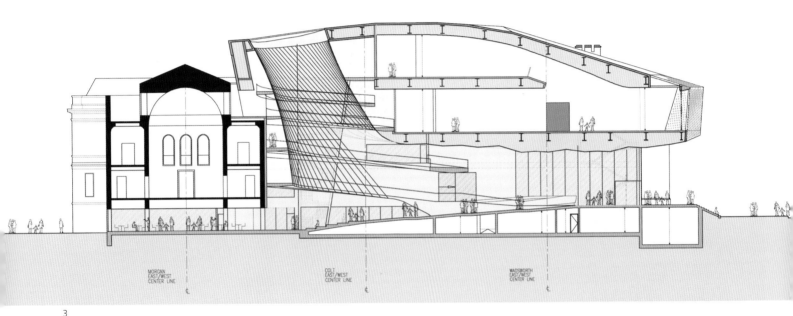

3

4

1 Model
2 Entry sequence
3 Section
4 Public landscape
5 Existing conditions
6 Diagram of complex
7 Before/after plans
8 Concept sketches

5

Hartford, Connecticut
Client: Wadsworth Atheneum Museum of Art
Completion: Pending

# Wadsworth Atheneum Museum of Art Master Plan and Expansion

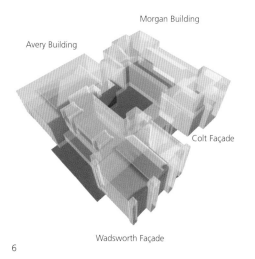

Morgan Building

Avery Building

Colt Façade

Wadsworth Façade

6

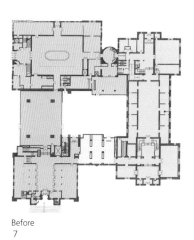

Before

7

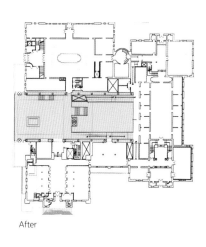

After

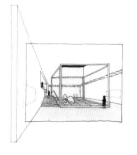
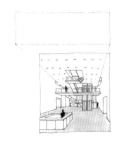
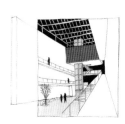

8

In 2000 the museum commissioned Fox & Fowle Architects to do a master plan for the entire complex. The mandate was to explore ways to meet the museum's needs for the coming century and evaluate the cost and phasing implications. Upon accepting key components of the master plan, the board of the museum initiated a comprehensive interview process for hiring a young architect for whom this commission would be a first major work on the East Coast. UN Studio of Amsterdam was selected and the Fox & Fowle Architects master plan was elaborated as the two teams collaborated on the design.

The Fox & Fowle Architects team posited that the transformation of the closed, static, and often confusing complex of structures into an open, linked sequence could be achieved by eliminating the problematic 1970s Goodwin Building. The openness between the buildings would be maintained by placing the circulation to the varying levels of the multiple buildings within this space. The contemporary exhibition gallery is located at the highest level of this new "courtyard." An open and inviting façade fronts the street to the north. A north/south axis from the street to the Morgan Building provides further linkage and overall building organization.

UN Studio and Fox & Fowle Architects developed this concept into a spatially rich "public landscape" entered from the north. The circulation evolved into a continuous sequence of stepped ramps that linked to each level of each building as they rotated their way up to the special exhibition and contemporary exhibition galleries. The ramps wrapped around a cone of light at the center of the complex. The continuity of the curved form was then animated by the changing levels of daylight from above. The entry level also folded down to the lower, concourse level, linking the museum and its north/south axis to the public park to the south, and creating a flexible event, exhibition, and meeting space.

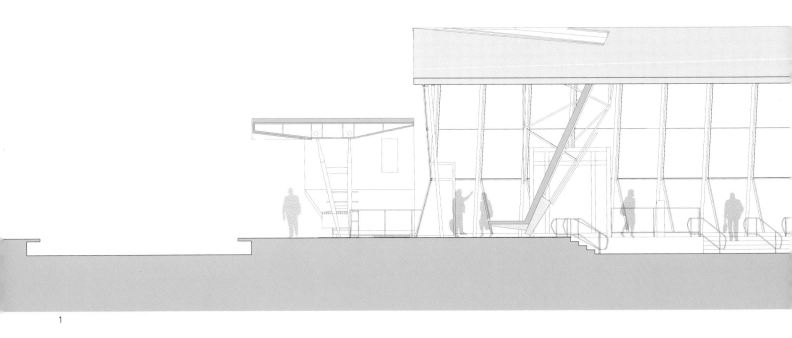

1

2

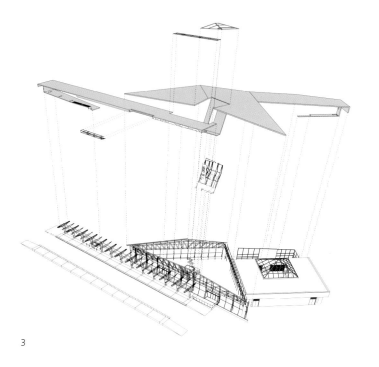

3

Camden, New Jersey
Client: New Jersey Transit
Completion: Pending

# Walter Rand Transportation Center

1  Section
2  Platform area
3  Exploded axonometric
4  Existing conditions and site plan

4

At the intersection of Mickle Boulevard and Broadway in Camden, the Walter Rand Transportation Center expansion project plays a part in the revitalization of this blighted satellite city, located across the river from Philadelphia. The project involves the design of an addition to the west headhouse and light rail and bus canopies on a site that currently houses abandoned mid-rise commercial and retail buildings. The existing transit system serves the New Jersey Transit Rail System, the New Jersey Transit Bus System, and the new Southern New Jersey Light Rail Transit System.

The addition is a steel and glass structure spanning an equilateral triangle floor plan. The building will shelter the transition between the existing train system below ground and the light rail and bus system above ground. The glass curtainwalls of the building maintain a highly transparent and easily secured environment.

Rather than engaging in structural gymnastics to create an icon, the design team created the primary form of the station by projecting its interaction with its occupants. The parti of the project is that of a folding roof, with portions peeled away to form canopies and skylights. The multi-functional wrapper represents a rethinking of the traditional notion of space formed by floors, walls, and ceilings. Using only the basic elements of the building, the team folded the skin perpendicular to major paths of travel. Light wells, benches, and information panels are interjected to add interest.

The idea is that the occupants become part of the architecture as they move through the station: the skin seems to mold around the travelers, as though the shed itself is not static but anchored by the movement inside itself. The combination of people, architecture, and the action of arrivals and departures at the intermodal station will create a sense of event that will provide identity and presence.

5

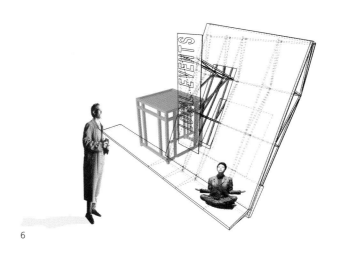

6

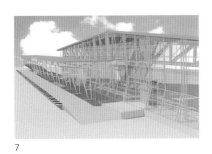

7

A

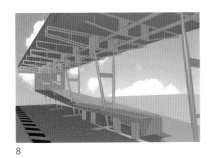

8

B

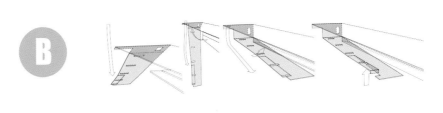

9

C

10

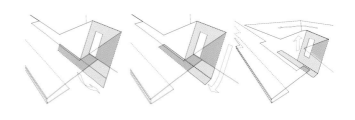

New
1  Waiting area
2  Platform
3  Auxiliary platform
4  East entrance

Old
5  Entrance to tunnel below
6  HVAC
7  Storage
8  Police station

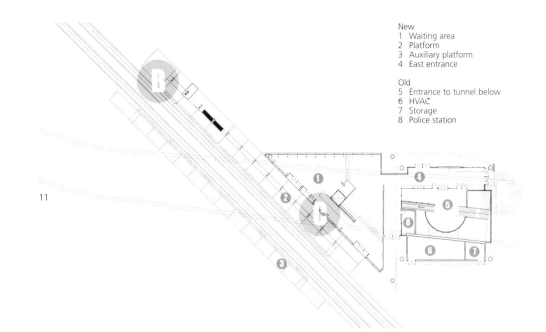

11

12

1 Canopy folded and unfolded
2 Rendering of L'Enfant Plaza
3 Hinged canopy
4 Exploded axonometric
5 Plan: roof level

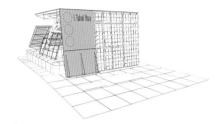

1

2

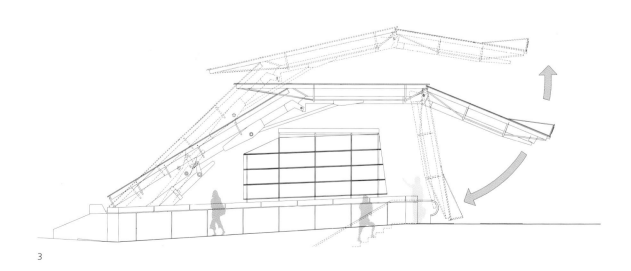

3

Washington, District of Columbia
Client: Washington Metropolitan Area Transportation Authority
Submitted: 2001

# Washington DC Transit Canopy Competition

4

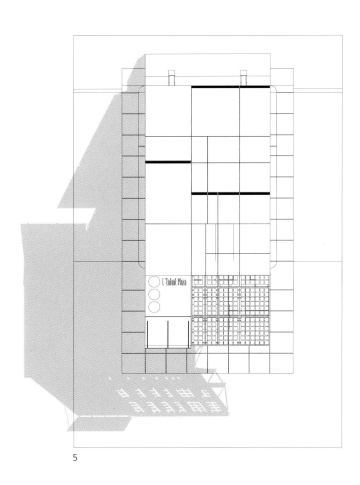

5

The Washington DC Transit Canopy Competition, for the Washington Metropolitan Area Transportation Authority rail system, gave the Fox & Fowle designers a chance to collaborate on a small but critical component of the city's transit system: the portal that riders must pass through before they descend below grade to use the system. The competition organizers sought a prototype design for 46 uncovered escalator entrances, to provide a recognizable identity and necessary protection from the elements. The passage to an underground environment is a critical transfer; riders would need to feel welcome, safe, and comfortable (even in a crowd). This transition can be an important element in the effort to assure riders that the overall system is safe, effective, clean, and user-friendly.

The concept for the canopies centered on the invention of a contemporary structure that could adjust to changing conditions. The designers aimed to create a solution that was multi-functional and self-supporting. The identity was formed through a tectonic approach and an honest expression of structure and materials.

The project was an exploration of a convertible envelope. The three-part hinged canopy was designed to fold into various positions according to weather and user traffic. On a sunny weekday, it could be wide open, doubling as vibrant signage and taking a more upright posture in its neighborhood. A less open position provides rain shelter, and the canopy can be closed and locked at night while the system is not operating.

The solution is adaptable to various entrance dimensions and site conditions. The metal structure incorporates tempered, modular, laminated safety glass. The modularity is an important part of making this canopy design efficiently and affordably adaptable to many locations. Entirely independent of the energy grid, the canopy derives its necessary power from integrated photovoltaic panels. Other aspects of the design, including lighting and signage, are also fully integrated into the structure.

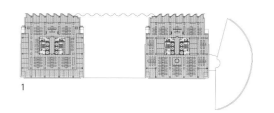

1

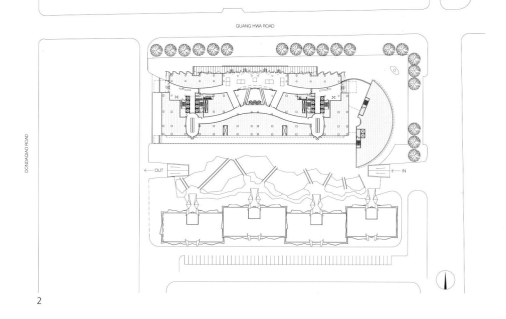

GUANG HWA ROAD

DONGBAQIAO ROAD

OUT

IN

2

3

Beijing, China
Client: Beijing Yi He Real Estate Development Company
Completion: 2005

# Yi He International Center

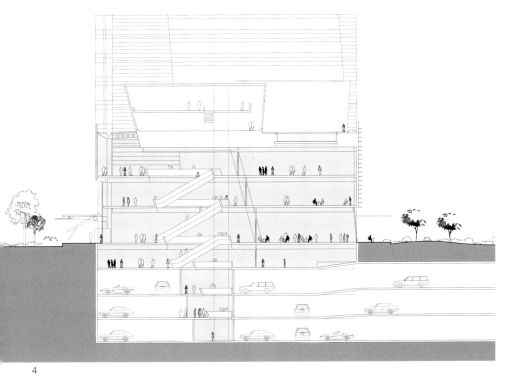

4

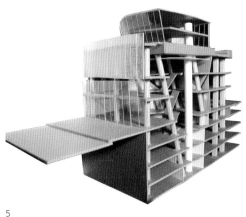

5

The Yi He International Center is located on a primary artery at the edge of Beijing's Central Business District, where it meets the fashionable Embassy District. Because of this prominent and visible location the owners wanted the two-tower office building to have a strong and attractive profile. Fox & Fowle Architects designed two 16-story office buildings connected by a four-story podium and an adjacent three-story pavilion. The design team created a diaphanous "wave wall" that covers the façade of each component of the complex and unites these masses into a cohesive whole.

The east and west façades are reflective glass for the hard-to-control horizontal light. The image is one of abstract sculptural form, celebrating the site's position as a district entrance. On the south side, a horizontal brise-soleil creates a modest, veiled image appropriate to the courtyard frontage that faces residential development.

This project represents the intersection and integration of solar and urban orientations. The north side is rendered in clear glass waves, letting in ample light. The sinuous, transparent façade acts as a sign on the boulevard frontage. Transparency into the various functions reinforces the urbanity of the context. This approach contrasts with much of what is built in Asia, where opacity is the rule.

1  Plan: tower level
2  Plan: ground floor
3  Rendering
4  Section
5  Sectional model details

Fox & Fowle Architects was founded in 1978 in New York City to provide architecture, interior design, planning, and urban design services to private and public clients. Today, 100 professionals including five principals and 16 associates make up the multidisciplinary firm. Each design team works closely and collaboratively with clients as integral participants of the project team to ensure that the work expresses their mission and culture.

The firm's rigorous exploration of fit and form involves a diverse and broad discourse and results in architecture and planning projects with strong social, environmental, and aesthetic integrity. The work has been recognized through local, national, and international design awards and articles in significant publications. Fox & Fowle Architects has always operated a single office in New York and has had the opportunity to work on many projects in its home city as well as in other parts of the United States and abroad.

The firm fosters a partnership between public and private interests, seeking to balance programmatic project concerns with an understanding of how that project interacts with the public domain. This concern permeates the work, which includes corporate, civic, cultural, educational, transportation, residential, hospitality, office, retail, and mixed-use projects on a variety of scales, from single story to high-rise, and small community to large urban center.

Each project benefits from principal and associate leadership. The work is organized so that teams with direct typological experience are supported by a broad internal network of talent: architects, interior designers, planners, and those with expertise in sustainable design, management, and technology. This structure fosters cross-pollination and interchange; bringing a wide range of expertise and experience to each project is a Fox & Fowle Architects trademark.

The intellectual basis of the design and planning process is paired with a dedication to working collectively, building trust-based relationships, engaging in activism, and exploring sustainability. In each of these areas, the firm has leveraged its knowledge and skills to become a leader in the community and the industry.

BRUCE FOWLE FAIA, LEED

Architect Bruce Fowle co-founded Fox & Fowle in 1978 on the philosophical basis that architecture must be conscious and respectful of context and utility while enriching the human experience. Since that time, he has guided his firm to international recognition for excellence in design and environmental responsibility.

Bruce's passion for architecture has been strong since he began work in the field 42 years ago. Today that passion is still in evidence; if anything, his perspective on the challenges facing contemporary society has heightened his belief that architects have a key role in creating a more humanistic and sustainable way to live. "Architects and planners have the ability—and the responsibility—to think about detail and about the large view in a very linked, connected way," he says. "We must find ways to apply our broad understanding about the many influences on the built environment."

Bruce's design leadership has shaped most of the firm's most recognized projects, ranging from high-rise, multi-use complexes to cultural institutions and private homes. His work has earned the firm a number of major awards, most recently a 2001 National Honor Award for Design, the highest honor that the American Institute of Architects bestows on a project, for the Condé Nast Building @ 4 Times Square. Many of Bruce's projects have been featured in major national and international publications including recent cover stories in *Architectural Record* and *World Architecture*. He has been seen in several national television broadcasts and heard on National Public Radio.

In 1985, Bruce was named to the AIA College of Fellows; in 1994 he was elected Academician of the National Academy of Design. His alma mater, Syracuse University, named him the 2001 recipient of the George Arents Pioneer Medal for excellence in his field. He is a member of the AIA Design Committee and a Fellow of the Institute for Urban Design. He is a former vice president of the AIA/New York Chapter and served as chair of the Planning and Urban Design Committee for 10 years. He received the AIA's 1994 Harry B. Rutkins Award for his contribution to re-zoning in

New York City, and he continues to lend his expertise to planning and urban design initiatives, a role he considers essential if architects are to have any influence over the broader context of our cities.

Bruce was a founder and chairman of the New York chapter of Architects, Designers and Planners for Social Responsibility, an advocacy group for social justice and a sustainable built environment. He is on the Advisory Boards of New School University's Eugene Lang College and the New York City Ballet, modern ballet being one of his favorite art forms. He has also served on the board of the Graham-Windham Childcare Agency, New York's largest organization helping abused and abandoned children. He is LEED accredited by the US Green Building Council.

Following the September 11 attacks on the World Trade Center, he helped create and mobilize New York New Visions, a coalition of organizations to help shape the planning and design response to the destruction.

From 1970 through 1977, Bruce was an associate in the firm of Edward Larrabee Barnes. Prior to that he worked for Brown Daltas Associates, Myller, Snibble and Tafel, Architects, and Willim B. Tabler Associates. A 1960 graduate of the Syracuse University School of Architecture, he currently serves as chair of the school's Advisory Board and was the recipient of its Sargeant Professorship in 1996. He is a frequent lecturer at various professional and academic institutions, and has served on many juries for student and professional design awards.

Bruce is married to Marcia Taylor Fowle, an environmental administrator/author and president of the Board of the New York City Audubon Society. Their three daughters are all involved in conservation or environmental planning and design.

DANIEL KAPLAN AIA

Architect Dan Kaplan joined Fox & Fowle in 1987, became a principal in 1996, and was elevated to senior principal in 2003. He has served in a design and leadership capacity for many of the firm's largest projects, crafting modern award-winning buildings that are distinguished by their imagination, responsibility, and sophistication. Dan has 20 years experience in the field. He excels in the design of complex, large-scale urban buildings. He leads the firm's work on commercial and residential projects and is accomplished at managing large teams of staff and coordinating with outside consultants.

Working toward a more socially, environmentally, and economically sustainable condition has been central to Fox & Fowle since the firm's inception, and Dan's work has pushed forward the technical and design rigor of the work as well as the firm's profile in the realm of architects who embrace this way of designing and building. "We have a keen understanding of sustainability," Dan says. "But we are just starting to create architecture that expresses a marriage of nature and culture. This is truly an exciting challenge. Sustainability is integral to creating work that is healthier and more effective over the long term—and is also more beautiful and more loved by those who see and use it every day."

Projects currently under Dan's direction include the *New York Times* Tower (in association with the Renzo Piano Building Workshop), The Helena, a high-rise residential tower on Manhattan's West Side, Yi He International Center in Beijing, and the renovation and expansion of the Roosevelt Avenue Station. He has been working closely with a broad team of industry leaders to develop the Liberty State Science Center's innovative working exhibit, "Skyscraper!"

Dan led the firm's participation in the Max Protetch Gallery's New World Trade Center exhibition in the months following the fall of the towers. The design that resulted was the firm's answer to the obligation to build an exemplar complex—an urban fragment that embodies the highest aspirations for the future of the city. The solution celebrates connections and mediates the rational uptown and organic downtown planning grids. Dan's team proposed that the tower footprints themselves be left as voids, as hallowed ground.

A number of Dan's projects have been honored by design organizations and others. The design for the Merrill Lynch Headquarters received a design award from the Society of American Registered Architects. The Reuters Building has been honored by the same organization and others. The Condé Nast Building @ 4 Times Square has received numerous accolades, including design awards from the AIA New York State, the National Honor Award from the AIA, as well as honors from the Alliance to Save Energy and the New York City Audubon Society.

With a growing reputation as an industry leader, Dan has spoken to many civic and professional organizations and published articles on the Times Square revitalization, the Condé Nast Building @ 4 Times Square, the Reuters Building, and other projects and subjects. He authored an article, "Manhattan's Green Giant," for *Lessons Learned: Four Times Square*, an extensive, multidisciplinary documentation of the project. That project has been published in many design and mainstream periodicals and Dan's design for the Roosevelt Avenue Terminal was covered in *Oculus* and other publications. He is also a visiting professor at New Jersey Institute of Technology's Graduate School Design Studio.

Dan is a member of the American Institute of Architects and the Urban Land Institute. He previously worked for Buro Raber & Seiber in Lucerne, Switzerland, and for Siris Combs Architects in New York City. A 1984 graduate of Cornell University, Dan received seven honors and medals for outstanding design work and scholarship during his tenure there.

SYLVIA SMITH AIA

Architect Sylvia Smith, named a principal in 1996, directs Fox & Fowle's educational and cultural work, which has won numerous awards for design excellence. Since joining the firm in 1982, she has been responsible for program-intensive projects of varying scope and size.

Sylvia is constantly cultivating new ways to make architecture more expressive and enriching. She is interested in design as a practical and poetic articulation of theoretical ideas, and is firmly committed to a sense of optimism at the heart of those ideas. "Every project, regardless of type or size, can make an architectural move that empowers it and enlivens the experiences of people who visit or pass by," Sylvia says. "The painstaking exploration of what spatial move will accomplish that is the joy of our work. Into that pursuit, we invest intellectual and emotional energy; it is a constantly rewarding process."

Her current work includes the new School of Management for Syracuse University, the redesign of the Lincoln Center public spaces (with Diller Scofidio + Renfro), a new building for the Wildlife Conservation Society, and renovations of The Spence School and The Calhoun School in Manhattan. Past projects include the New School University's Knowledge Union Technology Center, the Black Rock Forest Center for Science and Education, an award-winning renovation for the American Craft Museum, and a renovation/addition for the American Bible Society headquarters.

Architecture organizations and others have honored several Fox & Fowle projects led by Sylvia for their design excellence and other attributes. These include an AIA Award of Merit for the American Bible Society project, a Design Share/School Construction News award for educational innovation for the Black Rock Forest Center, and a Historic Educational Buildings Award from the Preservation League of New York State for The Spence School.

Several of Sylvia's projects have been published, such as the New School University's Knowledge Union in *Oculus* (magazine of the AIA New York Chapter) and the American Bible Society project

in *L'Arca* and *New York* magazine. Sylvia has authored articles for various design journals and other publications, including one for the American Craft Museum.

Teaching is an important part of Sylvia's own learning. She has team-taught a housing studio at the Parsons School of Design and a design/build studio and seminar at Ball State University School of Architecture. She is a frequent jurist at schools of architecture throughout the Northeast. She also teaches design and building skills at the Yestermorrow School in Warren, Vermont (and serves on its board of directors). She teaches, among other things, an intensive class for laypersons seeking a "hands-on" design and building learning experience. Her own interest in building began when she participated in the reconstruction of a village in western Ghana in a college summer abroad program.

She is an active member of the AIA and the AIA New York Chapter's Architecture for Education committee. She is a member of the Association of Real Estate Women, the American Library Association, the Society for College and University Planners, the American Association of Museums, the PENCIL (Public Education Needs Civic Involvement in Learning) program, and the Friends of Fort Tryon Park. In 2000, Sylvia was named one of the Women Real Estate Leaders for the 21st Century by the Association of Real Estate Women. She sits on the dean's advisory board for the University of Virginia School of Architecture.

Sylvia is a member of the American Institute of Architects. Sylvia earned a Bachelor of Arts degree in studio art and art history from Dickinson College, where she was named a Metzger Fellow. She received her Master of Architecture degree from the University of Virginia School of Architecture in 1979.

MARK STRAUSS FAIA, AICP

Architect, planner, and urban designer Mark Strauss joined as a principal when the firm he co-founded, Jambhekar Strauss, merged with Fox & Fowle in 2000. Mark now leads Fox & Fowle's planning and urban design work. A key aspect of his interest and talent lies in developing planning and design approaches to assist communities, institutions, and developers that are redefining properties in response to economic, transportation, and political conditions. He has developed a national reputation for the sensitive and viable repositioning of sites and communities.

Mark's planning background and interest in the contextual influences on architecture provides the basis for much of his work. Related questions are central to his inquiry: What are the economic magnets for communities? What brings people to a place? Genuine concern about why and how people get to and from communities and what kind of architecture is appropriate for the uses that have been defined are the drivers for Mark's work. He thinks about connectivity and place-making simultaneously.

Recent work includes a comprehensive plan for Downtown New Rochelle, New York; planning and development of the Nassau Hub Major Investment Study for Nassau County; transit oriented development planning for Metro-North; and the redevelopment of the Pitney Bowes manufacturing plant site in South Stamford.

The master plan for the Jamaica Station Area Urban Strategy received a merit award from the New York State AIA. The Midtown East Development Plan was honored with a special citation by the Boston Society of Architects/AIA New York Chapter Urban Design Awards. Mark recently led the winning entry for a master plan, Gloucester Green, for Gloucester, Massachusetts, in a Boston Society of Architects' Density Competition. Several of Mark's projects have appeared in *Planning* magazine. Mark authored a Viewpoint column on transit-oriented development in the May 2004 issue of *Urban Land* magazine.

As an architect, urban designer, and certified planner, Mark has melded his multidisciplinary skills to improve the built environment and influence public policy. He helped organize New York New Visions following the September 11 attacks and he was chosen to lead the long-term planning efforts for the alliance. Mark used his professional urban design and planning experience to develop a process that integrated the diverse talents and skills.

Mark served as board member of the New York Foundation for Architecture. In that capacity, he helped organize multiple seminars and events to highlight issues related to architecture and planning in New York, including the celebration for the new Center for Architecture. He was named 2005 vice president/president elect for the AIA New York Chapter and was the recipient of the 2004 Harry Rutkins Service to the Profession honor award. Mark also serves on the boards for the Citizens Housing and Preservation Coalition and the City College Architectural Center. He is also the co-chair of the Urban Design Committee for the American Planning Association New York Metro Chapter.

Mark is a professor at Baruch College's Newman Institute of Real Estate, where he teaches a course entitled: Introduction to Architecture, Planning and Construction in New York. He has also taught an urban design studio at Pratt Institute and has lectured at New York University, City College of New York, Columbia University, Virginia Tech, New York Tech and the University of Pennsylvania.

Prior to the formation of Jambhekar Strauss, Mark was Director of Planning and an Associate Partner at Kohn Pedersen Fox. He received a Bachelor of Architecture from Cornell University in 1976 and a Master of Urban Planning from City College in New York in 1977. He is a registered architect in New York, New Jersey, Connecticut and Pennsylvania and a member of the American Institute of Certified Planners. He is a member of the American Institute of Architects and was named to the AIA College of Fellows in 2004.

SUDHIR JAMBHEKAR AIA

Sudhir Jambhekar joined the firm in 2000 as a principal when the firm he co-founded, Jambhekar Strauss, merged with Fox & Fowle. He is an architect and urban designer with 35 years of experience on a wide variety of project types and scales. Sudhir's passion for design, art, and intellectual exchange with the next generation contributes a valued diversity to the design dialogue at Fox & Fowle.

Sudhir approaches design as a perceptive search for meaning and usefulness, narrowing the infinite possibilities for a project to an idea that balances the various forces at work in each. His approach is rooted in the belief that all elements are part of the larger whole, and each element of the built environment is not only worthy of, but requires, design excellence.

"Conceptually, there is a search for meaning and usefulness that is rooted in the belief that all elements are part of a larger whole. This search involves balancing opposites," he says. "At the physical level, the pursuit is a matter of aesthetics. For me, it is simplicity, abstraction of ideas, and modern compositional strategies that govern the aesthetics."

This belief has made Sudhir a design leader in a variety of typologies, including the firm's infrastructure and public work. His major projects include the design of Manhattan's new Second Avenue Subway Line, the Communications and Multimedia Centers at Lehman College, and the new LCOR office building in Jamaica, Queens. He led the design of the award-winning competition entry for the Queens Museum of Art expansion, chosen as one of five finalists, as well as the firm's innovative entry for the new Perth Amboy High School competition.

Sudhir's projects have won several major design awards, including a 2002 design award from AIA New Jersey for the Walter Rand Transportation Center Expansion and a 2001 Award of Merit from AIA New York State for the Jamaica Transportation Center. The Society of American Registered Architects granted design awards to the Queens Museum of Art competition entry, Hudson-Bergen Light Rail Transit System, and

Williamsburg Community Center competition entry. In addition, his designs for the Midtown East Development Plan and the Washington DC Metro Station Canopy Program competition were also honored with awards from the Boston Society of Architects in 2001.

Many of these and other projects have been published in the leading design publications, including Oculus (journal of AIA New York Chapter), Architectural Record, Architecture, and Competitions. The Korean publication Concept featured the Queens Museum of Art competition in April 2002. His design for the Perth Amboy High School won an AIA New York Chapter design award in 2004.

Sudhir has lectured and served on design awards juries at several AIA chapters, the Indian Institute of Architects in Bangalore, and the Urban Design Research Institute in Bombay. He is a visiting professor at New Jersey Institute of Technology's Graduate School Design Studio. He has participated on numerous design juries at architectural schools in the Northeast, and served on the board of directors for the Forest Hills Gardens Corporation and the Jamaica Center for Arts and Learning (JCAL). Sudhir's deep interest in sixteenth- to nineteenth-century Indian painting, as well as contemporary art, furniture, product design, music, and history, further enhances his contribution to the design dialogue at Fox & Fowle.

Sudhir is a member of the American Institute of Architects and the Society of American Registered Architects. Prior to the formation of Jambhekar Strauss, Sudhir led the design of a variety of large scale commercial, mixed-use, and institutional projects around the world at Kohn Pedersen Fox. He also worked at John Carl Warnecke & Associates and I. M. Pei & Partners. He received a Bachelor of Architecture degree from the University of Bombay in 1964 and a Master of Architecture and Urban Design from Columbia University in 1979.

# Associate Principals

HEIDI BLAU AIA

TIM MILAM AIA

Heidi Blau joined Fox & Fowle Architects in 2002 as a senior associate and was named associate principal in 2004. With many years of experience behind her, Heidi's particular strength lies in providing insightful program development, project management and attentive direction for educational, cultural, and municipal projects. She finds great fulfillment in contributing to each project from concept through completion.

Some of her recent projects include the renovation and expansion of the Brooklyn College Library, which was awarded a 2003 Building Brooklyn Award, the Wallach Study Center in Columbia University's Avery Architectural Library, the Mill Neck Deaf Educational Center, the Spence Lower School, and the Dana Discovery Center at the Harlem Meer in Central Park. She is currently directing the Lincoln Center and Juilliard projects that Fox & Fowle is completing in collaboration with Diller Scofidio + Renfro.

Because of her extensive library design expertise, Ms Blau was a featured speaker at the 2003 "Building the 21st Century Library" seminar, sponsored by the Metropolitan New York Library Council. In May 2004, she was recognized as a Woman of Achievement by the Professional Women in Construction.

Before joining Fox & Fowle Architects, Heidi spent 16 years at Buttrick White & Burtis, rising from a junior designer to job captain, project architect, associate, and partner in 1999.

Heidi is an active member of the American Institute of Architects, the Society of College and University Planners, the American Library Association, and the Cobble Hill Neighborhood Association. She received her Bachelor of Arts from Smith College in 1980 and a Master of Architecture degree from Columbia University in 1983.

Tim Milam joined Fox & Fowle in 2001 as business manager with 14 years of experience as an architect, planner, and manager. In 2003, he became managing director, and the following year was named an associate principal.

Tim is responsible for contract administration, project management oversight, and general management of the firm. His duties include strategic planning, contract negotiation, human resources, as well as staffing and recruiting. He also leads the firm's steering committee.

Before joining Fox & Fowle, Tim was a project manager at the City University of New York where he was responsible for oversight of projects at several college campuses, including the Brooklyn College Library renovation and expansion and the Lehman College Multimedia Center. Prior to that, he was an associate at Jambhekar Strauss Architects (since merged with Fox & Fowle), participating in management of the firm and with key commissions including the Hudson Bergen Light Rail System, the Hunts Point Center Master Plan, the Lehman College Communications Center, and the Queensborough Community College Master Plan.

Tim is a member of the American Institute of Architects. He earned his Bachelor of Architecture degree from the University of Kentucky in 1986 and completed a Master of Urban Planning degree at City College, City University of New York, in 1995.

# Associates

Carl Nolan, Director of Finance

Anna Ortega, Office Manager

Kirsten Sibilia Assoc AIA, Marketing Director


Elizabeth Finkelshteyn, Senior Associate

Frank Lupo AIA, Senior Associate

Ann Rolland AIA, Senior Associate

Nicholas Tocheff AIA, LEED, Senior Associate

Rodney VenJohn AIA, Senior Associate

Peter Weingarten AIA, LEED, Senior Associate


Susan Dunlope Masi LEED, Associate

Theresa Genovese LEED, Associate

Erica Joltin AIA, LEED, Associate

Alex Leung AIA, Associate

John Loughran AIA, LEED, Associate

Peter Olney AIA, LEED, Associate

Peter Pesce AIA, Associate

Gerald Rosenfeld AIA, Associate

John Secreti LEED, Associate

Daniel Schmitt LEED, Associate

# Collaborators

Over the years, Fox & Fowle Architects has worked with hundreds of professionals in all aspects of the design and building process. Without the commitment, talent, and effort of these individuals and teams, it would have been impossible to realize the potential of each project. We are grateful for these collaborative, creative exchanges and look forward to continued opportunities to pursue innovation and excellence together.

This list represents those who participated on the projects featured in this volume of our work.

21st Century Rail Corporation

Abel Bainnson Butz

Accord Engineering

AG Consulting Engineering

Altieri Sebor Wieber

AMEC

Amman & Whitney

Anastos Engineering Associates

Ann Kale Associates

AP3D Consulting

Arup

Athwal & Associates

Atkinson Koven Feinberg Engineers

B Five Studio

B2A/Survsat Consultants

Barry Hersh

Bergmann Associates

Bovis Lend Lease

Business Methods

Cambridge Seven Associates

Cantor Seinuk Group

Carbone Smolan Agency

Carlos Dobryn Consulting Engineers

Carrier Corporation

CBM Engineers

Centre Scientifique et Technique du Batiment

Cerami & Associates

Cornelia H. Oberlander

Corporate Interiors Contracting

Cosentini Associates

Cosentini Lighting

Dagher Engineering

David Harvey Associates

DeSimone Consulting Engineers

Development Consulting Services

DMJM+Harris/ARUP

Domenech Hicks & Krockmalnic Architects

Domingo Gonzalez Associates

Don Todd Associates

Dongbu Engineering & Construction Company

DVI Communications

Earth Day New York/E4

Earth Tech

East China Architectural Design Institute

Economics Research Associates

Edwards & Zuck

Eley and Associates

Empire Soils Investigation

En-Chuan Liu

Entek Engineering

Ernst & Young

Eustance and Horowitz

F. J. Sciame Construction Co.

Fisher Dachs Associates

Fisher Marantz Stone

Flack + Kurtz

Flynn Battaglia Architects

Fried, Frank, Harris, Shriver & Jacobson

Gabor M. Szakal Consulting Engineers

Gage-Babcock & Associates

Gardiner & Theobald

Gensler

Gerard Associates Consulting Engineers

Goldman Copeland Associates

Goldstick Lighting Design

Gottlieb Skanska

Green October Foundation

Haipo & Associates

Handler Grasso Durfee Bridges

Harman Jablin Architects

Harvey & Marshall Associates

Harvey Marshall Berling Associates

Hayden McKay Lighting Design

Heitmann & Associates

Herbert Levine Lighting Consultant

HM Brandston & Partners

HM White Site Architects

Hopkins Food Service Specialists

Hueber Breuer

Hutton Associates

Israel Berger & Associates

J.T. Magen & Company

Jaffe Holden Acoustics

Jam Consultants

Janet R. Duggan & Associates

Jaros, Baum & Bolles

Jenkins & Huntington

Jerome S. Gillman Consulting Architect

JHR Acoustical Consulting

John P. Stopen Engineering Partnership

Joseph R. Loring & Associates

Kallen & Lemelson, Consulting Engineers

Kiss + Cathcart, Architects

Kreisler Borg Florman General Construction Company

Kroll Schiff & Associates

Lakhani & Jordan Engineers

Langan Engineering & Environmental Services

LeChase General Construction

Lehr Associates Consulting Engineers

Leslie E. Robertson Associates

LK McLean Associates

Lo Yi Chan FAIA

LZA Technology

Maitra Associates

Margie Ruddick Landscape

Martin Rose Associates

Matthews Nielsen Landscape Architects

McHugh, DiVencent & Alessi

Morse Diesel International

Mottola Rini Engineers

Mueser Rutledge Consulting Engineers

Mullaney

Natural Logic

Natural Resources Defense Council

New York State Energy Research & Development Authority

No. 3 Engineering Construction Company

North Broadway Construction

Office for Visual Interaction

Olin Partnership

P.A. Collins

Parsons Brinckerhoff Quade & Douglas

Paul, Hastings, Janofsky & Walker

Paul, Weiss, Rifkind, Wharton & Garrison

Pentagram

Philip Habib & Associates

Phillips, Preiss, Shapiro Associates

Plaza Construction

Quennell Rothschild & Partners

R G Roesch Architecture & Landscape Architecture

Renfro Design Group

Renzo Piano Building Workshop

Richard Gluckman

Richter + Ratner Contracting Corporation

Riser Management Systems

RKG Associates

Robert Gaskin

Rocky Mountain Institute

Rolf Jensen & Associates

Romano Gatland

Rosenman & Colin

Rowan Williams Davies & Irwin

Saccardi & Schiff

SBLD Studio

Schnadelbach Partnership

Severud Associates

Shen, Milsom, & Wilke

Skanska USA Building

Slattery Skanska

Solar Design Associates

Space

Stadtmauer Bailkin

Stearns & Wheler

Steven Winter Associates

Storm King Contracting

Structure Tone

STV Group

Swan Drafting Services

Team for Environmental Architecture

The Clarett Group/Steven Weinryb

The Urbitran Group

Thomas Balsley Associates

Thomas Thompson Lighting Design

Thornton-Tomasetti Engineers

Tishman Construction

Todd Berling Design

Tor Smolen Calini & Anastos

Transolar

Turner Construction Company

UN Studio

URS Corporation

USCapitalInvest Bancorp

Van Deusen & Associates

Van Real Estate/Elisa Liu

Vanderweil Engineers

Vernon Hoffman

Verticon

VJ Associates

Vollmer Associates

Wallace Roberts & Todd

Washington Square Partners

Weidlinger Associates

Weiskopf and Pickworth

Whitehouse & Company

William Vitacco Associates

Wing Associates Landscape Architecture

Winthrop, Stimson, Putnam & Roberts

Wolf & Co.

Yorke Construction Corporation

Zimmer Gunsul Frasca Partnership

# Bibliography

Bagli, Charles. "Durst May Put Up a New Skyscraper on Times Square." *New York Observer* 21 Aug. 1995: 1+. [Condé Nast Building]

Bagli, Charles. "Bullish on Times Square Neon." *New York Times* 20 Aug. 1998, late ed., sec. B: 1+. [Condé Nast Building]

Bagli, Charles V. "A Project 30 Years in the Making." *New York Times* 16 Mar. 1999, late ed., sec. B: 1+. [One Bryant Park]

Bagli, Charles. "Battle of the Unbuilt Billboard." *New York Times* 21 May 1999, late ed., sec. B: 1+. [Condé Nast Building]

Bagli, Charles. "The Skyscraper Above, the Cracks Below." *New York Times* 1 Jan. 2000, late ed., sec. E: 29. [Condé Nast Building]

Bagli, Charles V. "Sale of Building on 42nd Street Brings 30-Year Feud to an End." *New York Times* 6 Dec. 2001, late ed., sec. D: 4. [One Bryant Park]

Bagli, Charles V. "35-Story Tower is Planned For Last Open Times Square Lot." *New York Times* 22 Oct. 2002, late ed., sec. B: 3. [Times Square Plaza]

Bagli, Charles V. "Bank of America Nears Agreement with Developer to Build 42nd Street Skyscraper." *New York Times* 27 May 2003, late ed., sec. B: 8+. [One Bryant Park]

Balfour, Alan. *World Cities* New York. Ed. Maggie Toy. New York: John Wiley & Sons, 2001.

Baldassini, Niccolo. "La Transparenza Come Segno, American Bible Society, New York." *L'Arca Maggio* 2000, pp. 60–63. [American Bible Society Renovation and Addition].

"Banking on Collaboration." *Space* Aug. 2000, pp. 52–57. [Industrial and Commercial Bank of China]

Barhydt, Matthew. "Field Reports." *Oculus* Sept. 1995: 3–4. [Herman Miller Showroom]

Bergsman, Steve. "'96 in Review: A Year of New Deals." *National Real Estate Investor* Feb. 1997: 46–50. [Condé Nast Building]

Berk, Michael. "Connecting as High Art." *Competitions* Jan.–Mar. 2002, pp. 50–61. [Queens Museum of Art Competition Entry]

Beverly, Robert. "A Tall Tale of Success." *Engineered Systems* Oct. 1999: 72–78. [Condé Nast Building]

"Bible Society Reaches Out." *New York Times* 21 Dec. 1997, late ed., sec. 11: 9. [American Bible Society Renovation and Addition]

Binder, Georges. *Sky High Living: Contemporary High-Rise Apartment and Mixed-Use Buildings*. Mulgrave: Images Publishing Group, 2002. [235 West 51 Street, Le Modrian]

Blau, Heidi. "An Enriching Place." *American School & University* Nov. 2004, 361–362

*Brick in Architecture*. Reston: BIA, 2002. [Fingerlakes BlueCross/BlueShield Headquarters]

Cappelleri, Alba. "Tre Torri [Three Towers]." *Domus* Apr. 2001, pp. 65–68. [*New York Times* Headquarters]

Capurso, Rossana. "Sede Della Condé Nast Building a New York." *L'industria Delle Construzioni Maggio* 2001: 40–47. [Condé Nast Building]

Cardani, Elena. "Le Torri Ecologiche Di Fox & Fowle [Fox and Fowle's Ecological Towers]." *Eco Enea L'Arca Supplement* May 1999, pp. 3–4. [Condé Nast Building]

Chaszer, Andre and Buro Happold. "Sign of the Times." *Steel Design* July–Sept. 1999: 6–9. [Condé Nast Building]

Cho, Aileen. "*New York Times* News Fit to Print." *Engineering News Record* 23 Oct. 2000: 16. [*New York Times* Headquarters]

Croxton, Randolph R. "Sustainable Design Offers Key to Control." *Architectural Record* June 1997: 76. [Condé Nast Building]

Cuozzo, Steve. "Showing Respect for the Past." *New York Post* 17 Oct. 2000: 35. [Reuters Building]

Cuozzo, Steve. "No Tenants Yet for Times Tower." *New York Post* 31 July 2001: 32. [*New York Times* Headquarters]

Cuozzo, Steve. "Too Much Space on Market: New Construction Could Create Glut." *New York Post* 30 Oct. 2001: 34. [Midtown East Redevelopment Plan]

Cuozzo, Steve. "Unnamed Pols Pushed for 42nd Street Deal." *New York Post* 11 Dec. 2001: 36+. [One Bryant Park]

Cuozzo, Steve. "The Times is Right." *New York Post* 22 Feb. 2002: 29+. [*New York Times* Headquarters]

Cuozzo, Steve. "Tower to Fill Gap in Times Sq." *New York Post* 4 June 2002: 6. [Times Square Plaza]

Davenport, Peter. "Hotel, Skyrises in Soho's Riverfront Future?" *The Hour* [Norwalk] 29 July 1999: 1. [Norwalk Development Plan]

David, Charles. "The Big Green Apple." *Multifamily Trends* Apr.–Jun. 2001: 16+. [Condé Nast Building]

Davidson, Judith. "Times Square." *World Architecture* Feb. 1997: 1. [Condé Nast Building]

Davis, Cheryl. "Silicon Alley—Smart Buildings." *CIO* 15 Dec. – 1 Jan. 1996: 20. [New York Information Technology Center at 55 Broad Street]

Denitto, Emily and Amy Feldman. "Downtown is Booming." *Crain's New York Business* 24 June 1996: 1+. [New York Information Technology Center at 55 Broad Street]

Denitto, Emily. "Environmentally Sound Properties Help Owners Seed Greener Fields." *Crain's New York Business* 21–27 Apr. 1997: 1+. [Condé Nast Building]

"Details." *Architecture* Sept. 1993: 27. [Industrial and Commercial Bank of China]

Deutsch, Claudia H. "On Electronic Highway, Manhattan is a Destination." *New York Times* 23 July 1995, late ed., sec. 9: 1. [New York Information Technology Center at 55 Broad Street]

Deutsch, Claudia H. "Leasing Real Space to Denizens of Cyberspace." *New York Times* 26 May 1996, late ed., sec. 9: 7. [New York Information Technology Center at 55 Broad Street]

Donoff, Elizabeth. "Daylight! Daylight! Read All About It." *Architectural Lighting* Jun. 2004, 32–35. [*New York Times* Headquarters]

Dorris, Virginia Kent. "Newsroom Circuitry: the Reuters Building." *GRID* Oct.–Dec. 1999: 67–72. [Reuters Building]

Douglas, Kristin Ralff. "AIA Honors Fox and Fowle for Condé Nast Building." *Environmental Design and Construction* Mar.–Apr. 2001: 17. [Condé Nast Building]

"Energia: Ora Tocca Al Vento." *Focus* April 2000: 181–182. [Condé Nast Building]

Forgey, Benjamin. "On Times Square, a Tower with a Tall Order to Fill." *Washington Post* 26 Feb. 2000: C01+. [Condé Nast Building]

Fowle, Bruce. "Due Culture a Confronto: Connections Between European and American Architecture." *L'Arca*, May 2000, Issue 148: 2.

"Fox & Fowle Architects, New York, USA." *Batiment* Oct.–Nov. 1995: 11. [Industrial and Commercial Bank of China]

"Fox & Fowle Architects: Designing Shanghai's Next Century." *China Building Development* 1995: 55–59. [Industrial and Commercial Bank of China]

Frankel, Elana. *Design Secrets: Office Spaces.* Gloucester: Rockport, 2001. [Skanska New York Offices]

Frankel, Elana. "Disorderly Conduct." *Interior Design*, Jan. 2000: 59–60. [Skanska New York Offices]

Gair, Cristina. "Architectural Trends: a Delicate Balancing Act." *National Real Estate Investor* Feb. 2002: 16–23. [*New York Times* Headquarters]

Ganga, Elizabeth. "Revitalized Downtown Planned." *The Journal News* 21 Nov. 2002, sec. B: 1+. [New Rochelle Downtown Revitalization Plan]

Garbarine, Rachelle. "Condominium Developers Expand Boundaries of West Village." *New York Times* 12 Mar. 1999, late ed., sec. B: 8. [99 Jane Street]

Garbarine, Rachelle. "Two Luxury Projects May Cast Shadows on the West Village." *New York Times* 8 Aug. 1997, late ed., sec. B: 5. [99 Jane Street]

Garreta, Ariadna Alvarez. "Arquitectos de Rascacielos." *Ganduxer: Atrium*, 2003. [Condé Nast Building, Reuters Building]

Garreta, Ariadna Alvarez. "Skyscrapers." *Fresas: Atrium*, 2002. [Condé Nast Building]

Gault, Ylonda. "Meat District Doesn't Make Cut for Retailers Moving to West." *Crain's New York Business* 19 Apr. 1999: 26+. [99 Jane Street]

Giovannini, Joseph. "Acing the Deuce." *New York* 21–28 Jan. 2002: 77–78. [Condé Nast Building]

Glave, Judie. "Things Will Soon Become Transparent at Times New Headquarters." *Associated Press* State and Local Wire 13 Dec. 2001. [*New York Times* Headquarters]

Goldberger, Paul. "Busy Buildings: Post Iconic Towers Invade Times Square." *New Yorker* 4 Sept. 2000: 90–93. [Reuters Building]

Goldberger, Paul. "Spiffing up the Gray Lady." *New Yorker* 7 Jan. 2002. [*New York Times* Headquarters]

Gould, Kira L. "Get a Little Closer." *Metropolis* Jan. 2004: 46. [Gloucester Green]

Grant, Peter. "Rudins' Downtown Man. Plans Developing Nicely." *Daily News* 5 Sept. 1995: 26. [New York Information Technology Center at 55 Broad Street]

Hart, Sara. "Guess Who's Going Green?" *Architecture* Aug. 1998: 116–119. [Condé Nast Building]

Healy, Peter. "City Offers Prime Sites." *The Advocate* 7 July 1998: A9+. [Norwalk Development Plan]

"Herman Miller." *Interior Design* Aug. 1996: 84–93. [Herman Miller Showroom]

Hetter, Katia. "Jamaica Economy Jump-start?" *Newsday* 8 May 2001. [Jamaica Transportation Center Master Plan]

Hochstein, Marc. "Queens' High Card." *Grid* Oct. 2001: 66–69. [Jamaica Transportation Center Master Plan]

Holtzman, Anna. "UN Studio: Wadsworth Atheneum Museum of Fine Art/Hartford." *Architecture* Aug. 2002: 34–35. [Wadsworth Atheneum Expansion]

Holusha, John. "A Corporate Headquarters Next to Bugs and Mickey." *New York Times* 6 Sept. 1998, late ed., sec. 11: 9. [Reuters Building]

Holusha, John. "Commercial Property/42nd Street and Broadway; Technology in the Front Seat at 4 Times Square." *New York Times* 30 March 1997, late ed., sec. 9: 7. [Condé Nast Building]

Holusha, John. "New Technology Enhances Marketing and Design." *New York Times* 7 June 1998, late ed., sec. 11: 7. [Condé Nast Building]

Holusha, John. "Wiring as the Tip of the Telecommunications Iceberg." *New York Times* 11 Apr. 1999, late ed., sec. 11: 9. [New York Information Technology Center at 55 Broad Street]

Holusha, John. "Turning Buildings Into Telecommunications Hubs." *New York Times* 10 Oct. 1999, late ed., sec. 11: 11. [New York Information Technology Center at 55 Broad Street]

Holusha, John. "Office-Building Plans Come Off the Shelf." *New York Times* 7 Oct. 2001, late ed., sec. 11: 1+. [One Bryant Park]

Iovine, Julie V. "Moving Day Angst at the Citadel of Chic." *New York Times* 26 Feb. 1998, late ed., sec. F: 8. [Condé Nast Building]

Ivy, Robert. "Another Pair of Eyes." Editorial. *Architectural Record* Dec. 2002: 17–18. [Condé Nast Building]

Jacobs, Karrie. "Gimme Some of That New-Time Religion." *New York* 1 June 1998: 16. [American Bible Society Renovation and Addition]

Jacobs, Rebecca. "The Greening of America's High-Rise Home." *Financial Times* 13–14 January 2001 XIV. [Condé Nast Building]

Jenkins, Janet K. "New Times Square Station Lights Up Broadway." *Passenger Transport* 22 Sept. 1997: 72. [Times Square Subway Entrance]

Johnson, Kirk. "Battery Park to Get a 'Green' High-Rise." *New York Times* 21 June 2000, late ed., sec. B: 5. [Battery Park City Sustainable Design Guidelines]

Kamin, Blair. "Skyscraper Exhibit Falls a Little Short." *Chicago Tribune* 29 Aug. 2000, sec. 5: 1+. [Reuters Building]

Kwang Young, Jeong. New York World Trade Center Competition. New Town Project 2. Seoul, Korea: *Archiworld*, 2003. [Max Protetch Gallery Show Entry]

Kujawski, Wojciech. "Zielony Gigant" *Inteligentny Budynek* Mar.–Apr. 2000: 52–55. [Condé Nast Building]

Lacayo, Richard. "Buildings that Breathe." *Time* 26 Aug. 2002: A36–A38. [Condé Nast Building]

Lange, Alexandra. "White Out." *Metropolis* Apr. 2002: 104–107. [*New York Times* Headquarters]

Lerner, Kevin. "UN Studio Brings Clarity to Atheneum." *Architectural Record* Sept. 2002: 34. [Wadsworth Atheneum Expansion]

Levine, Jeff. "Green Buildings: Planted In." *ABO Developments* Jan.–Mar. 2001: 13. [Battery Park City Sustainable Design Guidelines]

Lewis, David L. and Stephen McFarland. "City Aims for Hi-Tech Downtown." *Daily News* 30 Oct. 1995: 22. [New York Information Technology Center at 55 Broad Street]

Lewis, Julia. "Carpet Diem." *Interior Design* May 1999: 100. [Collins & Aikman Showroom]

"Light Rail Extension to Hoboken Opens." *New York Times*. 30 Sept. 2002, late ed., sec. B: 5. [Hudson-Bergen Light Rail Transit System]

Linn, Charles. "Signs of the Times." *Architectural Record* June 1997: 85–91. [Condé Nast Building]

Lipton, Eric and James Glanz. "9/11 Prompts New Caution in Design of U.S. Skyscrapers." *New York Times* 9 Sept. 2002, late ed., sec. A: 1+. [*New York Times* Headquarters]

Lloyd, Alan. "The Power Plant in Your Basement." *Scientific American* July 1999: 80–86. [Condé Nast Building]

Lloyd, Ann Wilson. "Architecture For Art's Sake." *Atlantic* June 2001: 85–88. [Wadsworth Atheneum Expansion]

Lohr, Steve. "New York Area is Forging Ahead in New Media." *New York Times* 15 April 1996, late ed., sec. D: 1+. [New York Information Technology Center at 55 Broad Street]

Louie, Elaine. "Desks Go West." *New York Times* 22 Aug. 1996, late ed., sec. C: 3. [Herman Miller Showroom]

Lueck, Thomas J. "Blue Ribbons and Black in Times Sq. Celebration." *New York Times* 28 Oct. 1997, late ed., sec. B: 7. [Times Square Subway Entrance]

MacFarquhar, Neil. "Times Sq. Entrance Opens Up the Underground." *New York Times* 16 July, 1997, late ed., sec. B: 3. [Times Square Subway Entrance]

Mays, Vernon. *Office and Work Spaces: an International Portfolio of 43 Designers.* Gloucester: Rockport, 1999. [Herman Miller, Nortel Networks]

Marks, John. "Wired Women Make the Cyberscene." *U.S. News & World Report* 16 Oct. 1995: 75. [New York Information Technology Center at 55 Broad Street]

McNally, Owen. "Museum Plans a Welcome Change." *Hartford Courant* 17 June 2001: 1+. [Wadsworth Atheneum Expansion]

McNally, Owen. "State of the Art: Oldest Public Art Museum Planning to Free Itself With Ambitious Redesign." *Hartford Courant* 16 July 2000, sec. A: 1+. [Wadsworth Atheneum Expansion]

Messina, Judith. "Rudin's High-Tech Building a Plug for Downtown Plan." *Crain's New York Business* 18–22 October 1995: 1+. [New York Information Technology Center at 55 Broad Street]

Moed, Andrea. "Sensurround." *Metropoli*, Sept. 1996: 53–57. [Black Rock Forest Center for Science and Education]

Murphy, Cathy. "How Green Are You?" *Structural Engineer* Aug. 2001: 30–37. [Condé Nast Building]

Muschamp, Herbert. "Smaller Is Better: Condé Nast in Times Sq." *New York Times* 18 May 1996, late ed., sec. 1, pp. 21+. [Condé Nast Building]

Muschamp, Herbert. "One Way to Get Taller in a City of Giants." *New York Times* 16 May 1999, late ed., sec. 2: 31. [Condé Nast Building]

Muschamp, Herbert. "A Rare Opportunity for Real Architecture Where It's Needed." *New York Times* 22 Oct. 2000, late ed., sec. 2: 1+. [*New York Times* Headquarters]

Muschamp, Herbert. "Architectural Order Graces a Chaotic Hub." *New York Times* 8 Mar. 1998, late ed., sec. 1: 37. [Reuters Building]

Nash, Eric P. *Manhattan Skyscrapers*. New York: Princeton AP, 1999. [Condé Nast Building]

N.C. "Four Projects to Show Energy Savings." *Architecture* December 1996: 35. [Condé Nast Building]

"Netting New York—http://manhattan." *The Economist* 25 May 1996: 90. [New York Information Technology Center at 55 Broad Street]

Neuwirth, Robert. "Trashprofit." *Metropolis* Sept. 1996, p. 67+. [Condé Nast Building]

"New York's Dynamic New Media." *New York Times* 16 Apr. 1996, late ed., sec. A: 20. [New York Information Technology Center at 55 Broad Street]

Norris, Floyd. "1999: Extraordinary Winners and More Losers." *New York Times* 3 Jan. 2000, late ed., sec. C: 17+. [Condé Nast Building]

O'Brien, Michael F. "Officials' Reaction Optimistic: Urban Renewal Needs City Approval." *The Hour* [Norwalk] 29 July 1999: 1. [Norwalk Development Plan]

Oser, Alan S. "A Housing Program's Next Generation." *New York Times* 21 Dec. 1997, late ed., sec. 11: 1+. [American Bible Society Renovation and Addition]

Overbye, Dennis. "50 Years of Guiding Policy by Persuasion." *New York Times* 1 May 2001, late ed., sec. F: 1+. [Black Rock Forest Center]

Owen, David. "Green Manhattan." New Yorker 18 Oct. 2004: 111–123. [The Condé Nast Building @ 4 Times Square]

Paganelli, Carlo. "Una nuova immagine." *L'Arca* Nov. 1996: 56–59. [Condé Nast Building]

Pearson, Clifford. "Developer Brings Green Ideas to the Spec Market." *Architectural Record* June 1997: 73–75. [Condé Nast Building]

Pande, Taani. "An Affair to Remember." *Mantran* Apr. 2002: 68+.

Platter, Dave. "The Big Apple Turns Green." *Urban Land* Feb. 2000: 41. [Condé Nast Building]

Polner, Robert. "Reimagining a Hub." *Newsday*. 11 May 2003: A6+. [Roosevelt Avenue Intermodal Station]

Rice, Andrew. "Back to the Drawing Board." *Architecture* Jan. 2002: 14. [Times Square Plaza]

Richards Kristen. "Durst They Do It? Condé Do It? They Dare! They Can!" *Interiors* Aug. 1996: 12. [Condé Nast Building]

Rogers, Christina V. "Finalists Announced in Queens Museum of Art Competition." *Architectural Record* 5 Oct. 2001. [Queens Museum of Art Competition Entry]

Rogers, Josh. "Silicon Alley Finds a Foothold in Refurbished 55 Broad St." *Downtown Express* 2–15 Apr. 1996: 12+. [New York Information Technology Center at 55 Broad Street]

Rothstein, Mervyn. "A New Information Technology Center in Lower Manhattan Has So Far Leased a Third of its Space." *New York Times* 10 Jan. 1996, late ed., sec. D: 18. [New York Information Technology Center at 55 Broad Street]

Rothstein, Mervyn. "With a Major Tenant Lost, Upgrading Plan Pays Off." *New York Times* 11 Mar. 1998, late ed., sec. B: 8. [Fingerlakes BlueCross/BlueShield Headquarters]

Sandler, Linda. "Mechanic's Skill is Wrenching Lease Deals." *Wall Street Journal* 27 Oct. 1999: B4. [Condé Nast Building]

Scheinbart, Betsy. "Meeks Unveils New Plans for Downtown Jamaica." *Jamaica Times* 10 May 2001. [Jamaica Transportation Center Master Plan]

Schmertz, Mildred F. "Saved by the Stock Market: Condé Nast on Times Square." *Oculus* Dec. 1999: 8–9. [Condé Nast Building]

Schulze, Franz. "Towers for Tomorrow." *Art in America* May 2001: 161–167. [Condé Nast Building]

Siegal, Nina. "Bronx Museum Plans to Renovate Old Space and Create New One." *New York Times* 24 Sept. 2000, late ed., sec. 14: 6. [Bronx Museum of Art Master Plan]

Slatin, Peter and Paul Tharp. "Condé Nast Seals $11M Tax Deal for Times Square Move." *New York Post* 8 May 1996: 2. [Condé Nast Building]

Slatin, Peter. "Durst Buys Location for Tower on 43rd." *Crain's New York Business* 12 Feb. 1996: 14. [Condé Nast Building]

Slatin, Peter. "Times Sq. Tycoon Climbs to the Top of the Heap." *New York Post* 19 May 1996: 62. [Condé Nast Building]

"Solar Energy in Times Square?" *Urban Land* June 1997: 12. [Condé Nast Building]

Smith, Sylvia J. "Blending Old and New." *American School & University* August 2000: 156+.

Smith, Sylvia J. "Crafting the Visionary Master Plan." *American School & University*, August 2003.

Sommerhoff, Emilie W. "Design Focus: University Hall Cultural Center, New York City." *Architectural Lighting* Sept/Oct 2004: 73. [New School University Arnold Hall]

"Special: Sudhir S. Jambhekar." *Archiworld* Apr. 2002: 56–97

Stanley, Sarah. "Taking Flight." *Urban Land* Nov.– Dec. 2001: 49–53. [Jamaica Transportation Center Master Plan]

Stanley, Sarah. "Discussing Ground Zero at Pratt." *Oculus* Mar.–Apr. 2002: 20–22. [Reuters Building]

Stephens, Suzanne. "Fox & Fowle Creates a Collage in Four Times Square, Using Skyscrapers Past and Present and a Touch of 'Green.'" *Architectural Record* Mar. 2000: 91–96. [Condé Nast Building]

Strauss, Mark E. "New Jersey's Watefront: Doing It Right." *Oculus* Summer 2004: 32–33.

Strauss, Mark E., and Larry Rosenbloom "Making TOD Real." *Urban Land* May 2004: 14–17.

Tatum, Rita. "Shapes of Things to Come." *Building Operating Management* July 1997: 49–58. [Condé Nast Building]

Thompson, Glen. "Optimism Reigns at Unveiling of Times Tower Design." GlobeSt.com 14 Dec. 2001 21 Aug. 2003. [*New York Times* Headquarters]

Thompson, John. "Green Design: Going Mainstream?" *Urban Land* July 2003: 10–17. [Condé Nast Building]

"Times Picks Designer for Tower's Interior." *New York Times* 10 Feb. 2001, late ed., sec. B: 3. [*New York Times* Headquarters]

"The Top 200 Architectural Practices/Design Firms." *World Architecture* 1995: 11+.

"The Two Faces of Times Square: One Façade's Limestone, the Other One's Glass." *New York Times* 19 May 1996, late ed., sec. 9: 1. [Condé Nast Building]

Traub, James. "The Dursts Have Odd Properties." *The New York Times Magazine* 6 Oct. 2002: 110–113. [Condé Nast Building]

Truppin, Andrea. "At the Crossroads of the World, a Facelift is in Full Swing." *Architectural Record* May 1998. [Reuters Building]

Tugel, Von Hanne. "The Age of Solartechnology." *GEO* Mar. 1999: 73–90. [Condé Nast Building]

Turner, Nicola. "4 Times Square–Breaking New Ground." *World Architecture* Feb. 2000: 56–63. [Condé Nast Building]

VenJohn, Rodney and Michael Stark. "Healthy, Productive & Green Offices at Little or No Extra Cost." *Corporate Real Estate Executive* Apr. 2001: 22–25. [Skanska New York Offices]

Vercelloni, Matteo. *New Showrooms & Art Galleries in USA*. Ed. Silvio San Pietro. Milano: Edizioni L'Archivolto, 1999. [Herman Miller Showroom]

Vogel, Carol. "Christie's Offers Prized Cezanne." *New York Times* 4 Apr. 2003, late ed., sec. E: 36. [New School University Arnold Hall]

"Watching the Construction." Editorial. *New York Times* 12 Dec. 1997, late ed., sec. A: 34. [Condé Nast Building]

Weiss, Lois. "Milsteins Win the Lot." *New York Post* 17 Jan. 2001: 35. [Times Square Plaza]

Weiss, Lois. "All-out Effort to Build Offices." *New York Post* 3 Oct. 2001. [Jamaica Transportation Center Master Plan]

Weiss, Lois. "Curtain up on Theatre Plan." *New York Post* 12 Dec. 2001. [*New York Times* Headquarters]

Weiss, Lois. "The Green-ing of New York." *New York Post* 01 May 2002: 36+. [Reuters Building]

Williams, Alex. "Wall Street Wonderland." New York 4 Nov. 1996: 32+. [New York Information Technology Center at 55 Broad Street]

Zukowsky, John and Martha Thorne, eds. *Skyscrapers: the New Millennium*. Munich: Prestel, 2000. [Condé Nast Building, Reuters Building]

FOX & FOWLE ARCHITECTS FOUNDED IN
New York, New York

EBERSTADT RESIDENCE
Walter and Vera Eberstadt,
Massachusetts

CHRISTIE'S EAST AUCTION HOUSE
Christie's, New York, New York

KLEIN RESIDENCE
Robert and Elaine Klein,
Massachusetts

MUSEUM OF CONTEMPORARY CRAFTS
American Craft Council, New York,
New York

767 THIRD AVENUE OFFICE BUILDING
The William Kaufman Organization,
New York , New York

VAN ZON HOUSE
Aaron and Gabrielle Van Zon,
Massachusetts

MOBIL TECHNICAL CENTER
General Services, Warehouse, and
Library Facilities, Mobil Oil
Corporation, Pennington, New Jersey

1978                    1979                              1981                           1982

ZIEGLER RESIDENCE

Henry and Patricia Ziegler,
Connecticut

150 EAST 52ND STREET

Royco Property Mgmt. Corporation,
New York, New York

45 BROADWAY ATRIUM OFFICE BUILDING

HRO International, New York,
New York

NATIONAL WESTMINSTER BANK USA
CORPORATE HEADQUARTERS

National Westminster Bank/HRO,
New York, New York

ONE EXCHANGE PLAZA OFFICE BUILDING

Exchange Plaza Partners, New York,
New York

TOWER 56 OFFICE BUILDING

HRO International, New York,
New York

MOBIL TECHNICAL CENTER, CENTRAL
RESEARCH DIVISION RENOVATION

Mobil Oil Corporation, Pennington,
New Jersey

1983

1984

WINNER, SOUTH FERRY PLAZA MIXED USE COMPLEX

South Ferry Associates/Zeckendorf Corp/World-Wide Holding Corp., New York, New York

527 MADISON AVENUE OFFICE BUILDING

Louis Dreyfus Property Group, New York, New York

AMERICAN CRAFT MUSEUM

American Craft Council, New York, New York

BROAD FINANCIAL CENTER OFFICE BUILDING

Aetna Life Insurance Company/HRO, New York, New York

MOBIL TECHNICAL CENTER, NORTHEAST COMPUTER CENTER EXPANSION

Mobil Oil Corporation, Pennington, New Jersey

THE SPENCE SCHOOL RENOVATION AND EXPANSION

The Spence School, New York, New York

650 MADISON AVENUE OFFICE BUILDING EXPANSION

The Hiro Real Estate Company, New York, New York

1985          1986                                        1987

7 WEST 34TH STREET OFFICE BUILDING
CONVERSION & RESTORATION

Devon Properties, New York,
New York

MESIVTA YESHIVA RABBI CHAIM BERLIN
COMMUNITY CENTER

Mesivta Yeshiva Rabbi Chaim Berlin,
Brooklyn, New York

NEW YORK CLEARING HOUSE COMPUTER
CENTER

New York Clearing House,
Weehawken, New Jersey

1675 BROADWAY OFFICE BUILDING

The Rudin Management Co.,
New York, New York

222 RIVERSIDE DRIVE APARTMENT
BUILDING

Royco Property Corporation,
New York, New York

40 FULTON STREET OFFICE BUILDING

Kalabi Realty Company, New York,
New York

WINNER, UNITED TECHNOLOGIES
CORPORATION HEADQUARTERS
COMPETITION

United Technologies Corporation,
Hartford, Connecticut

1989

380 MADISON AVENUE OFFICE BUILDING
RENOVATION

HRO International, New York,
New York

EMBASSY SUITES TIMES SQUARE HOTEL

Silverstein Properties/Embassy Suites,
New York, New York

MELVILLE CORPORATION HEADQUARTERS

Melville Corporation, Rye, New York

UNITED STATES TRUST COMPANY BANK
HEADQUARTERS

United States Trust Company,
New York, New York

CORE STATE FINANCIAL CENTER STUDY

JMB/Urban Development Co.,
Philadelphia, Pennsylvania

733 THIRD AVENUE LOBBY RENOVATION

The Durst Organization, New York,
New York

THE DALTON SCHOOL ATHLETIC FACILITY

The Dalton School, New York,
New York

1990

1991

JUPITER RESIDENCE

Harold and Tina Jupiter, Connecticut

THE POWERS OFFICE BUILDING
CONVERSION AND RESTORATION

Value Properties, Rochester, New York

101 AVENUE OF THE AMERICAS OFFICE
BUILDING

Edward J. Minskoff Equities/32B/32J
Service Employees Union, New York,
New York

401 FRANKLIN AVENUE OFFICE BUILDING
RENOVATION

Rockrose Development, Garden City,
New York

BERKELEY CARROLL SCHOOL ADDITION
AND RENOVATION

Berkeley Carroll School, Brooklyn,
New York

FINALIST, MADISON SQUARE GARDEN
OFFICE TOWER COMPETITION

Olympia & York, New York, New York

LE GRAND PALAIS APARTMENT BUILDING

Benenson Capital Corp./Loews
Corporation, New York, New York

1992

ROTHSCHILD HALL RENOVATION
Sarah Lawrence College, Bronxville, New York

THE SPENCE SCHOOL SCIENCE TEACHING LABORATORIES
The Spence School, New York, New York

WINDWARD SCHOOL EXPANSION
Windward School, White Plains, New York

WINNER: SOUTH CITY FIRST CENTRAL COMPETITION
Wuhan Guan Tong Real Estate Development Co., Wuhan, China

SOCIETY OF JEWISH SCIENCE RENOVATION
Society of Jewish Science, New York, New York

PHILADELPHIA NAVAL BASE RE-USE PLAN
City of Philadelphia Planning Commission, Philadelphia, Pennsylvania*

BAUSCH & LOMB CORPORATE HEADQUARTERS
Bausch & Lomb, Rochester, New York

COURT STREET PARKING GARAGE
City of Rochester, Rochester, New York

1993

1994

1995

*Projects led by Jambhekar Strauss PC, prior to merging with Fox & Fowle Architects.*

242

NEW YORK MEDICAL COLLEGE LEARNING CENTER

New York Medical College, Valhalla, New York

PILGRIM STATE CENTER MASTER PLAN

Empire State Development Corporation, Central Islip, New York*

DOWNTOWN MASTER PLAN

City of New Rochelle, New Rochelle, New York

THE SPENCE SCHOOL LIBRARY RENOVATION

The Spence School, New York, New York

UNITED TECHNOLOGIES AIRPORT OFFICES

United Technologies Corporation, Hartford, Connecticut

WINNER: WAYTOFUND FINANCIAL CENTER COMPETITION

Shanghai Waytofund International Financial Center Real Estate Company, Shanghai, China

AMTRAK 30TH STREET STATION MASTER PLAN

Amtrak, Philadelphia, Pennsylvania*

1996

BAY NETWORKS REGIONAL OFFICES
AND EXECUTIVE BRIEFING CENTER

Bay Networks, New York,
New York

GLEN COVE CREEK REVITALIZATION
PLAN

City of Glen Cove, Glen Cove,
New York*

QUEENSBOROUGH COMMUNITY
COLLEGE MASTER PLAN

City University of New York,
Queens, New York*

HERMAN MILLER OFFICES AND
SHOWROOM

Herman Miller, New York,
New York

TENNECO EXECUTIVE OFFICES AND
CONFERENCE CENTER

Tenneco Corporation, Greenwich,
Connecticut

UNITED STATES MILITARY ACADEMY
MASTER PLAN

United States Military Academy,
West Point, New York*

444 MADISON AVENUE LOBBY
RENOVATION

The Realex Corporation, New York,
New York

1997

*Projects led by Jambhekar Strauss PC, prior to merging with Fox & Fowle Architects.*

244

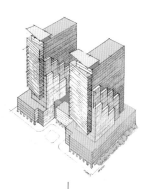

KNOWLEDGE UNION

New School University,
New York, New York

TIMES SQUARE INTERIM RETAIL
PROJECT

Times Square Center Associates,
Prudential/Park Tower Realty,
New York, New York

TIMES SQUARE SUBWAY STATION
MAIN ENTRANCE

Metropolitan Transportation
Authority, New York, New York

AMERICAN BIBLE SOCIETY ADDITION
AND RENOVATION

American Bible Society, New York,
New York

BUFFALO INNER HARBOR MASTER
PLAN

Empire State Development
Corporation, Buffalo, New York*

COLGATE CENTER RESIDENTIAL
MASTER PLAN

Colgate Real Estate, Jersey City,
New York*

COLLINS & AIKMAN OFFICES AND
SHOWROOM

Collins & Aikman, New York,
New York

MIDTOWN EAST REDEVELOPMENT PLAN
Arete Group, Queens, New York*

NORRISTOWN DOWNTOWN ECONOMIC STRATEGY
Montgomery County Commissioners, Norristown, Pennsylvania*

N.Y. INFORMATION TECHNOLOGY CENTER AT 55 BROAD STREET
Rudin Management Co., New York, New York

THE FOUNDATION CENTER OFFICES
The Foundation Center, New York, New York

99 JANE STREET APARTMENT BUILDING
Rockrose Development Corporation, New York, New York

SKANSKA NEW YORK OFFICES
Barney/Skanska, New York, New York

BLACK ROCK FOREST CENTER FOR SCIENCE AND EDUCATION
Black Rock Forest Consortium, Cornwall, New York

1999

*Projects led by Jambhekar Strauss PC, prior to merging with Fox & Fowle Architects.

THE CONDÉ NAST BUILDING @ 4 TIMES SQUARE

The Durst Organization, New York, New York

FINGER LAKES BLUECROSS/ BLUESHIELD HEADQUARTERS

Finger Lakes BlueCross/ BlueShield, Rochester, New York

INDUSTRIAL AND COMMERCIAL BANK OF CHINA REGIONAL HEADQUARTERS

Industrial and Commercial Bank of China, Shanghai, China

THE JORDAN COMPANY CORPORATE OFFICES

The Jordan Company, New York, New York

LABADIE HOUSE

Michael and Anne Labadie, Connecticut

PEEKSKILL ARTISTS' LIVE/WORK LOFTS PROGRAM STUDY

Insite/The Sheldrake Organization, Peekskill, New York

JAMBHEKAR STRAUSS ARCHITECTS PC MERGES WITH FOX & FOWLE ARCHITECTS

BRONX MUSEUM OF THE ARTS MASTER PLAN

NYC Department of Design and Construction/Bronx Museum of the Arts, Bronx, New York*

2000

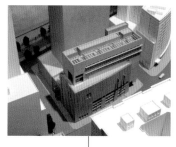

BUFFALO INNER HARBOR MASTER PLAN

Empire State Development
Corporation, Buffalo, New York*

JAMAICA TRANSIT ORIENTED
DEVELOPMENT PLAN

Greater Jamaica Development Plan,
Queens, New York*

FINALIST: MUSEUM OF WOMEN
COMPETITION

Museum of Women, New York,
New York

NORWALK CENTER COMMERCIAL MIXED-
USE DEVELOPMENT STUDY

Fred F. French Investing, Norwalk,
Connecticut

THE ROBERT J. MILANO SCHOOL

New School University, New York,
New York

SHANGHAI JAHWA TOWER OFFICE
BUILDING

Jahwa Real Estate Company/
Industrial and Commercial Bank
of China, Shanghai, China

SOUTH WILMINGTON DEVELOPMENT PLAN

Mentmore Holdings/Republic
Properties, Wilmington, Delaware*

*Projects led by Jambhekar Strauss PC, prior to merging with Fox & Fowle Architects.*

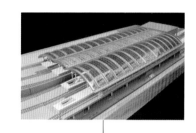

SUSTAINABLE DESIGN GUIDELINES FOR RESIDENTIAL DEVELOPMENT

Hugh L. Carey Battery Park City Authority, New York, New York

900 THIRD AVENUE LOBBY RENOVATION

The Paramount Group, New York, New York

COOPER SQUARE CENTER FOR ARTS AND CULTURE MASTER PLAN

The Buhl Foundation, New York, New York*

THE REUTERS BUILDING, 3 TIMES SQUARE

Rudin Mangement Co./Reuters America Holdings, New York, New York

STILLWELL AVENUE TERMINAL STUDY

Metropolitan Transportation Authority, Brooklyn, New York*

32 AVENUE OF THE AMERICAS RENOVATION

Rudin Management Co., New York, New York

AVAYA HEADQUARTERS RENOVATION

Avaya, Basking Ridge, New Jersey

2001

2002

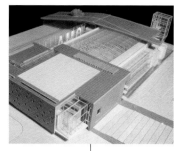

BERKSHIRE SCHOOL DORMITORIES

Berkshire School, Sheffield, Massachusetts

DUKE FARMS MASTER PLAN

Duke Farms Foundation/ The Conservation Fund, Somerville, New Jersey

NEW YORK ATHLETIC CLUB RENOVATION AND EXPANSION

New York Athletic Club, Pelham Manor, New York

FINALIST: QUEENS MUSEUM OF ART EXPANSION COMPETITION

Department of Design and Construction/Queens Museum of Art, Queens, New York

SUSTAINABLE DESIGN GUIDELINES FOR COMMERCIAL AND INSTITUTIONAL DEVELOPMENT

Hugh L. Carey Battery Park City Authority, New York, New York

COMMUNICATIONS CENTER LEHMAN COLLEGE

City University of New York, Bronx, New York

ARNOLD HALL CULTURAL CENTER

New School University, New York, New York

2003

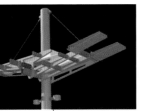

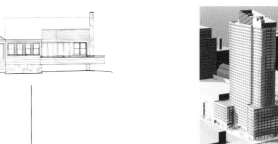

DOWNTOWN NEW ROCHELLE
DEVELOPMENT STUDY

City of New Rochelle, New Rochelle,
New York

EBERSTADT HOUSE ADDITION

Walter and Vera Eberstadt,
Massachusetts

HOBOKEN LIGHT RAIL STATION

New Jersey Transit, Hoboken,
New Jersey

FINALIST: PERTH AMBOY HIGH SCHOOL
COMPETITION

New Jersey Schools Construction
Corporation/City of Perth Amboy,
Perth Amboy, New Jersey

SCHAPIRO HOUSE

Donald and Linda Schapiro,
Massachusetts

THE CALHOUN SCHOOL ADDITION

The Calhoun School, New York,
New York

THE HELENA APARTMENT TOWER

The Durst Organization/
Rose Associates, New York, New York

2004

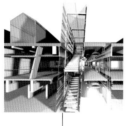

TUNNEL STATION, HUDSON–BERGEN
LIGHT RAIL

Union City, New Jersey

MARTIN J. WHITMAN SCHOOL OF
MANAGEMENT

Syracuse University, Syracuse,
New York

MULTIMEDIA CENTER, LEHMAN COLLEGE

City University of New
York/Dormitory Authority of the
State of New York, Bronx, New York

NEWARK–ELIZABETH LIGHT RAIL

New Jersey Transit, Newark,
New Jersey

ROOSEVELT AVENUE INTERMODAL
TERMINAL

Metropolitan Transit Authority,
Queens, New York

THE SPENCE SCHOOL MIDDLE AND UPPER
SCHOOL RENOVATIONS

The Spence School, New York,
New York

BRONX ZOO LION HOUSE CONVERSION

New York City Department of Design
and Construction/Wildlife
Conservation Society, Bronx, New York

SHELTER ROCK PUBLIC LIBRARY
EXPANSION

Shelter Rock Public Library,
Albertson, New York

2005

2006

# Photography Credits

**American Bible Society**

Jeff Goldberg/Esto: **30**(1); **31**(3); **32**(7,9); **33**(10)

Catherine Tigne Bogert: **32**(8)

David Sundberg/Esto: **32**(6)

**Avaya Headquarters**

Andrew Gordon: **34**(1); **35**(3,5)

**Berkshire School Dormitories**

David Sundberg/Esto: **36**(1,3); **37**(4,6); **38**(7); **39**(8,9)

**Black Rock Forest Center**

David Sundberg/Esto: **40**(2); **41**(4); **42**(5,6)

**Clinton Green Mixed-Use Project**

Scott Baumberger: **56**(1); **59**(7)

**Dongbu Headquarters**

Scott Baumberger: **66**(1,2)

**Durst-Strong Apartment**

David Sundberg/Esto: **74**(1); **75**(2,3,5)

**Herman Miller Showroom**

Marco Lorenzetti – Korab/Hedrich Blessing: **86**; **87**(2–5)

**Huntington Station Revitalization Plan**

Huntington Station Revitalization Committee: **94**(3)

**Industrial and Commercial Bank of China Headquarters**

Lu Yun Studio: **96**; **97**(2,3); **98**(4,8); **100**(13); **101**

**Labadie House**

Bruce Fowle FAIA: **106**(2–4); **107**(5); **108**(6–8); **109**(9–11)

**Lehman College Communication Center**

David Sundberg/Esto: **110**(2,3); **111**(5)

**Max Protetch Gallery: New World Trade Center Competition**

Mark Garten: **118**(1,4,5); **119**(7)

**New School University Arnhold Hall**

David Sundberg/Esto: **130**(3–5); **131**(6,7)

**New School University Knowledge Union**

Andrew Gordon: **132**(3,4); **133**(6)

**New School University Robert J. Milano Graduate School**

Chuck Choi: **134**(3,4); **135**(5)

**Rochester Revitalization**

Tim Wilkes: **152**(1–4); **153**(5)

**Roosevelt Avenue Intermodal Station Rehabilitation**

Lydia Gould Bessler: **155**(4)

**Skanska Offices**

David Joseph: **164**(1); **165**(2–4)

**The Spence School Master Plan**

Dan Cornish: **168**(2,3)

Christopher Wesnofske: **169**(4)

Peter Paige: **169**(5); **170**(6,7)

David Sundberg/Esto: **171**(9,10)

**Syracuse University Martin J. Whitman School of Management**

Roy Wright: **174**(4); **175**(5); **176**(7); **177**(14); **177**(15,16)

**Times Square Buildings**

Julian Olivas: **182–183**

**Condé Nast Building @ 4 Times Square**

Jeff Goldberg/Esto: **186**; **187**(2–4); **192**(15,16)

Andrew Gordon: **190**; **192**(17); **193**(19,20)

Bruce Fowle FAIA: **189**(9–12)

***New York Times* Headquarters**

Screampoint: **194**(1); **195**(2)

David Joseph: **197**(11)

**The Reuters Building**

David Joseph/Esto: **198**; **200**(3,9); **202**(4)

Raimondo Di Egidio: **201**(4,5)

Andrew Gordon: **203**(16)

**Times Square Plaza**

Jon Seagull: **207**

**Times Square Subway Entrance**

Andrew Gordon: **208**(1)

Roger Whitehouse: **209**(3,4)

**Wadsworth Atheneum Museum of Art Master Plan and Expansion**

7 UN Studio: **210**(2,4)

# Index

Jason Abbey  Sadiq Abdul-Kadir  Amy Acampora  Elizabeth Adams  James Adams  Diana Adelman  Brenda Agro  Ellen Albert  Douglass Alligood, Jr.  Hitoshi Amano  Yvonne Anzolone  Rebecca Arcaro  Francesca Aureli  Jonghyun Baek  Abigail Banker  Nsenga Bansfield  John Barbara  Winston Barker  Thomas Barry  Leila Battle  Efrem Belvin  Wayne Bennet  Venus Bernard  Reid Betz  Susan Bilenker  Vicki Bilenker  Maria Blanco  Daniel J.Blank  J. Daniel Blatt  Heidi Blau  Susan Bogaty  Pat Boles  Sheri Bonstelle  David Bootsman  Ania Bothe  William Bowick  Uwe Brandes  Darren Brathwaite  Kathleen Brettell  Sandra Briceno  Beverlee Brockdorff  Carl Brown  Charlene Brown  Elizabeth Brown  Mary Jean Brown  Tiffany Broyles  Peter Buendgen  Martha Burns  Kathleen Byrne  Michael Cala  Carlos Caldart  Chad Callis  Maria Canaves  Abigail Carlen  Christina Carlson  Carmen Casalta  Frank Casey Jr.  Russell Castle  Nicholas Cates  Rachel Cauvin  Walter Chabla  William Chalkley  Tanya Chamberlain  Kain Bon Albert Chan  Frank Chao  Elizabeth Chapparo  Stephen Chin  Teyana Chin  Biju Chirathalattu  Geraldine Chmil  Peter Cho  Paul Chovanec  Lisa Christie  Beth Clauss  Ethelind Coblin  Morris Coffey  Melissa Cohen  Orlando Conception  Philip Consalvo  Richard Cook  Tobie Cornejo  John Crellin  Patrick Crosgrove  Allison Cross  James Cudlip  PingPing Cui  Thomas Czarnowski  Zheng Dai  Denzil Davidson  Adesina Davis  Amy Davis  Brian Davison  Scott Davison  Catherine de Neergaard  Thalia Denis  Marilee Desiderio  Karen Devine  Francis DeVine III  Hughy Dharmayoga  Shirley Diamond  Ann DiFlora  Judith DiMaio  Peter Dixon  Susan Doban  Elizabeth Donoff  David J Dorfman  Michael Duddy  Sherwood Duffy  Sharon Leigh Dugel  Mathias Dujovne  Projjal Dutta  George Eberstadt  Charles Eldred  Eve Elmore  Laura Elterman  Donna Eng  Janet Eng  Terri Engberg  Elyse Engelhardt  David Ennis  David Enriquez  Gary Ensana  Ryan Enschede  Don Erwin-McGuire  Maximo Estrada  Julie Evans  Christine Everett  Bruce Fairbanks  Brian Fanning  Stephanie Feldman  Gabriel Fernandez  Harold Fine  Elizabeth Finkelshteyn  Irene Finkelshteyn  Christopher Finnican  Eileen Fisher  Jamie Fleming  Kaz Fleming  Ishmael Flores  Roger Flores  Maya Foldes  Owen Foote  Karla Forsbeck  Abigail Fowle  Margaret Fowle  Suzanne Fowle  Bernadette Fox  Thomas Fox  Robert Fox, Jr.  Francesca Franchi  Michel Franck  Margaret Freedman  Patricia Freedman  Douglas Freeman  Paul Freitag  Carol Frost  Ralph Frost  Karen Fuchs  Joanne Fuller  Carmela Fuluso  Robert Furno  Sandra Gambino  Kimberly Thomason Garcia  Mark Gausphol  Jeremy Gedes  Jennifer Gellin  Theresa Genovese  Valerie Giacomazza  Roberto Gil  Leila Gilchrist  Robin Gitomer  Deborah Goldreyer  Victor Goldsmith  Luciane Maia Goncalves  Griselda Gonzales  Robert Goodwin  Don Gorham  Jan Gorlach  Anjali Grant  Barbara Griffin  Deborah Griffin  Derek Griffith  Gary Todd Griggs  Ellen Hamilton  Annette Hammer  Joseph Hand  Susan Hanna  Julie Hanselman  Ellis Harding  Deniele Hartley  Bryce Hejtmancik  Donald Henderson  Nino Hewitt  Robert Hills  Renee Hammitt Hinton  Ervin Hirsan  Kristi Hirschman  Melanie Hobs  Preston Holmes  Kevin Hom  Samuel Hom  Joshua Homer  Henry Hong  Karen Howard  Danielle Hricay  Carol Hsiung  Doris Hughes  Carlton Hutton  Frederic Hyde  Marian Imperatore  Illiana Ivanova  Sallie Jackson  Lewis Jacobsen  Elizabeth Jahn  Peter Jensen  Li Jin  Michael Johnson  Erica Joltin  Dana Jupiter  Marisa Jupiter  Sylvia Juzwa  Michael Kally, Jr.  Scott Kamen  Duane Karlin  Robert Katchur, Jr.  Stephen Killcayne  Dong-Wook Kim  Gloria Kim  Kyung San Kim  Marjorie Lee Kim  Michael Kim  Michelle Kim  Paul Kim  Tami Kinsler  Allen Klein  Tomas Klopsch  Christina Holt Klumb  Scott Knox  Young Kim Koo  Edward Kopel  Steven Kratchman  Leon Kravhenko  Gretchen Kreuzer  John Kristovitch  Scott Kula  Victor Kung  Victor Lai  Eilleen Lamorte  Larry Lane  Michael Lanford  Robert Lanni Jr.  Lois Lazzarino  Cecelia Lee  David Da-Wei Lee  David Lee  Helena Lee  Kenny Lee  Omela Lee  Roger Lee  Woo-Hyoung Lee  Ronald Lem  Joseph Lengeling  Maybelle Leong  Wing-Shing Leung  Carl Lewis  Earl Lewis  Jeff Lewis  Lesley Carmona Lewis  Michael Lewis  Chang-Je Li